Year in Nam

Winner of the
1996
North American
Indian Prose Award

Year in Nam

A Native American Soldier's Story

Leroy TeCube

University of Nebraska Press
Lincoln and London

⊗

Library of Congress Cataloging-in-
Publication Data
TeCube, Leroy, 1947–
Year in Nam : a Native American
soldier's story / Leroy TeCube.
p.   cm.
ISBN 0-8032-4434-7
(cloth : alk. paper)
1. Vietnamese Conflict, 1961–1975 —
Personal narratives, American.
2. Vietnamese Conflict, 1961–1975 —
Participation, Indian.
3. TeCube, Leroy, 1947–   . I. Title.
DS559.5.T43   1999
959.704'3'092 — dc21   98-37668
CIP

To my family
(wife Angela, son Cordell, daughter Modina, son Frederic),
who gave me the reason to continue.

To my people,
the Jicarilla Apache Tribe,
who I am proud to be a part of.

To the Vietnam War veterans.
We did what we had to.

To the soldiers of the Americal
(Twenty-third Infantry) Division. Be proud.

Contents

Illustrations

Introduction

THE YEARS AFTER my military tour of duty in the Republic of South Vietnam were years of indifference. I felt that my experiences in the Vietnam War weren't of much importance, so I just kept them to myself. A few years ago an incident made me realize that I should share my personal experiences of the Vietnam War. A high school class invited several Vietnam veterans to talk about their time overseas. Although I strongly felt that my Vietnam War experiences were trivial, I agreed to attend.

I fully expected to lose my young audience within minutes. However, when well into my presentation, I was surprised to see the students sitting attentively, paying very close attention to me. After the session I thought that it might be worthwhile to put some experiences in writing. I felt that generations to come should have an idea of what happened in the Vietnam War from my perspective.

This early undertaking soon broadened into a major endeavor. I started writing in 1990, twenty-one years after returning from the Vietnam War. The writing process has been a major challenge for me, mainly because I had been just an average student in English class. I also debated with myself many times whether to continue, often setting the writing aside for months at a time.

During this time I tried to contact members of my former military unit in Vietnam. I was mostly unsuccessful, and the few members that I did speak with couldn't give me useful information. I am a member of several veterans associations, which were key sources of information. I wish to acknowledge the Americal Division Veteran's Association, the

196th Light Infantry Brigade Association, the First of the First Cavalry Association, the Americal Division Far West Chapter, and the Combat Infantrymen's Association. The newsletters of these associations were great aids for my recollections.

I served in Vietnam from January 1968 to January 1969. My MOS (Military Occupational Specialty; an army term for a job) was the infantry. Having an infantry MOS meant that you spent your time out in the "field," trying to locate the enemy. This was a hard task, because you were on the enemy's native soil.

You dealt with three types of enemies. The first was the Vietcong, who were called by several different names, including VC, Victor Charlie, gook, dink, and so on. The most common name was just plain Charlie. Charlie was usually of local origin and practiced guerrilla warfare. He rarely stayed around to engage you for any length of time in firefights, unless he had the upper hand. His preferred tactic, which was more deadly than bullets, was to use mines and booby traps to inflict casualties. He traveled light and maintained a vast network of tunnels, which could be miles long. When he was in danger, he could easily disappear into his surroundings or tunnel complexes.

The other main type of enemy was a member of the North Vietnamese Army (NVA), who was a highly trained soldier and part of a large military unit. He trained in North Vietnam to aid the Vietcong in their quest to overthrow the South Vietnamese government. He carried a heavy arsenal of weapons. If you happened to engage him, he would stay and fight.

A third type of enemy, at times more deadly than the other two, was the South Vietnamese people themselves. When among them, you had no way of knowing whether they were the enemy or not. The enemy could be a cleaning lady, a barber, a laundress, or even an innocent-looking child. These individuals aided the enemy in planting mines and booby traps, scouting, or providing useful information. Some had jobs inside U.S. military installations, working at tasks less preferred by the GIs, such as burning human waste, KP, cleaning, hauling garbage, and so forth. The enemy was all around you. The only territory you held was where you stood.

The enemy was a seasoned veteran who had been fighting throughout most of his life. He was on his home turf and knew every foot of it. On the other hand, the American GI was on the average about nineteen years old. He usually had little outdoor experience and had to engage and defeat his adversary with about four months of training. The situation could be considered a big mismatch in the enemy's favor. Without the vast firepower that we had, it would have been.

It was very important for the infantryman to know how to use the firepower to his advantage. When out in the field he had to be familiar with various terrain features and be able to read a map accurately. To survive, it was of the utmost importance to know your exact location. If the enemy happened to gain the upper hand, you could call in all types of firepower for support.

During the war I was very fortunate to be knowledgeable about various types of terrain features. I grew up in an era that required spending much more time outdoors. In those days our dwellings were very simply constructed with whatever lumber that might be found. They were small wooden structures that usually consisted of a room or two. In many instances canvas tents provided shelter. The dwellings mainly provided shelter during the night or bad weather. My average day was spent out in the countryside, which in reality was a natural learning experience of various terrains. Also during this time most of the people around me raised livestock as a livelihood. As young boys we often had to take care of them.

My childhood and youth had many twists and turns. I didn't grow up with any one family. My mother passed away when I was about a year old. After that my grandmother raised me until she left me when I was three years old. I then lived with other relatives until I was of age to start my schooling. When I was five years old, I entered, along with other school-aged kids, the local Bureau of Indian Affairs dormitory and Indian school. I spent most of my elementary school years there.

During my high school years I was fortunate to have spent more time with my aunt and uncle. It was during this time that I gained much of my knowledge of the great outdoors. My uncle took the time to teach me about my surroundings as well as how to hunt.

On hunting trips with my uncle and my cousins, I learned to orient myself when out in the woods by using various terrain features. Having this knowledge of the outdoors would become the most valuable asset I had while in the rice paddies, jungles, and mountains of South Vietnam.

I also loved hiking and different outdoor games. At every opportunity the youths took to the hills and countryside, their favorite playground. The natural surroundings drew them like a magnet and were part of them. They enjoyed engaging in mock battles using the natural terrain for concealment. In mock battles the idea was to outsmart your "enemy" by using strategy and cunning.

Various outdoor games popular with the youths included Follow the Leader, which was a favorite. The game often involved an older leader who made you try to do some seemingly impossible feat, such as jumping off a steep cliff. One game that was also popular was Kick the Can. This was a form of the old Hide and Seek game. The "it" person tried to locate the ones hiding, while at the same time guarding the can. If someone kicked the can without his knowledge, the ones already found were free to hide again. It was better to play the game at night with the can located next to a large fire. Then the kids sharpened up their skills in the art of concealment, using the darkness to great advantage.

All the outdoor games and the natural love of hiking were in reality a valuable learning experience. They taught us the art of concealment (day or night), how to encroach without being seen, how to recognize various terrain features (especially at night), and how to follow orders without hesitation.

We grew up full of discipline in our lives and understood the reason for it. We were expected to respect traditional values and our tribal elders. Jicarilla Apache was the main language spoken in the households, although most of the kids in my age group had to learn the English language before they started the learning process.

When I reminisce about the quality of education provided by the old Indian school, I realize how effective the teaching method was. In those days corporal punishment was used at times to aid the goal of teaching us. Teachers were also dedicated enough to show us how to survive in the outside world. Of course, it was up to us whether we wanted to learn, but the opportunity was there. When the Indian school era ended, the public school system continued to provide a very good education.

This early education process provided me with the knowledge and skills I needed to compete with the rest of the world. This was why I could carry out orders, read maps, understand world affairs, be aware of my surroundings, and give orders when I was in the Vietnam War.

Before I entered the military service, I was aware that a war was going on at a place called Vietnam. The news media provided daily coverage of the war, but I paid very little attention to it. However, when an older brother ended up being drafted, I quickly became more aware of the crisis. He often wrote to me from Vietnam and tried to explain how it was over there. I never fully understood the situation.

During this time the Selective Service System was in effect. All young men reaching the age of eighteen were subject for draft into the U.S. Army. After I completed high school I got a temporary exemption from being drafted by continuing my education. I attended Haskell Institute, a higher learning institution for Native Americans in Lawrence, Kansas, for two years. When I completed my training there, I knew that it would be a matter of time before I entered the military service.

Soon after I left school I passed my required physical examination for induction into the U.S. Army. I then had recruiters from all branches of the military come around to recruit me. At the time I was leaning more toward the air force and thought about enlisting with them. However, the marine recruiter was very persistent and eventually had got me to agree to enlist. He gave me a reporting date and location. However, fate intervened.

Before I was to report, I received my notice for induction into the U.S. Army. My reporting date for induction was a day before I was to enlist into the Marine Corps. I thought it over and chose to go with the induction notice and enter into the army. A difference of two years was the deciding factor. I would have had to serve four years in the Marine Corps versus two in the army.

During this time many young men from my hometown went into the military service. Some volunteered, although most entered the U.S. Army by way of the draft. Many of them ended up in Vietnam, and two didn't make it back alive.

I was sworn into the military service at Albuquerque, New Mexico, on August 17, 1967, and received my basic training at Ft. Bliss, Texas. While processing at the Ft. Bliss Reception Station I had to identify where I wanted to serve overseas. At the moment I had no real ambition, but I had often wondered what it might be like in combat. I had to find out what it was like at Vietnam, so I answered, "Vietnam" without hesitation.

At the time I was young, full of life, and had hardly any strings attached. There was no place that I could truly call home, having lived with relatives or in the boarding school most of my life. To top it off, an older brother was already in Vietnam.

After I completed my basic training I went to Ft. Polk, Louisiana, for jungle warfare training. I was in a platoon that also trained for antitank warfare. In December of 1967 I completed my training at Ft. Polk, whereupon I received orders to go to the Republic of South Vietnam after a one month leave.

My recollections are from an infantryman's point of view. It's said that out of all the GIs that served in the Vietnam War, about one in five were in the infantry. There were various nicknames for these guys, but the most common was grunt.

The grunts spent most of their time out in the "field," trying to locate and destroy the enemy. For their efforts they received the coveted Combat Infantryman's Badge (CIB), among other awards, after meeting certain criteria. In my unit, which was the American or Twenty-third Infantry Division, you had to engage the enemy where your outfit received a casualty in order to receive the badge.

The infantryman in most cases never engaged the enemy on a daily basis. There were long periods during which no hostilities occurred. When he went out in the field, he took everything that he needed to survive for weeks at a time. His main attire was jungle fatigues, which were a lot lighter than the normal fatigues. Jungle fatigues had a lot of pockets, which provided more places to carry items.

Over the fatigues he wore the web gear, which was merely a sort of harness attached to a pistol belt. With the web gear you carried such light necessities as a first aid kit, water canteens, hand grenades, a pistol, a flashlight, ammunition pouches, and so forth.

Over the web gear the infantryman carried other necessities in a large pack called a rucksack, a large pouch with smaller pouches on the sides and attached to a metal frame. Some items carried in it included writing paper, personal hygiene and shaving items, books, souvenirs, C rations, a poncho, a poncho liner (a light blanket to go inside the poncho), extra ammunition clips (magazines), water canteens, a claymore mine, machine gun ammunition (one hundred round belt), an entrenching tool, a rocket launcher, and a gas mask, among other things.

Although it was not required some GIs wore a flak jacket underneath the rucksack. This provided extra protection to the upper body, but it was bulky and heavy. Having to carry the combined weight of all these items was a great inconvenience.

Dealing with the elements required a great deal of stamina, often testing your limit of endurance. Some days the temperature would rise above the already sweltering hot conditions and reach 120 degrees. The humidity added to the unpleasant conditions. The liquid lost to perspiration had to be replenished quickly. At times it could rain for days at a time, causing a sharp drop in morale. The wet weather could also make it just cold enough to be uncomfortable. The different types of terrain were also a big factor in your daily survival. You had to walk through steaming hot jungles, in knee-deep mud, over steep mountains, on loose sandy soil, in thick vegetation, or in open rice paddies or negotiate large rivers. Each had its own type of inconvenience, and the hot sun was almost always present.

Insects, ants, poisonous snakes, leeches, wild animals, water buffaloes, and the fact that most of the plants had thorns on them were part of your daily environment. At night millions of mosquitoes came out to feast on you. When you tried to cover yourself with something it would get too hot and uncomfortable. Mosquito repellent helped to a certain degree, but it had an odor, allowing Charlie to detect your position. When you failed to take the required medication or use iodine tablets, malaria, dysentery, or other diseases could be contacted.

You learned to get by on a few hours of sleep, sleeping lightly and pulling guard duty every night while in the field. You cleaned yourself as best as you could by using your helmet (steel pot) as a wash basin. You often went weeks at a time without a change of clothing. It wasn't uncommon to have individuals wearing clothing with holes or large tears in them.

The infantryman coped with all the hardships mentioned and still had to worry about getting shot or stepping on a mine or booby trap. He had to do his share and hoped that the others did the same. He had to be sure that his weapon was always ready to fire at all times, especially during the rainy season.

I would guess that every infantryman did a lot of praying. In the very dangerous world he lived in, prayer was the ultimate source to turn to.

With the amount of time that has passed it was difficult to recollect everything. I did the best I could. There are periods when my mind is blank and I can't recollect. A friend from California told me about making a combat assault in a driving rain. I told him, "I don't remember, I probably was not there."

He said, "You were there. You were our leader." Perhaps it is best not to remember some instances.

Some recollections are based on my traditional views of the war. While in Vietnam, I found out that the local people there saw me differently from other GIs. They thought that I looked like they did. I was a source of great interest to them. At times while I was in Vietnam I would have flashbacks to similar situations that I had experienced as a youth on the Jicarilla Apache Reservation.

The Vietnam War was similar to the Indian Wars of a hundred years ago. I realize that my ancestors fought the same type of war against the United States. However, as would other American Indian tribes, they ended up fighting for the United States after treaties were made. Since then every succeeding generation continues to fight in our nation's wars with a feeling that the land is still ours to fight for. We still live on it.

The tradition of our people fighting side by side with other Americans goes back to World War I. Then one or two went into the military service to fight for our country. In World War II there were many more. They fought in all theaters of the war. Some fought in the South Pacific, some in Europe; some were paratroopers; some hit the beaches of Okinawa, Tarawa, and Iwo Jima, some in North Africa; and some hit the Normandy beaches on D-Day. Our young men also fought in the Korean War, similar to Vietnam in that their goal was to stop Communist aggression. In the end they succeeded in getting freedom for South Korea. Many told of the bitter cold they went through. Our forebears fought the wars with quiet distinction. In our youth we were aware of what these men did. They instilled a pride in you, knowing that one day you would be in their shoes. This is the way of my people. We have to carry on the warrior tradition.

From an American Indian viewpoint, it might be said that one does not put his life or parts of it in writing. This might be so, but I feel that it is best to do this for future generations. This is the only way for them to know of our past. And because of my experience and having assumed a leadership role in Vietnam, I believe that I can offer something to the youth of today and of future generations.

In a sense, as infantrymen, we all died in Nam. Views about ourselves were forever changed in a period of time that was an eternity to us. For some the change was positive. For many others it was negative.

It is my wish that whoever reads my book understands the Vietnam War from my point of view. The following are some recollections.

1. Getting There

THE ROCKETS AND MORTAR ROUNDS are exploding all around as I desperately try to keep my jeep under control. Seated behind me are two GIs, next to a 106 recoilless rifle. I swerve to my right as a round explodes in front of the vehicle. A GI seated next to me yells, "Look out!" as I somehow keep the vehicle under control.

We are a team trained in antitank warfare and are desperately trying to get into a fighting position. Time is of the essence, and we are well aware of approaching enemy tanks. Suddenly, I hear automatic rifle fire directly to my left as the rounds hit the side of the jeep. In the next instance I feel pain and a hot sensation running down my left leg. The jeep then comes to an abrupt halt inside a crater left by an exploded round. I check my leg and realize that I am bleeding badly from multiple wounds. The blood keeps running, and I am unable to stop it. I look at the GI seated next to me as he slowly fades from view.

At that instant, I suddenly woke up. I was at my aunt and uncle's house, in Dulce, New Mexico, where I resided. After sitting up I realized that I had had a bad dream that seemed all too real. I looked at the red glow coming from the gas heater and felt its warm heat. My hometown, set in a very high altitude, has weather that is very severe during the winter months.

It was January of 1968, and the temperature outside was well below zero. A few weeks earlier I had received orders at Ft. Polk, Louisiana, for overseas duty in Vietnam. I had now spent most of my leave, and the time to depart was rapidly approaching.

Ironically, that winter was one of the worst on record as far as snowfall. It snowed a lot throughout the Four Corners area. Many people were stranded in the rural areas. The thick blanket of snow made it impossible to go anywhere I wanted, but it did allow me to spend time with as many friends and relatives as I could.

Sitting beside the heater, I thought about the bad dream. It gave me an uncomfortable feeling knowing the dream might not be too far from reality. I tried to forget what I heard of dreams sometimes coming true. I stayed awake for some time before I went back to sleep.

When I awoke again it was to the smell of home cooking, the type of food I would miss in the year ahead. I had lived with my aunt and uncle since my high school years, and I was used to my aunt's traditional way of cooking. After I cleaned up and sat at the kitchen table, my aunt asked, "Son, is there something bothering you?"

After she poured me a cup of coffee I said, "I had a bad dream about being shot and all that. Why did you ask?"

My uncle spoke, "We heard you last night, and you seemed to have stayed up most of the night."

I replied, "The time is getting close before I leave. Perhaps, something in the back of my mind is telling me something."

My aunt said to me after I finished eating, "Son, don't go anywhere this evening. Be home before it gets dark."

During my leave I turned twenty-one years of age, which gave me new freedom as an adult. However, at times it was hard to understand how the adult system worked. A popular song of the time said, "You're old enough for dying, but not for voting." Young men in the prime of their lives were dying, in a far-off country, before they could vote.

The local tavern was one place I went to exercise my new freedom. The people there were aware that their young men were again going off to war. Many of my people served in World War II and the Korean War. I felt their genuine sincerity when they wished me a safe return.

That evening, obeying my aunt's wishes, I was home early. I sat in the living room and watched the evening news on TV. I watched with interest as the Vietnam War dominated the screen. Walter Cronkite suggested that the South Vietnamese were winning the war, although they suffered a lot of casualties.

The evening news was still on when a vehicle stopped outside. My aunt went to see who it was and a minute later welcomed our visitors. I recognized the elderly couple at the door, one of whom was a tribal medicine man.

"Son, we hired this man to pray for you, since you're going to where a war is going on," my aunt said. "That is why I asked you to be home early tonight."

After the couple ate we all retired into another room for the very important ceremony. Until then, something of this nature had never crossed my mind. It became clear to me that the ceremony that would take place would be a very significant event in my life.

The medicine man explained that the prayers went back into time immemorial. The prayers were for someone leaving for an unknown place. I nodded my head that I understood and sat through the prayer session with utmost respect. I was taught to respect traditional doings by elders.

When the prayer session ended, the medicine man gave me instructions for what to do. He looked at me and said, "You think you know in your mind what happened here tonight. Not totally. You'll know when the time comes. It'll happen when you are across the big water. When the time comes, don't be afraid to admit that you are scared. Everyone is afraid of the unknown. Just don't let your fears control you in a bad way. Be brave. Above all believe in the power of prayer."

A few days later I bid farewell to most of my friends and relatives. I had to report to Oakland, California, for overseas duty. On January 12, 1968, I began a journey that would dramatically affect my life. I had on Class A military attire, and my duffel bag was full of military necessities that would be suitable for the hot, humid weather ahead. The only non-military items I carried were good luck charms and what was in my pockets. Around my neck were GI dog tags with my name, military ID number, and religious preference.

On the bus, I gathered my thoughts. People would be killed or wounded where I was headed. At Ft. Polk were soldiers that had already gone through combat experiences of the war, and they prepared us mentally. I thought of how real the war games were during our last week there.

I also thought of my traditional ways and what was expected from me along those lines. I already knew that my upbringing was different from other youths I met in the military. I thought back to how my native culture was a great part of my upbringing. Prayer was always conducted when situations warranted it. My earliest recollection was of my grandmother saying prayers around our tent before we retired for the night.

In the early morning hours of January 14 I reached Oakland. There in a hotel I salvaged what was left of the night. In the morning as I was leaving I noticed a football game on TV. It was the Super Bowl. I wanted to watch the game, but I had to be at the processing center at noon.

Arriving at the processing center, I had with me several copies of orders, which I presented to the personnel there. They took what they needed and gave the rest back. The packet of orders had to be shown to other personnel at other places along the way. More GIs bound for Vietnam arrived when I did. After being assigned barracks, the overseas processing procedure started immediately. We were processed as quickly as possible. The whole procedure took about two days.

Just as quickly as we arrived, we were ready to be transported to Travis Air Force Base. While waiting for buses to arrive someone called me from across a room. I looked and recognized Leon-Guererro, a good buddy from basic training.

When I walked over to him, he asked, "You ready to take on the Vietcong?"

"I guess I'm about as ready as I'll ever be," I answered. "I see you're headed to the First Infantry Division."

"Yeah, I'll be with the Big Red One. What about you?"

I shrugged. "I don't really know. All I see on my orders is 22 AG or something like that. None of the units posted all over the place at Ft. Polk is mentioned."

Leon-Guererro then introduced me to his parents, a Polynesian couple from Guam. We all chatted for a few minutes before we had to board the buses. Unfortunately, my friend would fail to return home, becoming one of many fatalities of the Vietnam War.

The brief encounter with him and his parents will always hold a special place in my heart. It reminds me of how much we were willing to sacrifice to help another country. That was the reason we headed to an unknown country halfway around the world. I know many other parents shared a similar anguish.

Several buses then took us across the bay to Travis AFB, where we waited for less than an hour before boarding a commercial jet. I sat next to a good friend from Ft. Polk named Ulenkott. I remember him saying, "I guess we'll make it there whether we want to or not."

When the plane lifted off there was a heavy atmosphere of uncertainty and fear of the unknown. I also felt a strange feeling of excitement. The young soldiers on the plane were silent. Some tried to take a last look at the mainland.

We departed on January 16, 1968, with our first stop scheduled for Honolulu, Hawaii. Initially, I looked out the window at all the water below. Occasionally, through the clouds, I observed a ship headed somewhere. However, I soon became bored and tried reading a paperback I had with me.

Unfortunately, our plane had no movies in flight. I tried to get as much sleep as possible, knowing I would soon be deprived of it. Every few hours the stewardesses fed us. I ate even though I wasn't hungry. Somehow I knew that my main diet in the year ahead wouldn't match the meal given us.

The flight to Honolulu seemed short, although it took about five hours. The weather was clear when we landed at the Honolulu International Airport. A four-hour delay gave us time to stretch our legs and buy souvenirs.

From Honolulu we headed for Clark AFB in the Philippine Islands. Again I tried to sleep, but the thought of getting to our final destination was sinking in. Somewhere between the two groups of islands, we crossed the International Date Line. When we did, the captain informed us that we would be losing a day when traveling in a westerly direction. January 17, 1968, was the day we lost. We arrived at Clark AFB in a very short time.

After a brief stopover we departed for Bien Hoa in the Republic of South Vietnam. This was a time to prepare yourself mentally for the final destination. You naturally tried to think of more pleasant circumstances far away. However, the thought of shortly being in a war zone drove away other thoughts. The flight took about an hour. On this last leg of our journey everyone was wide awake.

Bien Hoa, our final destination, was about twenty-five miles north of Saigon, the capital of South Vietnam. It was dark when we approached a very large array of lights below. This I assumed to be Saigon. As we circled the city a stewardess said, "On some nights you can see all the explosions where the fighting is going on." She pointed out the window. There were indeed some explosions here and there.

In the early morning hours of January 18, 1968, we landed at the Bien Hoa airport. When we disembarked, the hot and humid air hit us immediately, even though it was nighttime. This was quite a change from the sub-zero weather at home a few days earlier. The area looked very secure, but I knew that no place in a war zone was entirely safe. Hereafter, we would be subjected to all types of hostilities.

Retrieving our duffel bags, we went to a place under a makeshift canvas shelter. A rope divided the space under the shelter in two. We sat on chairs on one side of the barrier. Already seated on the other side was another group of soldiers. They smiled big at our arrival. We soon realized why they were there. The plane that had brought us here was to be their "Freedom Bird" back to the "World." There was no verbal communication between the two groups. The departing soldiers knew what was ahead of us and let it be. Our tour of duty was just starting. We had to learn to cope with our situation as quickly as possible and could only pray to be in their shoes in a year's time.

After a short orientation we boarded buses to the Ninetieth Replacement Center, a preliminary staging area to process replacements coming into the country. Upon arriving there, although late at night, we started the in-country processing. What I recollect about this process is getting in-country ID cards and converting our money into Military Payment Certificates (MPCs). MPCs were paper money used in lieu of U.S. currency and coins in the Vietnam War. They ranged in denomination from fifty cents to twenty-dollar bills. No one could keep U.S. currency or coins, although some did.

After getting ID cards, MPCs, and so forth, we hauled our duffel bags to our barracks (billets). There we tried to salvage as much sleep as possible. The billets were built to allow air to flow freely through them. This helped a little, but the air remained hot and sticky. In time we would partially get used to it.

Just as quickly as I dozed off it was time to get up again. All the GIS that trained together back in the states formed small groups. The guys in my platoon at Ft. Polk did the same. We all stuck together for moral support. When we checked our orders most of us were going to the 22nd AG, wherever that was. One person had orders for the 1st Infantry Division. Another had orders for the 199th Light Infantry Brigade.

After cleaning up and having breakfast, we stood in formation in the sand for instructions on what to do for the day. After that, we went to various places to continue our in-country processing. As I stood in different lines, I wondered when weapons might be issued to us.

KP and other duties still had to be assigned. Most of our group evaded these responsibilities by knowing who to keep away from. Only Sommers wasn't so lucky and got picked. We watched from our hiding place as he was led off for some sort of duty.

After a few hours Sommers came back exhausted and said, "Boy, you guys are lucky. You think KP is the worst duty in the military. I'll tell you there is an even worse one."

"What are you talking about?" Kastern said. "There isn't anything worse than KP."

"You know what they do with all that crap in those outhouses? They burn it. That's what some of us had to do," Sommers lamented. "You have to take the stuff out of the houses and mix it with diesel fuel. Then you light it and have to keep mixing until it burns up."

After that we all made double sure not to get caught.

While at the Ninetieth Replacement Center we got our first close look at the Vietnamese people. I soon realized how small in stature they were. On average they seemed less than five feet tall. The Vietnamese were hired to perform various duties inside military installations. However, at night they were required to leave.

Wilcox, a GI from Ft. Polk, muttered, "I don't trust all these Vietnamese roaming all over the place. Who knows what they could do." Kastern and I agreed with him.

We spent about two nights at the Ninetieth Replacement Center. On the second night several of us went to an enlisted men's club. I arrived back at my bunk late that night and drifted off into a good sleep. Sometime past midnight I woke up to boisterous voices and excitement. Incoming rounds were exploding in the distance and were coming closer. When the sound got very close, we all took cover under our bunks.

A sergeant stationed there came around and scolded us, "Get up, get up, the rounds are too far away." It was easy for him to say, but we were new.

Before long we had completed the initial in-country processing and were now ready to head to our assigned units. On the last morning at the Ninetieth Replacement Center each man reported to someone from his assigned unit. Most of the major units had personnel there to pick up their new replacements. Some units there were the 1st Cavalry Division, the 1st Infantry Division, the 9th Infantry Division, the 25th Infantry Division, and the 199th Light Infantry Brigade. Those like myself who were assigned to the 22nd AG had to go farther north to Chu Lai.

We were to fly to Chu Lai that day, so we waited at the Bien Hoa airport. Our flight was delayed several times before we walked out to a waiting C-130 aircraft. I assumed that we would board the aircraft in an orderly manner. That didn't happen. We poured into the large open area in the back of the plane as a large mob. Some managed to find a seat on the side of the plane. The majority put their duffel bags down in the center and used them as seats. There were well over a hundred men. Most of them were enlisted men, along with a few officers. We were all new in-country as we sat wearing our brand new jungle fatigues.

2. Chu Lai

WE FLEW NORTH. A few minutes into the flight we all settled down, using our duffel bags as backrests. I tried to imagine what it might be like where we were headed. The conversations were short. Mostly it was quiet, and I dozed off. An hour or so later I was awakened by a change in the sound of the airplane engines as we descended. We grabbed onto anything we could, because a landing by a C-130 wasn't smooth by any stretch of the imagination. We bounced all over the place, hanging on for dear life.

When we landed the hot sun was well above us, blazing down on the sprawling Chu Lai base. Upon disembarking I protected my eyes with my hands. The bright glare took some time to get used to. When my eyes became accustomed to it I looked around. Chu Lai was located in a large, flat area between the mountains to the west and an ocean to the east.

From the airport we rode on trucks to a large replacement center next to the ocean. Someone asked, "Do you know what that ocean is?"

"I'm not too sure but I think it's the Indian Ocean," I answered.

Ulenkott, within hearing distance, turned and said, "I believe it's the South China Sea." Others agreed.

The place turned out to be the Twenty-second AG Replacement Center, and it appeared to still be under construction. We stood next to large tents in a row. The site, being close to the ocean, had sand everywhere. Beyond the row of tents and farther away from the beach and among large sand dunes were more permanent buildings. Most of them had sandbags around them.

We hauled our duffel bags next to the tents and set them in the sand. The tents housed the new replacements who were constantly coming and going. A sergeant came around and said, "Grab a cot in one of the tents as they become available. For now just leave your bags and follow me."

We followed the sergeant to an area where there were small sand dunes. Out in the open was a large sign that had a blue patch with four white stars. Across the opening were larger sand dunes with some sort of trees among them. Shortly after that an officer came around and stood next to the sign, looked at us, and said, "First of all, you guys are probably wondering what this patch represents. It's for the Americal Division and will be your outfit from now on. I would assume most of you aren't aware of it. It was reactivated about three months ago. Anyway I want to welcome you to the Americal Division.

"I'll give you a brief history of the division. It formed during World War II on the Island of New Caledonia. It is the United States Army's only named division. The name comes from American and New Caledonia. The division has a proud history. It was the first army division to take on the offensive against the Japs in the Pacific. And did so at Guadalcanal. It also served at Bougainville, Leyte, the Solomon Islands, and the Philippines during World War II. It was in the Korean War. It is now part of the Vietnam War. It is the army's most decorated outfit.

"The division presently has three main elements. They are the 196th Light Infantry Brigade, the 198th Light Infantry Brigade, and the 11th Light Infantry Brigade. The brigades are supported by the 1st of the 1st Cavalry, an armored outfit, and various aviation groups. There are also various other support groups. Chu Lai is the home base of the division." The officer went on to explain what we would be doing for the next few days and told us to wait for further instructions later in the day.

We finally knew what division we would be with, but we still had to be assigned to one of the brigades. I was familiar with the 196th from training at Ft. Polk. The 198th and 11th had recently arrived in-country. I wasn't familiar with them.

After the welcome speech we were given some free time to find a cot in a tent. By this time many individuals had completed the in-country processing and left for their units. We quickly claimed their empty cots. Unfortunately, when we left our bags in the sand, there had been a brief shower. We hauled our dampened bags to our tents, which would be our temporary housing for the next few days.

The Chu Lai base was one of the larger bases in South Vietnam. The large air base could deploy all types of aircraft to support the men in the field. The base had a large division hospital. Medical evacuation (Medivac) helicopters could be deployed to all parts of the division Area of Operation (AO) to bring in wounded GIs within an hour. Other organizations on the base were the United Service Organization (USO), Sea Bees, U.S. Marine units, Post Exchanges (PXs), and other military units affiliated with the Americal Division.

All the major units mentioned had a sector around the perimeter that they had to secure. A perimeter is the distance around your unit, no matter how large. The Chu Lai perimeter was several miles long, from the ocean to the mountains and back. The size of the base with all its vital functions made it a major target for enemy attacks, usually by rockets.

That afternoon we again waited in the sand for further instructions. During this time a scrawny GI who resembled Barney Fife from TV's *Andy Griffith Show* came over to a buddy he recognized and said, "You just get here? Me, I'm getting out of this place. I'm headed further north. This joint is for the birds."

"What's up north?" his friend asked.

"I don't know," the scrawny GI replied, "but anything is better than this place."

Some within hearing distance had no choice but to listen as the guy went on, "The VC [Vietcong] know all about this place and exactly how many GIs are here. They also know that there is a bunch of GIs without weapons."

"Hey you, shut up," someone sitting nearby interrupted. "We don't want to hear any more of your nonsense."

Mr. Know It All looked down at him and said nothing. He got the message, told his buddy, "I'm outta here," and left.

Someone from the replacement center came over and told us what to expect for the next few days. As he talked, we began to realize that the information given us was word for word what Mr. Know It All told his buddy earlier. When he got to "the VC know that there are lots of GIs without weapons," the guys looked around for Mr. Know It All. However, he had already beat a hasty retreat.

For the next few days we put up with the classic military adage of "hurry up and wait." Our day started very early and ended late. We waited in long lines to take care of personal effects. This included what to do with our monthly pay. I felt there was no place to spend money, so I just requested twenty dollars a month. The rest was to go to a bank back home.

With each passing day I became more familiar with my surroundings. You realized the place was as secure as you would find. The living conditions weren't modern, but you had hot meals and a roof over your head. The permanent buildings were constructed to keep out the tropical rain, with sandbag walls around them. This provided some security from incoming rounds. Bunkers were located in strategic places to provide security. They had thick walls of sandbags on top and at the sides.

The food at the center was as good as could be expected. It was served three times a day and was canned, dried, or instant. The water was seawater that was purified to make it potable. It was tasteless.

Overhead, various types of helicopters were constantly coming and going. I was fascinated by the largest one, named Chinook, with its large rotary blade on each end. The double blades would twirl as the machine glided across the sky.

Helicopters were more commonly called choppers. They were the workhorses of the Vietnam War. There were various types, ranging from the Chinook to the small reconnaissance chopper called Cayuse. The most common type was the Huey. It resupplied the men out in the field, evacuated the wounded, airlifted men for combat assaults, provided firepower during combat operations, flew reconnaissance missions, or transported materials and supplies.

During our stay at the replacement center KP duty and burning human waste had to be done. You had to be very careful not to be chosen for these duties. Every morning we all got in a long line to police the area for litter. However, only the larger pieces of litter were picked up. You used your jungle boots to cover the cigarette butts with sand.

Another one of our responsibilities was filling sandbags, a necessity that could save someone's life. Once when doing so, I worked close to Martinez, a Puerto Rican, and his fellow countrymen. They were busy working and talking in their own language. Someone asked Martinez if his Spanish was the same as that spoken in the states. Martinez replied, "Hell, I don't even know what the guys from Texas are talking about." To me it sounded the same.

Sweating in the hot sun, filling sandbags, caused tempers to flare. Martinez got on one guy's case. This individual was not helping with filling sandbags and was just looking at us. Finally, Martinez said, "Hey guy, you better get with it" and threw him an entrenching tool. Very reluctantly the guy started filling a sandbag, so Martinez and the rest of us sat for a brief break.

A moment or two later a sergeant came over. Observing the guy working and the rest of us sitting, the sergeant said to us, "You guys get off your butts and get to work." He turned to the guy working and said to him, "You can take off. You seem to be the only guy working."

Despite all the waiting in line we still managed to find some free time to write home or check out parts of the base. During some free time Wilcox and I checked out the division PX. It was located on the northeast part of the perimeter, about a mile north of the replacement center. A PX is the military equivalent of a store. It can be large or small depending on the need.

The division PX had to serve the Americal Division and so was very large. It appeared to have a little of everything. The chips were in sealed canisters to protect them from the humidity. Wilcox saw a camera that he liked and purchased it. I thought of buying one but decided against it.

We still had a lot to learn about the humid weather and how to protect everything of value from the dampness. The humid condition along with the salt air was very corrosive to metallic objects, including watches, pocket knives, cigarette lighters, pens, and so forth. Wilcox quickly learned to protect his new camera from the damp air.

About halfway between the PX and the replacement center was the Sea Bees. Farther toward the ocean was the USO. There was a large beach area between the replacement center and the USO.

Some of us had never seen the ocean before. Wilcox and I headed for the beach at our first opportunity. We stood on the sand, fascinated by the waves coming and going. Large military trucks were traveling next to the incoming waves without sinking.

When I strolled farther down the beach, Wilcox yelled, "TeCube, come over here and check this out. Look! When you press down on the wet sand with your boot nothing happens. If you press down and twist your foot the sand gets soft enough so your foot sinks in."

When looking at the incoming waves, you could become hypnotized. You could momentarily forget where you were and think of the more pleasant surroundings of home. However, reality would quickly return. You could look out past the incoming waves beyond the horizon and realize that somewhere halfway around the world was home. My tour of duty was just beginning, and a year was already becoming an eternity. The dominant thought in my mind was to make it home alive and in one piece.

The incoming processing at the Twenty-second AG Replacement Center soon ended. During this time my MOS changed from 11H10 (antitank) to 11B10 (infantry). I had a strong feeling that this would happen. Common sense told you that tanks were hardly used by the enemy. This meant that I would be spending a few more days at the replacement center. Infantry personnel had to repeat what they already learned in the states.

Before we started our refresher course an instructor said, "Forget what you learned back in the states. We do things different here." All the instructors were infantry personnel who had already spent time out in the boonies. The key instruction was to pay attention. You would have a better chance of coming out of the field alive.

The instructors gave us a good idea of the nature of the war and where the VC and North Vietnamese Army (NVA) were operating. While in training at Ft. Polk we thought the war was conventional in nature, which meant the enemy was on one side of a line and you on the other. We quickly learned this was not the case. Stressed to us was the fact that the only territory that we controlled was where we stood. The enemy controlled all the rest. Our task would be to locate the enemy and eliminate him. This would be our main objective for the rest of the time we were out in the boonies. The instructors reminded us that the enemy was not only the VC or NVA but could also be the people themselves, including women, children, and elderly men.

Our in-country training repeated some instruction we had already had. An instructor said, "I know that you already had training in setting up a claymore, but I'll show you again. I also know that one of you clowns will set up the mine in the reverse." When he was through he selected some GIs to demonstrate what he had just taught.

One was Voss from our platoon at Ft. Polk. Voss apparently paid very little attention to the instructor. We watched as he went through the motions of setting up the mine. At the end he lay on the ground and set up the mine pointing toward himself. When he was ready to blow himself up, we looked at him with embarrassment. Others around us were more amused and began laughing.

On one training session we went to the west end of the perimeter, close to the mountains. When we took a break, I overheard some GIs talking. "I wonder what it is really like out there," one guy said. "I know one thing for sure. We will all end up killing a VC or two," another replied.

A lone GI quietly listened to the conversation as he sat on a large boulder. Someone asked him, "What about you, soldier? What would you do if the time comes to shoot a VC?"

The GI just looked at them and said softly, "Me, I don't want to kill anyone."

I would become close to that young man in the year to come. His name was Ladd, and he exemplified the average GI in the Vietnam War. He had been drafted. He was white and about nineteen years of age. He was of medium stature, and you could tell that he had had a proper upbringing. Upon seeing him for the first time you got the impression that he might not be reliable in a firefight. Volunteering for a dangerous mission seemed out of the question for him.

Individuals such as Ladd, however, would eventually become the ones we relied on when the chips were down. They had the discipline needed to carry out orders. The more aggressive types carried a heavier burden, but they needed the support of steady soldiers such as Ladd. Ladd was from Michigan, and I often referred to him as "the lad [Ladd] from Michigan."

Toward the end of our in-country training several military trucks arrived where we were trained. The military personnel in them were from the different battalions of the Eleventh Brigade. By now I knew that I would be with the Eleventh Brigade and with the Fourth of the Third Infantry Battalion. I was the only one from my platoon at Ft. Polk assigned to this battalion. Most of the guys were assigned to the Eleventh Brigade and to the other two battalions, the Third of the First Infantry and the First of the Twentieth Infantry.

When the trucks stopped we were taking a break, sitting in the hot sand. A GI got out of one vehicle and looked our way. Another joined him from the passenger side. He looked our way and shouted, "All you guys with the Fourth of the Third come over here." Several of us walked over and were each issued a brand new M-16 rifle.

"Remember to carry the M-16 with you at all times, even to use the latrine," the driver said. "Get in the habit. It could save your lives. Your training will end in a couple of days. We'll pick you up then."

"What about the ammo?" someone answered. "You guys forgot to give us some ammunition?"

"That comes later, when the time comes for you to go out in the field," the driver replied. "Just don't rush it. The time will come soon enough."

The M-16 rifle was a lightweight weapon especially designed for close jungle warfare. It could fire about 150 rounds per minute. When I had the brand-new weapon in my possession I felt more secure, despite having no ammunition.

During most nights I saw tracer rounds going into the air not too far from the perimeter. This spectacular display meant that I was a lot closer to the war than I had realized. Watching the red rounds hit the ground and streak into the air made me wonder what it was like out there.

A tracer round is a bullet with a tip designed to glow red when fired. This enabled the person using the weapon to see where his rounds were going. A person could use tracer rounds in his M-16 if he wished, but they were mostly used by the machine gunner. The machine gunner carried an M-60 machine gun and usually relied on the tracer rounds to pinpoint his target. At times he fired from the hip and adjusted his fire using the tracer rounds. Unfortunately, using tracer rounds could backfire, because the enemy could pinpoint your position.

On the last night of training we had to go on a night patrol to where the tracer rounds were going off. "We'll go out of the perimeter tonight to apply some of what we tried to teach you," our instructor said. "We'll be making a patrol. If you make it back alive you graduate."

Just as quickly as it began our in-country training ended. We had been in-country for about ten days by this time. When the time came, the men who had issued us our rifles picked us up. About eight of us went by truck to the battalion sector, which was close to the mountains. We were very close to going out in the field.

3. Landing Zone Uptight

FROM THE REPLACEMENT CENTER we went by truck to the Fourth of the Third Battalion sector. It was close to the mountains on the southwest side of the perimeter. Here we learned that we would be joining our company later in the day. Our company, B Fourth of the Third, was somewhere south of Chu Lai. Before doing that we received the necessities for going out in the field. These we loaded along with personal belongings into a rucksack. We also left our duffel bags, extra jungle fatigues, and any personal belongings we couldn't carry.

While waiting for a chopper, we filled our rifle magazines with ammunition. We were all eagerly loading our magazines when a sergeant came over and said, "I suggest that you put only eighteen rounds into each magazine. If you load twenty, it could very likely jam on you. For now I suggest you load at least twenty-five magazines. Later on take as much as you can handle. You might feel you're loaded down. Wait until you get in a firefight. Then you'll never have too much." We all took the sergeant's advice and loaded twenty-five magazines.

We hauled our loaded rucksacks and weapons to a chopper pad. While we waited in the available shade, I felt apprehension from the group. The time to go out in the field was rapidly approaching. We were a green bunch with our new jungle fatigues, new gear, and new camouflage helmet covers. We felt every bit as green as the color radiating from us.

I already knew a few individuals by sight but not yet by name. One was Ladd. Another was Espinosa, who was more vocal than the others. Others who would be in my platoon were Karaba, Brown, Winston, and

Geary. Our group was a broad racial and ethnic mix. Karaba, Ladd, and Geary were white. Winston and Brown were black. Espinosa was Hispanic. Everyone had his own idea of what it would be like out there.

The chopper taking us to our company arrived in the late afternoon, stirring up large cloud of dust while landing. Once aboard, we sat looking out the open sides. We all double-checked our gear and weapons. We were ready to go.

When ready, the two chopper pilots and door gunners communicated above the noise with headsets. The chopper hovered and lifted up in a rocking motion, slowly gaining altitude and then heading south, past the Chu Lai perimeter. The chopper flew low over a countryside dotted with hundreds of rice paddies, clusters of trees and vegetation, and a village here and there. The people below were working in rice paddies or walking along large trails. Some stopped what they were doing and looked up at us. The terrain was flat with an occasional large hill. After a few more minutes we passed a large river. The South China Sea was off to our left and plainly visible.

As we continued flying south the replacements silently eyed the terrain below. We kept quiet for the duration of the trip. Whatever was below would alter our lives forever. After about twenty minutes we approached a small outpost situated on a large hill. It seemed to be in the middle of nowhere. From the air the outpost appeared to be well secured.

"Hey, this place looks very secure," someone remarked. "I wouldn't mind spending all my time here. I have no intentions of going out into all the stuff we just flew over."

I kept quiet and knew that it was wishful thinking. The place we had just flown over was where we would be spending more of our time.

We landed inside the perimeter on a landing pad at the high point. When we got off we assembled off to the side. The chopper was swiftly unloaded and then flew back toward Chu Lai.

An older-looking sergeant met us at the landing pad and said, "I'm First Sergeant Dahner. I want to welcome you to Bravo Company. Before I turn you over to your platoons I have to get some information out of you."

We soon learned that Sergeant Dahner was nicknamed "Top." Top wore a Third Infantry Division patch on his right shoulder, meaning he had seen combat with the outfit. Harlow told me Top also served in World War II and the Korean War. Top was about twenty-five years older than the rest of us, but he could hump with the younger men. He had good rapport with the men in the company. Eventually Top would receive his third Combat Infantryman's Badge (CIB). This made him one of a handful of soldiers in this category.

After that a captain came over. The first sergeant said, "I want you guys to meet our company commander (CO), Captain Michles."

"Welcome to the company," the captain said. "I suggest that you pay close attention to your platoon and squad leaders. Learn as quickly as possible. First sergeant, get these guys taken care of. We have a busy day ahead of us tomorrow."

Captain Michles had arrived with the Eleventh Brigade from Hawaii. To me he seemed a very capable leader with a no-nonsense approach. At times he became very aggressive and gung ho. For this reason, the guys came to call him "Mad Dog."

After a brief orientation we all went to the Third Platoon. We followed a sergeant down an incline to the south sector of the perimeter. The guys in the third platoon were aware that replacements might be arriving. They looked from bunkers before some guys started making their way toward us. When we arrived at the command bunker we met our platoon leader, Lieutenant Carter.

Lieutenant Carter reiterated what the first sergeant and captain had told us. He introduced the two squad leaders, who were Sergeants Jordan and McCloud. The platoon sergeant was Sergeant Williams.

Sergeant Williams was black and very tall and big boned. He had a bad rapport with the platoon and was considered a "lifer" by all. He often would make a big issue of a trivial matter. I never developed any positive relationship with him and just let him be.

"Why are there only two squads instead of the four in a normal platoon?" someone asked.

"We found out that we have better control of a situation having just two squads," Jordan answered. "It's just something that we feel comfortable with." After that Sergeant Jordan assigned us to a squad.

Our new company had three line platoons and one weapons platoon. The line platoons conducted search and destroy operations and ambushes. The weapons platoon provided mortar support.

The platoons had a platoon leader, a platoon sergeant, two squad leaders, and team leaders. The squads broke down into fire teams, and each had an M-60 machine gunner with an assistant. Each fire team also had an M-79 grenadier and several riflemen. All members of the fire team carried at least one hundred rounds of machine gun ammunition, a claymore mine, and trip flares. A machete, entrenching tool, and light antitank weapon (LAW) were divided among the teams.

When we joined the platoon, we joined the group that we would spend the year with. The platoon was the unit where you became close to a group of guys. The bond developed had to be strong to ensure your chances of survival out in the field. In direct contrast to some recent movies about the Vietnam War, the guys were very supportive and helped us to settle into the platoon. Some checked out our field gear to ensure that we had everything we needed. This was a commonsense approach and stood to reason. To have a strong unit every soldier was important.

The guys we joined were fairly new in-country themselves. They had arrived on a ship from Hawaii about six weeks earlier. Military personnel from the Fourth Infantry Division and the Australian Army gave them on-the-job training after they arrived.

When I joined the company, the personnel knew how to conduct a military campaign, although they were still learning. Their situation compared to the first military units that arrived several years earlier. They had to start from scratch. The military campaign was mainly against the local VC. The company's AO was considered a VC stronghold, with many VC sympathizers.

Sergeant Jordan, my squad leader, assigned me to Sergeant Hadaway's team. Hadaway, who was team leader during the initial part of my time with the platoon, was white, from Iowa, and prematurely balding. He would turn out to be one of the most capable leaders our platoon had. He seemed to have a natural knack for leadership. I always felt secure when he was in charge. He was his own man and got carried away at times in dealing with the enemy or villagers. For his antics, the platoon nicknamed him "Animal."

After we settled in, members of the platoon came over to check us out. When I joined the platoon it consisted mostly of white GIs, followed by blacks and Hispanics. I was the only American Indian. Someone asked, "What race are you? You look like an Indian."

"That's right," I replied. "I'm Jicarilla Apache from the state of New Mexico."

A tall, lanky white GI sitting nearby said, "Is that right. My name's Guthrie, and I'm from Alamogordo, New Mexico. I'm familiar with the Mescalero Apaches."

"I've been to Alamogordo a number of times," I said, "and I have some Mescalero friends."

"Are you a descendent of the Apache chief Geronimo?" someone asked.

I smiled. "No. I believe Geronimo was a Chiricahua Apache, and he was not a hereditary chief."

As the men continued to discuss chiefs, Hadaway spoke up. He said, "In that case we'll call you 'Chief.'"

I said simply, "In my traditional way the title of chief is earned and shown respect."

Most of the guys would call me Chief from then on, although a handful of individuals called me by my real name. Up until that moment throughout my training no one even suggested calling me Chief. I wondered why that was so. Perhaps because as trainees we were used to being treated as animals and were addressed by our last names. Now here in Vietnam everyone had an identity.

I met most of the guys that afternoon, but it took some time to get to know them well. Guthrie took a special interest in me and offered me a can of beer. I opened the warm can of beer and took a sip. I wondered if I would ever get used to drinking it warm.

Sergeant Jordan came over again. "By the way, we get two cans of soda or beer as a daily ration," he said. "The resupply chopper brings them in wherever we might be. If you new guys want sodas or beer it'll cost you ten dollars a month. If you guys need anything on the resupply chopper let me know. We'll get you resupplied as soon as possible."

Some individuals that I remember talking with that first day were Guthrie, Jordan, McCloud, Hadaway, Harlow, Willingham, Espinosa, Ladd, Karaba, and Whitaker. We sat on a bunker and looked out over a commanding view.

We were situated on Landing Zone (LZ) Uptight, a small artillery outpost. It was on top of a small knoll that protruded out of the east end of a large hill covered with tall grass. A steep incline angled down on the north, east, and south sides of the knoll. The west end had a dip before it extended onto the large hill. This was the area where an attack would be most likely to occur. The perimeter was slightly larger than a track field and elongated in shape. There were bunkers all around the perimeter joined by a narrow trench. The bunkers had heavy wooden frames that supported several layers of sandbags on top and at the sides. I understood that the bunkers could withstand a direct mortar round. For rockets and rocket-propelled grenades (RPG) it was something else. The area past the perimeter on the north, east, and south sides was heavily mined. The perimeter had several strands of concertina wire around it. Concertina wire, like the musical instrument, is stretched apart to use. It is a coil of wire about four feet in diameter with razor-sharp points. The wire is a deterrent for the enemy seeking to gain an easy access into military installations. One coil of wire could be stretched for several yards.

Our infantry company provided security for Fire Support Base (FSB) Uptight, which is another term used instead of LZ. The Sixth of the Eleventh Artillery provided fire support for infantry units with its 105 howitzers. Our company provided security for LZ Uptight when we joined them. The average stay at places such as LZ Uptight was about two days. This gave the troops out in the field a brief rest. However, the company providing security still sent out day patrols and night ambushes. The 11th Brigade was the most recent unit to occupy LZ Uptight. It followed a long succession of units that occupied the place. These units included the U.S. Marines, the 1st Cavalry Division, the 101st Airborne Division, the Republic of Korea (ROK) Marines, and so on. The unit before the 11th Brigade was the 4th Infantry Division. It moved to Pleiku in the Central Highlands after the 11th Brigade arrived.

The terrain below to the south and east was dominated by rice paddies. Here and there were clusters of trees and vegetation. To the southwest were more hills, and far beyond that were hazy blue mountains. The hill we were on was mostly tall grass that extended farther west and north. Several large trails crisscrossed the terrain below. Smaller trails branched out from them. A large river in the distance met the South China Sea to the southeast. Farther on, past the river, the terrain disappeared into a hazy horizon. The villagers and animals among the rice paddies and on the trails appeared as tiny specks.

Gazing at the scenery, I asked, "I wonder how many villages are below? From up here there seems very little."

"From here it appears that there is nothing down there," Harlow answered. "The villages are where all the vegetation is. There must be hundreds of villages down there."

"The local villagers are still influenced by the French occupation era," Whitaker added. "The French ruins are still intact in many places."

Before it got dark I had a chance to write a letter to my brother back home. He had already completed a tour of duty in Nam and had been stationed in the Qui Nhon area. I asked him to send me a camera, a definite necessity. I reassured him that so far I was doing fine. I would get my first real taste of the field in the morning.

Sergeant Jordan set up a guard schedule. He told us to get used to pulling guard every night and getting by with a lot less sleep. There would be times when we might even have to stay awake all night. I was to follow Hadaway, who was the first one on guard duty.

When everyone turned in for the night I stayed awake thinking of some close friends and relatives. I wondered what they were doing. It was the latter part of January, and I had been in-country for almost two weeks. Now I was on the eve of my first day out in the boonies. Tomorrow I would leave the safety of the perimeter wire and head into Charlie's domain.

Before long Hadaway came into my bunker and said, "Chief, are you awake? It's time for your guard." I was still awake when Hadaway handed me a watch. I already had a watch, but we all shared one on guard duty.

"Although the place looks secure, don't take anything for granted," Hadaway warned. "Keep alert. Get into the proper routine."

I then grabbed my m-16, took several bandoleers of ammunition, and left the bunker. Outside, Hadaway stood by me as we looked out into the darkness below. While we did, Sergeant Williams came around checking the guards. He and Hadaway talked for a few minutes as I listened.

The three of us looked out at the specks of light engulfed by the darkness. While we did the artillery personnel sent out a round. A few seconds later a flare round lit up the area directly south. After a few minutes, more flare rounds went off, illuminating the area even more. We anxiously waited for something to happen. Nothing did.

"A platoon has an ambush somewhere out there. Maybe they might make contact," Sergeant Williams said.

"It seems like the illumination is getting hung up in some clouds," Hadaway answered.

"Yeah. It won't do much good if the platoon does make contact, the way they are losing the illumination."

"That's the same area we will be going to tomorrow. Did you hear anything from the co?"

"Nothing definite. Only that he knows Charlie is definitely down there and will continue fighting his guerrilla type of warfare. No one has to remind you to watch out for mines and booby traps. Charlie's hard to trap. He's a crafty little devil."

"If you go further north, you go into nva territory," Hadaway said.

Williams nodded. "Up there the fighting is a half-ass conventional warfare. I heard someone mention the nva used tanks in one battle. Anything is possible. Then again all the fighting is mostly a guerrilla type."

I listened as the artillery sent off more rounds, but not flare rounds, below. Soon the intensity of the rounds escalated. Hadaway observed, "That's a fire mission. Someone must be getting it bad somewhere."

The artillery continued sending rounds off and on for the rest of the night. Nothing different happened during my watch. When it ended I drifted off to sleep thinking about what might happen in the morning.

All too soon we were up and getting ready in the early morning light. As I cleaned up I looked down to the south. The place was still swimming in a sea of haze.

I ate a breakfast of C rations, my main diet for the rest of my tour of duty. Although there were a variety of C ration meals available, I would eventually grow tired of each one.

We started getting ready for our day operation. The area we had to go to was directly south and about two klicks (two kilometers) away from LZ Uptight. We would be returning the same day. All we had to take was our web gear. I filled two plastic canteens with water, thinking this might be enough. The day had barely begun, with the sun just above the horizon. It was already hot and humid. I had second thoughts about taking more water canteens but for now decided against it. We all had a first aid pack with us. It contained a large gauze pad about four inches square and two inches thick with a long strap on each side, which stopped the bleeding from large wounds by direct pressure. Everyone carried one with the idea of using it on a large bodily wound. However, in reality most of the wounds received were multiple in nature. When that happened everyone shared first aid packs.

As for hand grenades I just grabbed two. Sergeant Jordan advised, "Bend the pin back on the hand grenade. This is to avoid accidentally pulling it out. I guarantee if the time comes to pull the pin it won't be hard."

Sergeant Hadaway came around and handed each new guy a hundred rounds of M-60 ammunition. "I can't tell you how many M-16 clips to take," he said. "Take as much as you can, even though it's only a day operation. We might get pinned down. Then you might fall short." I tied several bandoleers of ammunition to the web gear and around me.

When we were ready to move I noticed how the leaders seemed to know what to do. They checked out their guys and assured that everyone was ready to go. I thought to myself that I wanted no part of that type of responsibility in the year ahead. I was content to be just a rifleman during my tour of duty.

Circumstances would prove otherwise. Little did I know at the time that in reality leaders get killed, wounded, go to the rear, get sick, or complete their tours of duty. Someone has to take their place.

Sergeant Jordan came around and said, "Hadaway, your squad will be bringing up the rear. Saddle up, we're moving out."

Saddle up meant to put on your gear. It reminded me of putting on a football uniform. You made sure that your equipment was in proper order before you went to do battle on the football field. The only difference was that in football you had referees to make sure you played by the rules. In the present situation, you knew that the rules of the Geneva Convention wasn't going to apply out in this field. You would be fair game once you left the perimeter. With this thought in mind I locked and loaded my M-16. With a mixture of butterflies in my stomach and excitement I was ready to leave the perimeter.

After we joined the platoon it was considered at full strength. Each squad had two M-60 machine gunners with an assistant. The fire teams had several riflemen and a grenadier. I don't recall everyone who was in my squad as we left the perimeter that day. Some that I remember were H. P. on the machine gun; Brooks, his assistant; a grenadier named Wright, nicknamed Topcat; Whitaker, a rifleman; and Hadaway, our team leader.

It was still very early when the point element of the platoon left the perimeter. They were followed by the command group or command post (CP). This group consisted of the platoon leader, platoon sergeant, the radio telephone operators (RTOs), and the medic.

Our fire team brought up the rear. We left on the west end of the perimeter where a saddle connected the knoll to the rest of the hill. We took a path through the concertina wire, following countless GI footsteps.

When we left the perimeter we headed into tall, waist-high grass. There were different trails that led down the hill. I first thought of the possible mines Charlie might have set. All the trails crisscrossed as they headed down in different directions. I was second to the last with Whitaker bringing up the rear. When I reached the edge of the hill the point man was already well down the hill. He slowly headed forward and seemed aware of mines, as he changed directions several times before reaching the bottom.

Heading down the hill Jordan said, "You guys be sure and maintain a distance of fifteen feet between each other. We don't want one mosquito to give you all malaria." This was a joke; he really meant that one mine could inflict multiple casualties.

When we descended we took short standing breaks. At those times, I would take a better look at where we were headed. Upon reaching the bottom the point element was well into abandoned rice paddies. The villagers didn't farm this area because it was directly below LZ Uptight. We followed the rest along a narrow rice paddy dike.

We were soon moving along a large trail that was quite visible from the top of the hill. Although this trail could be considered a main road for the villagers, it couldn't handle large vehicles. I knew of only two roads in Vietnam that were large enough to handle military vehicles. One was Highway One, which ran along the coast. The other was Highway Two, which ran through the Central Highlands. The rest were mostly pedestrian trails linking the large and small villages. Bicycles or scooters could travel the larger trails linking the larger villages. The trail we were on was one such large trail.

We stayed on the trail as it headed west. By this time I had become uneasy and kept expecting something to happen. The hot, humid weather was starting to bother me. I gulped water at every opportunity and soon realized that two canteens weren't going to be enough. The hot weather caused you to drink excessively.

After going another hundred meters we got off the main trail and headed south on another rice paddy dike. The rice paddies were full of water on each side. We continued, keeping a distance from each other and following the point man. Up ahead I noticed figures in the middle of the rice paddies. When we got closer they became more clear. They were clad in black pajamas and white cone-shaped hats. They were exactly what I thought the Vietcong were supposed to look like.

I became more alert. Just then Hadaway murmured, "See those gooks out there. Keep an eye on them. You can't trust any of them even though they might just be planting rice." I also instinctively looked to my right, left, and rear and gripped my rifle tighter.

About a dozen villagers were bending up and down doing something. Every now and then one of them would look up and check us out. They weren't too far away as we slowly went past them. From there we headed more to the southwest. After passing them I still kept an eye on them. I fully expected them to try something.

We continued to the southwest on the rice paddy dikes. Most of these dikes were about a foot wide, which left very little room to maneuver and required a balancing act. We found that some dikes were very shallow and narrow, while others were wide and deep. The main trails often served as rice paddy dikes. During this early part of my tour of duty most of the rice paddies had water in them. This was the time when the villagers spent much time planting or transplanting the rice plants.

When we passed the people in the rice paddies, the point element entered a grove of palm trees and dense vegetation. Soon we entered the grove of trees, but we headed out just as quickly. After the trees was a small stretch of rice paddies that headed directly into a village. The village was nestled in palm trees and dense vegetation and seemed large. I was sure Charlie would now make his presence known.

Just before the point element entered the village little kids of all sizes came swarming out to greet us. The kids were saying, "GIs number one," or whatever English they could muster up. They blocked the trail trying to get the GIs' attention any way they could.

"Pay no attention to the kids. Just hurry on into the village," Lieutenant Carter yelled. He obviously knew more than we did.

We continued after the point element. Just as the rear element entered the village shooting erupted from the front. The rear element found cover next to a stone wall about four feet in height. I had my rifle pointed to the rear as did Whitaker. We were ready to fire.

Meanwhile, the shooting continued with machine gun and rifle fire. A chopper appeared out of nowhere and flew in circles above us. Every now and then it would shoot a volley of fire. The chopper, I found out later, was called Warlord. It resembled a large glass bubble.

The shooting died down to sporadic fire, and we maintained a sharp lookout to the rear. I looked at Whitaker next to me. He must have noticed my uncertain look. He motioned with his hands not to worry. After another half an hour the shooting stopped.

"It looks like there was a skirmish up ahead," Whitaker said. "We'll just have to wait and see. Were you scared?"

"I'd be lying if I said no," I admitted. "I really expected something from the rear. The fighting seems to have quieted down."

"You get used to it to a certain extent," he reassured me. "Just keep alert. All that shooting wasn't for nothing."

Whitaker was a tall, lanky black man from Detroit and was proud of being from Motown. He had a way about him that made you take a liking to him. He often mentioned that he wanted out of the army. However, his actions told you differently. I thought Whitaker would have been an excellent career soldier. The army needed men like that.

Coincidentally, when the shooting ended we were also at our destination. Our orders were to check out several villages. We also set up a blocking force on the west end of the village. Lieutenant Carter told us to set up in twos behind the hedgerow. If we saw a gook running, we were to shoot first and ask questions later.

Willingham and I set up a position where we could see through the hedgerow and also to our right and left. At first we expected Charlie to come running, so we kept a sharp lookout. However, after an hour it appeared that Charlie had all but disappeared. I then took time to look closely at my immediate surroundings. The bamboo stand that concealed us was full of thorns. After about an hour or two we broke up the blocking force.

Sergeant Jordan came over and told Hadaway, "We'll spend the rest of the day here. Have your guys check out the place thoroughly. Don't let the guys wander off by themselves or bunch up."

When we began checking out the village it came back to life. The villagers came out from whatever hiding places they had disappeared into. Soon we had little kids surrounding us again. Some guys were talking to them and didn't bother checking out the area. I figured that it wasn't a bad idea to get in good with the villagers. Their full cooperation could make life easier.

I was interested in how the villagers lived. All the villages appeared identical. They had at least one well, usually in the center of the village. A cemetery might be at the edge of a village, where large and small mounds of earth were the grave sites. In addition, all the villages had tunnel complexes and small gardens.

Their dwellings (hootches) were made of a bamboo frame covered with straw mats for walls. Bare earth was the floor. The roofs were made of straw (thatched). The interiors were very simply furnished with a bed here and a table there. The furnishings too were made out of bamboo and straw. At corners of the dwellings were places to build a fire and cook. The dwellings were raised about two feet above the ground. In the center of the dwellings holes were dug deep into the ground to serve as bomb shelters or escape routes.

Their standard of living could be considered on the primitive side. Most of the work required manual labor. Water buffaloes or other cattle performed harder tasks. Their whole livelihood appeared to revolve around growing rice, farming, or fishing. Besides cattle and water buffaloes other domestic animals were dogs, chickens, ducks, and pigs.

Other common food included rice, coconuts, bananas, breadfruit, and others. The bananas were smaller and more round than those we were familiar with. They grew in bunches at the top of the trees. The banana trees had very large leaves, the size of a man, and were very soft; they could be felled with one whack of a machete. The breadfruit had a rough outer edge and was white on the inside.

I was especially intrigued by the coconuts. When I first observed them clustered high above in the coconut trees, I wondered how the villagers got them down. They were about fifty feet above the ground. One day Wilson and I asked a young boy to climb up a coconut tree for us. He agreed to in exchange for a can of C rations. Then he scrambled up the tree in his bare feet, using the rough rings around the trunk as steps. When he reached the top he twisted coconuts loose and dropped them to the ground. The coconut was large, green, and smooth, not like the ones I had seen in grocery stores. The boy descended, asked for a machete, and used it to slice off one end of the coconut. Wilson and I both drank the milk from the hole. It didn't taste too bad. Then the boy cut off the rough outer bark. What remained looked more familiar—about the size of a softball, brown, and hairy. Some GIs later invented a drink we called Jungle Pop, made by pouring a packet of soft-drink mix into a coconut and mixing it with the milk.

The villagers burned a lot of incense, the smell of which was evident when entering their dwellings. A few years earlier I had read about or seen on TV that Vietnam had many Catholics. Here in the villages there was no evidence of that. The dwellings all had a place inside to practice Buddhism.

The time went by quickly. I soon realized that I was running out of water. I said to Willingham, "I'm getting low on water. I don't think it'll last me for the rest of the day."

Willingham directed me to a well inside the village. He reminded me to put iodine tablets in my canteens. The iodine killed the bacteria in the water, but it made the water taste terrible.

Before noon we made our way across a short pathway to another village to the south. Here, Sergeant McCloud motioned with his hands and said, "Chop chop."

We sat against a stone wall and opened up our C rations. Some little kids came over for a handout while we ate. Sitting against the wall, I checked out the kids more closely. I noticed for the first time that they could pass for some kindergarten kids back home. The resemblance was strong. Some kids came over to me, and one said, "You same-same Vietnam." This was the first of many times that expression would be directed at me. For the rest of my tour of duty these people considered me a lot like them.

The kids sat down as some shared C rations with them. The older girls, although still small, cared for their younger brothers and sisters. They carried the young siblings on their hips for long periods of time. One said, "Babysan chop chop," pointing to her baby brother on her hips. I handed her some chocolate candy that was in a C ration can. Both had a big smile as the girl said something in her language, which I interpreted as a thank you.

When I finished eating, Guthrie motioned me over with his hand. "Chief, come over here. I want to show you something."

I followed him across a small clearing and through a hedgerow. When we came to another clearing he pointed to a dozen dead bodies on the ground. "This is what all the shooting was about this morning."

"What is going to become of the bodies?" I asked.

"I don't know," he replied. "Just leave them here. Their mamasans will take care of them."

At that instant I fully realized what war was all about. In the most simple terms it was merely kill or be killed.

For the rest of the day, we continued checking out the area. In late afternoon we headed back to LZ Uptight by a different route. I still felt vulnerable as we left the villages, and so I kept checking out the rear. As we slowly approached LZ Uptight I became more secure.

Soon we were climbing the large hill. I was gulping from the canteens with the iodine tablets. The heat was terrible, and I wondered if I could ever get used to it. To survive the heat you would definitely need plenty of water. The sun was well above the horizon when we arrived safely back into the perimeter.

At our sector we discarded our web gear and took off our sweat-soaked shirts. We had some free time to do whatever we wanted.

I sat in the shade next to a bunker and chatted with Harlow. I said, "I didn't get shot at today. At least I survived my first day out in the field. I hope all the rest will be the same. I ran out of water. Luckily the water seemed okay from the well."

"The water is okay from the wells," Harlow agreed. There may be times when even that won't be available to you."

Harlow, a white soldier, was from Huntington Beach, California. Early on we became good buddies. He was one that I would often talk with about the world. He is also one that I kept in touch with when we returned to the states.

While we sat around and chatted Jordan came around and said, "All you team leaders make sure your guys are ready to move out in the morning. We will have an extended stay out in the field."

I checked all my gear. I made sure that I had everything I would need, including extra canteens. When I was through I set my rucksack off to the side, ready to go. The idea of war was sinking in. I was actually there. This was what I had fantasized about as a kid and had trained for.

There was still some daylight when I opened some C rations. I ate as I looked east toward the South China Sea. The ocean seemed about three klicks away. Harlow, Willingham, and some others came over and we sat looking out toward the ocean.

Willingham spoke up, "I'm from Newnan, Georgia. I came over with the Eleventh Brigade from Hawaii. Here, you can have one of my sodas." When you looked at and talked to him you felt he wasn't the military type.

"Guess what, I got my stripes yesterday when you arrived," Harlow said.

"I know, now you're just a buck sergeant with no time and grade," Willingham joked.

"How have you guys been doing for the past few weeks?" I asked.

"The company just arrived to this area a few days ago," Harlow answered. "Before that we were somewhere closer to the mountains. We don't really know what it's like around here."

"How was it where you were, and how is our CO?" I asked him. "I heard someone call him Mad Dog."

"Let me tell you something about him," Harlow confided. "In our last AO, we were being harassed by a gook sniper when Mad Dog directed an attack to eliminate the sniper. They gave him the Silver Star for that, or rather he gave himself one."

Willingham laughed, "We call it the Battle of Champagne Valley."

When it got dark others came to where we sat and joined in the conversation. Willingham started singing, "People there's a train a coming. You don't need no baggage to get on board. All you need is faith to hear the diesel humming. . . ." Soon we all joined in as best as we could. Another song, sung to the lyrics of "Poison Ivy" went something like this, "Viet Caw aw aw aw ong . . . Viet Caw aw aw aw ong . . . Late at night while you're sleeping. Vietcong comes a creeping all around. . . ." Another song was, "Jingle bells, mortar shells, VC in the grass . . ." Singing would become a regular way for us to escape.

We turned in early knowing that we had a long day ahead of us. Afterward, I lay in my bunker and thought of the day's activities. I was thankful that we had no casualties. But it would be just a matter of time. The local people weren't very cooperative when we interrogated them. They seemed to know a lot more than they were willing to tell. In the villages we had seen only the elderly and the very young. I suspected that the villagers would be like this. In training at Ft. Polk, however, we had been told that the villagers would give us their full cooperation and that there were people of all ages in the villages.

I had made it through my first day out in the field and already knew a lot about surviving out there.

4. Task Force Barker

THE FOLLOWING MORNING, before daybreak, the company prepared to go out in the field. All around men were quickly getting their gear ready. I double-checked my gear from the day before. When ready I struggled to put on my rucksack, which seemed to weigh a ton. I realized that the weight would be an important factor out in the field. We were preparing for a lengthy stay that could last several weeks.

As the sun came up our company left the perimeter on the west end and went north. From there the trail we followed gradually went down the hill. Our platoon brought up the rear. When we descended the hill, the tall grass gave way to hedgerows and rice paddies. We were soon on the north side of the large hill in an area not visible from LZ Uptight.

From there we continued northwest on another main trail. The area had many abandoned hootches scattered here and there. I mistrusted my surroundings as I walked down the trail. It seemed that Charlie was just waiting for the right moment and all hell would break loose. I kept alert and looked around for Charlie's possible hiding places.

My thoughts flashed back to a time I herded sheep with an older Jicarilla Apache man. He was a World War II veteran who had been with the First Cavalry Division in New Guinea. He was very proud of his service to his country. He told me stories of his war experiences knowing I was very interested.

I was now in his shoes. I remembered him telling of possible places where the Japanese concealed themselves. The places he described were very similar to my present environment.

I recalled one day when the veteran and I sat under a tree as the sheep grazed peacefully below. I asked him the important things to know when in the war. He replied, "You have to know where you are at all times. Rely on gut feelings. Sometimes you could get turned around in the jungle. There is no sun and everything looks the same. Sometimes I walked way in front of the platoon. After a while you knew what to expect. When I was in front I might shoot to the top of coconut trees. Sometimes a Jap might come falling down."

I never tired of his stories. On that day, however, the black dog with us must have gotten bored. Soon it was sleeping off to the side. When my companion saw the sleeping dog, he whispered, "Be quiet, let's play a joke on the dog."

With that we quietly crept away from the animal, inching our way up the hill. When we got to the top of the hill, he laughed and said, "That's another thing you have to know. How to be sneaky." He then whistled to the dog, which barked loudly before finding us.

This was my second day in the field. I wasn't totally secure, but it gave me confidence to know that the whole company was out. Our task was to search for and destroy suspected vc hiding places, activities, and so forth, and if possible, to find the enemy.

Sergeant McCloud told us, "Check out the area thoroughly, especially for hidden tunnels. If you see anything suspicious let us know. Don't wander off by yourselves. Keep alert in two-man teams. Charlie is probably close by looking at you. The villagers in this area have ID cards. Check them out."

We entered a village that wasn't as populated as the one we had checked the day before. The rest of the company continued forward to check other villages. Coming upon some elderly men, I inspected their ID cards with their pictures on them. I pointed all around and asked, "You see vc?"

The answer was negative; the men folded their hands in front of them and nodded. When I observed them doing that, I knew getting information from these villagers would be impossible. The area had already been checked out many times by the military units mentioned earlier. The locals had grown leery of strange men, some twice their size.

We spent the better part of the day searching villages in the area. I took more notice of my surroundings. I eyed the coconut trees with great interest. They stood very tall, with coconuts clustered at the top between the large leaves. I wondered how the villagers got them down, as there were no branches to climb. The area also had hedgerows, rice paddies, bamboo stands, and the same types of domestic animals as we had seen before. A well in each village provided some good water.

When I filled my canteens I was already debating whether to continue using iodine tablets. I said to Whitaker, "The water tastes terrible with the iodine tablets. I wonder how it would be to not use them."

Whitaker grimaced. "I'm tempted to do that. But I'm afraid of getting the runs. It's up to you, Chief. If it gives you the runs, don't say I didn't warn you."

I noticed small gardens among the hedgerows. While checking out one with Willingham I inquired, "I wonder what these plants are? They are the size of a small potato. It is red on the outside and white on the inside. It looks like a radish and potato mixed."

Willingham looked at it and shrugged. "I don't know what it is. The gooks seem to use it a lot. They slice them up and put them out to dry on large mats."

When the day came to a close the company set up a defensive position for the night. The perimeter was on a small rise north of a village among the hedgerows. The company commander had the artillery forward observer (FO) call in marking rounds around the perimeter.

A forward observer was an artillery personnel assigned to an infantry unit. He went in the field with the infantry to call in artillery support when needed. Every night he preset the company perimeter by calling in marking rounds. Charlie knew this, and it helped keep him honest. The weapons platoon performed a similar task with their mortars. However, the weapons platoon had the mortar rounds with them out in the field.

When the perimeter was secured we took out our C rations. After the exhausting day any type of meal was good. Sergeant Jordan told us to be sure and dig a foxhole after we ate, because we never knew when Charlie might send in some rounds. Hadaway's fire team would go out on ambush that night.

Later Hadaway gave us instructions: "We'll be going about a klick to the east and set up an ambush on a side trail. Tie down any gear that might make noise. Make sure your weapons are working. You still have some time to clean it. Any questions?"

"What about face paint?" someone asked. "And do we put branches on our helmets?"

"We have some face paint, and there are plenty of branches," Hadaway acknowledged. "It's up to you if you want to use them."

When it was dark we left the perimeter for the ambush site. The RTO advised the perimeter of our leaving. We then walked into the darkness. The feeling of fear of the unknown quickly returned. I thought about the Vietcong coming out of their hiding places just ahead. Realizing that we were only a handful of men headed into Charlie's domain didn't help. I followed Topcat in the darkness with my rifle at the ready. To avoid detection we avoided the main trails. We kept quiet as we walked across several large open rice paddies and eventually reached our ambush site.

Hadaway whispered, "We're here, keep quiet. There's a small trail that meets the larger one up ahead. Set up claymores to cover as much of the trail as you can. Make sure you have them facing the right way. See the tall trees against the sky to the north? If we make contact and get confused, that'll be our rallying point."

Our position was behind some hedgerows overlooking the trail. The place seemed secure, and we hoped Charlie wouldn't detect our position. The claymore detonators were placed next to the positions overlooking the trail.

Hadaway continued, "If you see or suspect anything out there try to notify everyone. If you can't, just detonate the claymores."

With the ambush set I tried to get some sleep on the bare ground. Another problem quickly arose—mosquitoes. This was the time of night when they came out by the millions, so I covered myself with my poncho liner. It was too hot and uncomfortable. I thought of using mosquito repellent to ward off the hungry pests. However, the mosquito repellent could give away our position. Finally, I covered my face with my helmet in such a way as to allow air in and keep the mosquitoes to a minimum.

I went to sleep thinking of my friends and relatives back home. I knew that some were also thinking of me. I was dreaming of a more pleasant surrounding when I vaguely heard, "Chief, wake up. It's time for your guard." I quickly woke up. Topcat handed me the watch and detonators and said softly, "It's quiet. Keep alert and stay awake. I don't want Charlie cutting my throat."

A claymore mine is a command-detonated mine. A detonator controls it from a distance of a hundred feet. The claymore is about six inches by twelve inches with a curved shape. On the outside curve are several hundred small rounds. On the other side is an explosive charge. When detonated, the rounds are shot away from you like a giant shotgun. If used properly the mine could inflict many casualties. You had to be careful to set the mine in the right direction. Sometimes Charlie also switched the mine around on you.

I quickly became accustomed to the darkness and looked directly in front of me. A gentle breeze was blowing from the east, which caused the leaves to rustle. It helped keep the mosquitoes away. In the darkness I could make out the rice paddy dikes and the general area where the trail was. I thought of Charlie and how he might know where we were. If so he wouldn't be foolish enough to use any trail. He would go by another route. All kinds of possibilities crossed my mind.

I soon became aware of another strange phenomenon. To this moment I hadn't paid much attention to the stars above. Growing up I had spent a lot of time outside at night, so I was familiar with the night sky. As I sat there I looked up. The night sky was different here. The Big Dipper to the north was nowhere in sight. To the south, above the horizon, were four stars that resembled a cross.

Right then and there the reality of my situation finally dawned on me. I was sitting halfway around the world from home in a very hostile environment. The enemy out in the darkness had one objective—to kill you anyway he could.

Instantly, the words of the medicine man back home struck me. "You might think you know what happened here tonight. You don't know. You will when the time comes, and you'll know what to do."

There in the rice paddies of Southeast Asia I learned to pray. I had been aware of what prayer was. However, I had never said one sincerely. In our traditional way, as in the Christian way, we pray to a Supreme Being. The only difference is that we refer to the Supreme Being as our grandfather, not our father.

The words just came out. I prayed in my traditional way, saying, "Grandfather, I pray to you this day. You know of my situation and what is happening. It's only because you allow this to happen that it is. Watch over me and all my fellow soldiers here with me. Take care of us this night and the coming year. I pray that everything comes out good for us. I pray that whatever comes out of this place becomes a positive one to guide our lives with. Talk to all our relatives back home worrying about us. Grandfather, I beg of you to listen to my prayer. Thank you."

After that the breeze blew stronger, causing the branches to sway. I believed in my Creator. I didn't allow my mind to play tricks on me. Out in the distance I heard explosions. When my watch ended I quickly went off into a light sleep. I was learning quickly.

Before daybreak we were already on our way back to the company perimeter. When daylight arrived the villages were coming to life. There is that certain pungent smell and feel of the villages that is unique. The smell was a combination of smoke, decaying food and plant matter, stale water, manure from the animal pens, and human waste. A rooster crowed out in the distance. The fires from the villages formed a bluish haze throughout the countryside. The cooler night air was rapidly giving way to the rising sun as we returned safely into the perimeter. We finished a quick meal of C rations

The new day's activities were to be no different. We were to continue the search and destroy operation.

We came upon a place with many open abandoned tunnels. We threw hand grenades into them, yelling, "Fire in the hole!" Some hidden tunnels had to be checked out. Although it wasn't a requirement, most volunteered to be a "tunnel rat" at some time.

I watched with interest as Jordan went into a tunnel. He took off his shirt, grabbed a flashlight and a .45 caliber pistol, and lowered himself into the tunnel. Before he did Lieutenant Carter reminded him to put in earplugs, or his eardrums might rupture if he had to use the pistol.

Jordan disappeared into the tunnel. After some time he reappeared and told Lieutenant Carter he would go back in. When Jordan came out the second time he had a handful of documents with him. Lieutenant Carter and Jordan looked them over. Lieutenant Carter remarked, "If you see Dien Bien Phu on them we're too late." The documents were forwarded to the CO group.

When another tunnel was to be searched Jordan asked, "Chief, do you want to check out the tunnel?"

I hesitated. I was never fond of enclosed places. But my curiosity won over my better judgment. I just had to get the feeling of going into a tunnel.

After being instructed by Jordan, I lowered myself into the small opening and went straight down. About four feet down, the tunnel branched two ways. The tunnel to the right appeared more accessible. I headed in that direction. I had earplugs on, the .45 caliber in my right hand with the flashlight in my left. I put the pistol and light in front of me and started easing myself forward.

I quickly realized that tunnels were for very small persons, rather than my five-feet-eleven frame. The tunnel gradually became a tight squeeze as I moved forward. It appeared to have been out of use for some time. Large spiders were perched on top where roots were coming through. They scampered away in front of me, into the darkness. That alone gave me a creepy feeling and second thoughts about the whole affair.

The passageway continued to get smaller. The tunnel was pitch-black, and I could only see more tunnel fading into the darkness. Another frightening thought struck me, "What if I become wedged inside the tunnel with no way of getting help?" I became more afraid of this possibility than of Charlie waiting up ahead. However, I continued. After what seemed like an eternity I entered a room the size of a small bedroom.

When I was inside the room I could stand by bending down. I flashed around the room. My fatigues were soaking wet. It could have been from the heat or just the anxiety of being inside the tunnel. I checked the room thoroughly for hidden passages and signs of VC activities. Satisfied there were none I headed back out. I was glad when I saw daylight again.

I reported that the tunnel was out of use and empty. Jordan ordered me to throw a grenade inside. We all knew that this action would only deter Charlie temporarily. He'd soon have the tunnel repaired. At least it gave him some extra work.

Twice more I was a tunnel rat, but then I left that task for someone else. I knew that it took a very special person to go into the tunnels.

We had our gear with us always and took breaks to relieve the tremendous stress on our shoulders. The combined weight we had to carry on our backs was about sixty pounds or more. To put up with this and the heat required great stamina.

During the day I also got a feel for how to use the radio and the code system. While resting next to a well, Willingham was watching the radio. I was next to him when a call came for a radio check.

"Radio check, how do you read, over," the caller said.

"Lima Alpha Charlie, Hotel Mike (loud and clear, how me), over," Willingham replied.

"I hear you same."

Harlow explained that there was a periodic radio check among the units, and that the radio code for our company changed every now and then. Our company decided what code it would use to identify itself. Harlow also stressed the importance of brushing up on the army's phonetic alphabet.

That evening the night defensive position was at a different location. The FO called in marking rounds again to secure the perimeter. I was relieved our platoon was not going out on ambush after the exhausting day.

I asked Hadaway, "Do we have to dig a foxhole, or can we take our chances and let it go?"

"You heard the platoon leader," Hadaway said. "We all have to. It's to keep our butts alive," he explained. "I'll tell you something. Charlie is good at walking mortars into your perimeter. When he does that you at least have some warning and get into your foxhole. Sometimes he's good enough to land beau coup [French, for a lot] rounds inside your perimeter. If that happens you might not have a chance to react. It's very important to dig a foxhole every night you're out in the field. Just get in the habit of doing so, even if you're tired." With such advice in mind, I dug a foxhole with the entrenching tool.

For a few days our operation consisted of the same search and destroy routine. One day it changed. During a lunch break Lieutenant Carter said, "Squad leaders, have your guys ready to move out ASAP. The company is moving out shortly. Another unit is in trouble. Be ready for anything."

We were soon moving quickly along a large trail. I felt well protected to the front because the company was ahead of us. I was uneasy about the rear. We kept up a good pace.

We eventually entered a large clearing. Our platoon and part of another were still crossing the clearing when Charlie made his presence known. Automatic rifle fire erupted from our right. The rifles made a sort of cracking sound, accompanied by the sensation of something whizzing by you. We instantly took cover behind the rice paddy dikes.

This is the moment those with combat experience talk about. Baptism by fire. It is the moment we dream about as kids watching war movies. We all insinuate that we will fight when the time comes and leave it at that. However, it is easier said than done. No one knows how he'll react until that decisive moment arrives. Most will return fire, but some will hesitate and keep under cover.

I was lying behind a rice paddy dike. Charlie had the upper hand and sprayed bullets at us. In the next instant I raised my rifle above the dike and fired while lying down, aiming at the general direction of a wood line. I had my rifle in semiautomatic and sent as many rounds as I could. Others did the same. Everything seemed to happen instantly. I quickly went through one magazine and fumbled to put another into my rifle. Within minutes there was a tremendous amount of hot lead headed toward Charlie. He quickly got the message and left the area.

When the shooting subsided I felt a great sense of relief. Not from the idea of shooting to kill, but from being a team player. I knew then that I would do my part in a firefight.

Lieutenant Carter received a call from the CO when we gained control of the situation. "How's everything back there?"

"We received beau coup rounds," Carter reported. "No casualties.

Charlie was shooting from the village to our south. He appears to be gone. I think it was just for harassment. Do we go after him?"

"Go ahead and make a quick sweep of the area," the CO ordered. "We have orders to keep moving to our objective."

With that we advanced toward the wood line with fire teams abreast, ready to fire. Some fired at anything suspicious. The grenadier also fired into suspected areas. We reached the wood line and entered a small village. We quickly moved from hootch to hootch, hurrying because we needed to rejoin the rest of the company as soon as possible. As expected there was no sign of Charlie.

When we got back on the trail the rest of the company was progressing well toward the objective. We followed at a rapid pace, moving northeast. "I wonder what the big rush is," Hayes panted. "The heat and my pack are getting to me."

I took a big gulp of water as we briefly rested in place. I told him, "Maybe Charlie was trying to delay us in getting to our objective. The way we're going we might be playing into his hand. I don't trust the rear. I'll keep a sharp lookout in that direction."

After another klick or two we came upon a chopper shot down by Charlie. The crew had held him off until our company arrived. When our platoon arrived a large perimeter was already in place around the chopper, which had managed to land at the edge of a large clearing next to a wood line.

The CO cautioned, "Charlie is still in the area. He might be waiting with RPGs. A chopper is on the way to take in the crew members. Especially watch out when it arrives."

The rescue chopper came and took the crew without incident. After that we waited for another chopper to take in the downed chopper. Soon a chopper called the "flying crane" came and took the downed chopper back to Chu Lai.

After the excitement we returned to the LZ Uptight area and continued our operation.

Day by day, we steadily headed in a westerly direction. It seemed that we had been out there forever. One evening I asked Harlow and Willingham if they had any idea where we were going.

Both thought we were headed toward another LZ called Dottie. The place was west of LZ Uptight. No one was familiar with it. Harlow thought there might be a Non-Commissioned Officer's (NCO) club there. He let Willingham and I know that he would take advantage of his sergeant stripes if there was one.

The area we operated in became known as the Task Force Barker area. The task force formed in January of 1968 and was named after Colonel Frank Barker. It formed to control the VC in the area around LZ Uptight and LZ Dottie all the way to the South China Sea. The coastal area was the area most infested with VC.

The task force consisted of three infantry companies. They were B 4th Battalion 3rd Infantry (B 4th of the 3rd), C 1st of the 20th, and A 3rd of the 1st. A battery of the 6th of the 11th artillery located on LZ Uptight supported the infantry companies. To the north of the task force was the 198th Light Infantry Brigade. To the south was the Army of the Republic of Vietnam (ARVN).

We had been out in the field over a week. We experienced no major casualties, but we did come under sniper fire now and then. The daily routine of searches, night ambushes, and interrogation of suspected VC continued. It became clear that the villagers wouldn't talk under any circumstances. Talking meant brutal retaliation from the VC, so they chose to put up with GI methods of interrogation.

The hot weather was always a problem, though I was slowly becoming used to it. During this time I quit using iodine tablets and chose to take my chances. I now carried four canteens, which I felt were sufficient.

A chopper resupplied us daily. It located our position by a colored smoke grenade someone threw. A typical conversation with the supply chopper might go, "We see you now coming in from the horizon. Keep heading east. We are about a klick away."

"We are now in the approximate area."

"We are below. You should be able to see our smoke. We'll be using Goofy Grape."

"Okay, we see it. We'll land next to it."

The chopper brought letters from home with our daily rations of sodas and beer. At times some lucky GIs received a letter or two. Sometimes I received a letter, which bolstered my morale tenfold. Our daily ration of sodas and beer were warm. Drinking the warm sodas was okay, but the warm beer took some time to get used to. To make matters worse the choices of beer were Black Label, Pabst Blue Ribbon, and Ballantine Ale, none of the major brands.

One evening Mahr (Uncle Mickey) offered me a can of beer as we settled down next to our rucksacks.

I told him, "I don't mind if I do. Thanks."

He sat back and sighed. "Boy! What I wouldn't give to have a can of Shaeffer's. That's what we drink back in the world."

I took a sip and asked, "Where you from?"

"I'm from upstate New York," he said. "A place called Troy."

Uncle Mickey often received newspapers from Troy, which he would read from cover to cover. He often sang his favorite song, which went something like this:

> Baby now that I found you I can't let you go.
> I'll build my world around you, I need you so.
> Baby even though you don't need me, you don't need me.

Besides our C rations and resupply the chopper sometimes brought a large box for each platoon. The box was a sundry pack that contained cigarettes, cigars, chocolate bars, writing paper, mixed candy, chewing tobacco, chewing gum, toothbrushes, pipe cleaners, and various other items. The items were distributed among the platoons.

The daily routine of "humping," along with the hot weather, definitely took its toll. You had to get as much rest as you could or fatigue would set in. Charlie would take advantage of such moments of vulnerability and inflict serious casualties. To avoid this you had to psych yourself to get by on minimal rest. Somehow you got used to it, and you managed to get by.

You kept clean as best as you could. There was no daily change of clothing. You often wore clothing until it wore off. Washing your clothing quickly became an exercise in futility. Eventually you gave up and just didn't give a damn. However, you still shaved, brushed your teeth, and washed your hands and face. Now and then you washed your hair. As in all wars, you used your steel pot as a washing basin.

As the days went by I got to know more of the platoon members. A guy named Easterling was a machine gunner. Aubrey was an M-79 grenadier. The RTO for the platoon leader was Hatch, and for the platoon sergeant it was Navarri. Hayes and Caluchio, both being from the Bronx, were very close. In time I got to know all the guys except one individual. He was on the tall side and about average build. He had a crew cut and an air of confidence about him.

One day we were crossing a large open rice paddy area heading west. It was a typically hot day, and our objective was some hills with thick vegetation. We had had no contact for several days. The tall guy with the crew cut who I didn't know was on point. I was the last one in the platoon as we headed across the dry rice paddies.

Before the point man reached the wood line we came under an intense volley of automatic rifle fire. After we found cover Sergeant Jordan shouted, "Everyone in the rear hold your fire. You might hit someone in front. Wait until we get the fire teams abreast."

The front element was already returning fire. Lieutenant Carter shouted to them to keep up the fire while the rest of us got on line. We then quickly worked ourselves into position for an assault on the VC position. Fortunately, we had a lot of rice paddies to work with. Most of the rounds were going over our heads. However, before we could make an assault something overcame the point man. When the point element returned fire again he jumped up from the rice paddy cover and single-handedly charged the VC location. Sadly, Charlie cut him down before he got to his position.

Until that moment we had experienced no casualties. The cry "Medic, Medic!" rose from the front element. By now we had our fire power directed at Charlie's position. McCloud hollered, "One of our guys is hit. Let's move out."

In this situation our immediate concern was for the wounded. We headed straight into the line of fire. That day we had the fire power to quickly overtake the VC position. Doc Taylor reached the wounded man as quickly as possible, but he couldn't save him. The man had received a chest full of rounds. A Medivac chopper took away our dead comrade.

Charlie had casualties of his own. He retreated into the thick vegetation with his wounded.

I had witnessed my first friendly KIA (Killed in Action) after a few weeks in-country. The guys who came over from Hawaii knew the point man. As I listened to them talk, I thought of a remark made back in Ft. Polk. An instructor had said, "Be careful of becoming too close to anyone. Death is very real. You might blow your mind if you see a close buddy get killed and lose your sense of reality." This was the first incident of this sort for many of us. Charlie believed that such casualties caused us to fear him. In reality it only made us more resentful of him. None of us was scared, and we became intent on revenge.

Another thought, which you kept to yourself, was, "At least it wasn't me."

One evening as we settled behind some hedgerows Jordan informed Hadaway, "The First Platoon spotted some gooks heading our way. They appear to have uniforms. Get your guys and guard our rear." With that we took our gear across the open area to another hedgerow and strung out.

The light was fading when shooting erupted from the First Platoon. From the sound of the shooting it was our guys that were doing most of it. After the heavy shooting died down sporadic shooting followed, but that soon subsided. We kept a sharp lookout through the hedgerows, maintaining our positions until morning without any more incidents.

Word went around the next day that the First Platoon had spotted some VC headed their way. The platoon had waited for Charlie to get close, but that never happened. Somehow he became wise to our position. When Charlie tried to evade, the First Platoon opened up on him, but, like many other times, he used the darkness and thick vegetation to escape.

5. *Landing Zone Dottie*

AFTER DAYS IN THE BOONIES we were now much closer to the mountains. We heard the sound of large military trucks out in the distance, coming and going. Someone said, "Those trucks mean we're close to Highway One. We might be going into a base camp soon. I could sure use a shower and put on a clean set of clothes. These rags are about to fall off me."

We all felt the same. Again there was speculation that we might soon be going to LZ Dottie. However, we continued working our way west, still checking out the villages. The large trucks going north and south were now a few hundred meters away.

Here, I had my first contact with villagers who peddled wares. They knew we had been out in the boonies for a couple of weeks and awaited us some distance from Highway One. Most of the peddlers were on foot. A few had small carts and bicycles. The villagers had all types of wares to sell, including souvenir items, soda pop, and beer. I bought myself a can of Coke, giving the peddler a fifty-cent MPC. Harlow advised me, "Next time give them fifty piasters, which is their own money. It's not worth as much as ours." At the time buying a Coke out in the boonies seemed strange. I wondered how the peddlers got hold of some American-made items.

In another village the people were more open and responsive to us. They were better able to express themselves in English and had a larger vocabulary. Some could carry on a brief conversation rather well. One phrase the villagers commonly used was "di di mao" or "di di," which meant to get lost. Another favorite expression was "You number one GI.

49

You souvenir me C ration." This meant they wanted you to give them some C rations or whatever item caught their eye. When the villagers asked for souvenirs we usually just ignored them, unless we had a personal favorite. However, they often used a baby or small child to gain a favor. They would say, "You souvenir babysan." Most of the time if I could I would give the kids something. When that happened the villagers looking nearby would have big smiles on their faces. I still remember the elderly ladies with large smiles and teeth black from years of chewing betel nuts.

Navarri enjoyed teasing the villagers, who sometimes became upset with him. As a joke Navarri told a young lady, "You want me souvenir you C ration. I give you C ration if you give GI boom boom."

"Never happen," the young lady retorted. "You number ten GI. You want boom boom, you go see mamasan at village by road."

After we spent a few more days in the village, we received order to go to LZ Dottie. The company was soon strung out in a long line headed south on Highway One. Now and then a truck convoy passed heading north or south. It seemed more secure walking on the road than where we had just been.

You never could get used to the heavy rucksack. You tried different ways to relieve the tremendous pressure on your shoulders. During brief stops you might bend forward and briefly put the weight at the point of the shoulders. This momentarily relieved the pressure at the shoulder area. It was always a welcome sound when you heard "take five." Then you would discard your sweat-soaked rucksack or simply sit in place and use it as a back rest. We had a few such breaks as we continued south.

The weight you carried was great. You had to be alert at all times, but this wasn't always possible. The preferred way to carry your rifle was in front of you at the ready. However, at times you carried your rifle by the sling, by holding it by the handhold on top, over your shoulders, or whichever way you felt comfortable.

On the way in an older sergeant nicknamed "Pops" was evacuated due to heat exhaustion. He was the oldest member of our platoon and was in Korea and now Vietnam. Pops was well liked by the guys and came with the troops from Hawaii. I later learned from Jordan that Pops had bought some Japanese whiskey from villagers and put it in his canteen. The combined effects of alcohol and heat were too much for him.

After an exhausting march we finally made our way through a small village just outside LZ Dottie. Again vendors were here and there, trying to sell their wares before we entered the compound. We were more concerned with taking showers and putting on clean fatigues.

A short distance from the village was the main gate to LZ Dottie. The base camp was just off Highway One and on a small rise. The headquarters for Task Force Barker was here. When we entered the place it was a welcomed relief to be inside a secured installation again.

LZ Dottie had some large tents on the north side. A mess hall, a barber tent, and a large landing area for choppers were on the south side. On the west end was Highway One. Past the perimeter on the north, east, and south sides were rice paddies. The area across the rice paddies on the east and south sides was thick with vegetation and trees. This was where VC sappers often tried to penetrate the perimeter or heaved satchel charges. To discourage this activity nightly ambushes were conducted there.

Once inside, the platoons were given a sector of the perimeter to secure. Our platoon trudged to the southeast side of the perimeter, where the platoon leader assigned bunkers. We discarded our packs and sat down to rest.

A few minutes later Lieutenant Carter announced, "Squad leaders, when you get your men settled, there are clean fatigues at the mess hall area. Unfortunately, there are no hot showers. But there are places where you can take a cold shower. The mess hall will be serving hot chow shortly. I suggest that you get some clean clothes ASAP."

Harlow and I quickly headed to the mess hall, where clothes were piled on several tables. I had expected a more organized handout of clothes. We went through the piles of clothes and found a set that might fit. The clothes were ones that had already seen much wear, but at least they were clean. I wondered what had happened to the new sets of fatigues that I left back in Chu Lai. Following Doc Taylor's advice, I took a couple extra pairs of clean socks to keep my feet dry and prevent jungle rot.

After receiving clean fatigues I thought about taking a shower. At the few places where makeshift showers were set up, however, you had to wait your turn. You also had to take a five-gallon can of water and climb up a ladder to fill a tank with water. Instead, most of us just took "sponge baths" and cleaned up as best as we could. It was good to have on clean fatigues and feel clean, if only briefly.

The hot chow was a welcomed relief from our daily diet of C rations. It was better than the food we had in Chu Lai. When we left the mess hall I noticed a painted sign on the roof that read "4th Bn 3rd Inf, The Old Guard." I turned to Harlow and asked, "What does the sign stand for?"

Harlow filled me in. "The Old Guard is for the 3rd Infantry. It is the oldest infantry in the army. Our battalion, the 4th, is with the 11th Light Infantry Brigade. The 1st of the 3rd is in Washington DC serving as the official army unit guarding the nation's capital. The 2nd of the 3rd is with the 199th Light Infantry Brigade around Saigon. I believe the 3rd of the 3rd is inactive. The unit crest is a headwear from the Revolutionary War."

When we returned to the bunkers we learned from Whitaker that our platoon didn't have to go out on ambush that night. Whitaker always seemed to have the inside scoop about what was happening.

When some beer arrived we sat next to a bunker, drinking it. There was still some daylight left and the mail had arrived. The talk was of home and what might be happening. Some guys shared the latest news as they read letters from home. The warm beer relieved some tensions and anxieties we had picked up the last few weeks. As I listened I looked at the guys. I thought about how young most of them were.

The company had suffered minor casualties. I preferred that it remain that way for the rest of the year. My time to go home still seemed an eternity away. Our time to leave would eventually arrive, but we despaired to think of the many months until then.

Warm beer brought a temporary absence from the war. A more extreme way of coping was using drugs. On our way in some guys had bought marijuana cigarettes from the villagers. The stuff was called dope, grass, or more commonly dinky dow. It was very easy to get in Nam. Little kids sold the stuff at ten sticks for a dollar. The sticks were the size of a regular cigarette. When passing a bunker I came upon some guys smoking the stuff. As I stood in the doorway someone said, "Hey Chief, do you want to take a hit?" The guy inhaled the stuff and held it in as he passed it to the next person. I had no experience with dope and had no idea what to expect. Growing up I had heard of marijuana, but I had no idea how it looked or smelled.

I declined the offer. This was a very new experience for me, and I was cautious.

We all stayed up for a few hours before fatigue got the better of us. Sometime during our time in the field I had received an air mattress, which I blew up before going to sleep. It was a good feeling to be able to rest under more secure circumstances.

In the morning we had a good breakfast of eggs, bacon, cereal, juice, and coffee. The eggs were real instead of the powdered type. After our meal I asked Harlow, "Did you get a chance to go to the NCO club?"

"This place doesn't have much of anything, much less an NCO club," Harlow replied. "I guess I'll just have to wait until we get to Bronco."

The following day Captain Michles let us have a leisurely day. First Sergeant Dahner (Top) recruited some guys to go swimming with him. No one knew of a swimming hole nearby. We were in open rice paddy terrain with a river a distance to the south. Top remained close-mouthed, telling us only to make sure to bring weapons and plenty of ammunition, because we had to go a few klicks to the north.

At least a platoon-sized group left the perimeter and headed north. Traveling light gave you a better sense of security and mobility. As we walked we met all kinds of villagers walking or riding a scooter type of vehicle. Off the road in the rice paddies more villagers were working in their fields. The area north of LZ Dottie was mostly rice paddy. As we walked among the villagers I felt secure, knowing Charlie wouldn't risk hitting his own.

All types of bomb craters dotted the landscape. In our earlier excursion in the boonies I had become familiar with terrain such as this. The whole area evidently had been the target of repeated bombing missions. The craters left behind were small and large. Some were huge.

After trekking a couple of klicks we arrived at our destination, a large bomb crater filled with water. Top had noticed the crater the day before, and he believed it could serve as a swimming hole. Top divided the group in two and said, "This group will set up security and keep a lookout at the far wood line. The rest of you can take off your rags and jump into the water."

The water in the crater was clear like in a large swimming pool. At first we were reluctant to go in, not knowing what might be in the water. Top went in first, told us the water was fine, and ordered us in.

Soon the guys were frolicking in the water enjoying themselves. The "skinny dipping" GIs attracted the attention of the local villagers. The little kids came around as we continued our antics. They were very amused by GIs frolicking nude in the water. Top then showed his sense of humor. He swam on his back with only his private parts swaying above water. The kids and some villagers had a good laugh out of it. That day was a welcomed change from the days of humping the heavy packs.

After a few hours we headed back to LZ Dottie and returned to reality. Our platoon was to send an ambush out that night. Hadaway was ordered to send out a fire team a couple of klicks south. I was assigned to point.

Since we left LZ Uptight I had been walking point. This meant that you walked a ways ahead of the platoon and looked out for anything suspicious. If you were in doubt you alerted the platoon about possible danger. You walked with your weapon off safety, ready to fire, knowing that you would probably be the first one to make contact. The chance of your next step being your last increased substantially. Your first concern was getting shot, followed closely by the fear of stepping on a mine.

There was no way of telling accurately where a mine could be. To do this required a great deal of time. Ideally, you would have a mine detector and would slowly make your way forward, checking out every place the detector indicated something.

This was the exact way we dealt with mines early on. On top of the heavy load carried you also had to put on a headset and walk with a mine detector in front of you, a slow process. Charlie buried all kinds of empty C ration cans that gave false readings. Although there were times when a real mine was detected, the process slowed you down as well as prevented you from using your weapon effectively.

In the end the use of mine detectors was abandoned. After that, the point man had to move at a steady pace, trying to locate mines and detect possible ambush sites at the same time. You definitely did a lot of praying while on point, especially after someone got blown up.

Walking point at night was altogether different. You weren't concerned that much about mines but instead about close contact with the enemy. You walked just ahead of the group, maintaining contact, and made out the darkness while still being aware of your surroundings. This I didn't find too difficult. I grew up having to do just that at times. Night was the time when Charlie operated most. You suspected him to be behind every bush, tree, hedgerow, and so forth, as you negotiated the darkness.

When it became dark we headed out into the night with me on point. Highway One was strange without traffic (there was never traffic at night). We were the only ones around and had the whole road to ourselves. I was confident Charlie's night activities hadn't started. When we reached the trail heading east I used rice paddy dikes to get to our destination. Soon I whispered to Hadaway, "We are in the general area. Another trail branches off to the south."

"That's our trail," he whispered back. "We'll set up next to a hedgerow farther south."

We soon had claymores covering the trail. As I settled down I heard the sound of someone inflating an air mattress. Caluchio, sitting in the darkness next to me, was blowing one up. I asked softly, "Hey, Caluchio, is it necessary to go to the trouble of blowing up the air mattress?"

"What the hell, we won't make contact anyway," he grumbled.

I thought he was getting careless. It was too dangerous to become too lax. You had to sleep lightly. I told Caluchio, "Just make sure you don't get too comfortable, and pull your share of guard duty. Charlie might cut our throats if you fall asleep."

The night passed without incident. Before daybreak we were back at LZ Dottie. When we were in the mess hall Lieutenant Carter came in and announced, "Squad leaders make sure your guys clean their weapons.

Be ready to move out in a minute's notice. We are headed back to the boonies."

We would be making a combat assault (CA) with helicopters within the hour. We were heading east, somewhere toward the ocean. This would be a new experience for many of us. Several choppers would pick up our platoon simultaneously, with seven men to a chopper. The squad leaders and team leaders would be in charge of each group of seven. They would stand and hold up their rifle to signal the chopper pilot where to land. The rest of us would divide three on each side and were ordered to board quickly and face outward when the choppers landed.

Within a few minutes several choppers arrived. The two platoons on the first lift were ready at the landing area. We watched from a distance as the choppers created a large cloud of dust and the men scrambled onto them. Within a minute the choppers rose above the cloud of dust. They headed south, then turned east.

We were next, so we hurried to the landing area. There we set up horseshoe formations where the choppers would land. There was little time to gather thoughts about what might be ahead. I had to rely on my instincts. While we waited we double-checked our gear and weapons. There was very little conversation among the platoon. We all had the same thought and prayed that nothing drastic would happen. It was foolish to tell yourself that you weren't afraid, since your fear of the unknown was greatly enhanced.

Soon the choppers appeared and again came in for a landing, guided in by individuals holding rifles high over their shoulders. We crouched low and scrambled onto them, fighting the winds created. Just as quickly as they landed, the choppers lifted off. We all felt great danger lurking just around the corner.

6. Rain of Death

THE TERRAIN BELOW US first appeared to be hills but within minutes changed to rice paddies, as we flew parallel to a large river. LZ Uptight was plainly visible to our left. We were perhaps a thousand feet in the air as we flew toward the ocean, a blue haze ahead.

I looked at the other choppers. About ten were flying in a single unit, making a loud twirling sound. The sliding doors were missing from them, which enabled us to board the choppers within seconds when they landed. The door gunners had their M-60 machine guns ready to fire as they eyed the terrain below.

Also flying in formation were choppers that were painted to resemble sharks. These I gathered to be gunships. I understood that they had a Gatling gun mounted in front that could dish out a lot of firepower. Underneath the gunships and clearly visible were rockets ready to destroy large targets. These, along with the door gunner, provided gunships with a formidable amount of ammunition. They escorted all combat air assaults to provide as safe a landing as possible.

The terrain quickly changed again, as we began to fly over rice paddies among hedgerows. At this point we started losing altitude and neared the ocean.

I gripped my rifle tighter and noticed Willingham sitting at the edge of another chopper. I thought to myself that we would be the first ones out of the choppers when they landed. When we made eye contact his expression was indistinguishable, but he certainly wasn't smiling.

There is that certain look everyone has when making a combat assault. You are in a serious state of mind. You are aware of what is around you. At the same time you are also aware of what is about to happen. You know that everything will be happening fast once the chopper lands. Your main thought is to quickly get off the chopper no matter what. Others will be scrambling to get off behind you. You never get used to combat assaults. It is the same whether you are making your first or have already made dozens. No one in his right mind would wish the landing to be hot.

Colored smoke rose from the rice paddies ahead. With that signal the choppers descended and circled. The gunships now became very active, shooting into the trees and sending rockets into hootches. The first lift had landed in a different location. Our LZ wasn't secured yet.

The choppers started landing as each pilot found a suitable place near the colored smoke. I waited until our chopper hovered about a foot off the ground, then scrambled off as best as I could, using the chopper landing skid as a step. Doing so caused the chopper to rock, which made me lose my balance. However, I managed to land on solid ground with the heavy load I carried. I then raced toward some mounds in the open area. After reaching a large one I went into the prone position ready to fire. Soon others were next to me while Lieutenant Carter shouted to the leaders to get organized.

That day there was very little resistance as we landed. As soon as we regrouped, Lieutenant Carter ordered us to head toward the trees to our south, the source of some small-arms fire. We cautiously made our way to the tree line, expecting fire as we did. However, Charlie chose not to stay around and left the area.

This was the first of several combat air assaults we made to this area. The place was the responsibility of the ARVN or the South Vietnamese Army. However, the GIs often assumed responsibility from time to time. The region was a notorious VC stronghold totally supported by the local population.

For the rest of the day we conducted a search and destroy operation. The villagers here were more scarce, which made us extra cautious. We sensed that Charlie was waiting for the right moment to spring an ambush. As the day wore on the other platoons reported some enemy killed in action (KIA). One platoon also reported running into mines. The platoon's own wounded in action (WIA) were Medivaced out by chopper.

When night fell the company set up a perimeter in the open, as there were no hills in the area. Our platoon secured the south side of the perimeter. We quickly dug foxholes, anticipating the worst from Charlie that night. Listening posts (LPs) were established a few meters from the perimeter. We set up claymores and trip flares after the FO secured the perimeter. Four men were assigned to each guard position. This meant turning in early to get as much rest as possible.

The guard positions were situated among islands of trees in rice paddies. There were short stretches of rice paddies in the more wooded areas all around the perimeter. For the first time I felt that we were truly in Charlie's domain. My sixth sense told me he'd try something. I told Jordan about my premonition.

Jordan took me seriously. "I know what you are saying. This war is a guessing game. You never know when Charlie could hit you. On the other hand you also have to rely on your intuition. In a situation like this no one has to tell you to be alert."

I awoke to the familiar sound of, "Chief, are you awake?" I stayed next to my foxhole as I settled into my guard. Stars were overhead, but the terrain made the surroundings hard to see, so I stared into the darkness. After a while I made out the rice paddies and the tree line farther to the south. I thought of the other guards on each side of me and hoped that they were wide awake.

About halfway through my watch I thought I heard voices from the far wood line. I was certain there was no LP out in that direction. I wondered if the other guard positions also heard them and thought of alerting them when I heard the voices again. This time they definitely sounded like the enemy. At the same instant I heard thumping sounds. I had never heard the sound before, but instantly I knew that mortars were being launched.

Other guards soon started yelling, "Incoming, incoming." We were pummeled by a barrage of mortars. I hunkered down inside my foxhole with my helmet on. The mortar rounds seemed to land all around my position. The whole ground shook. One mortar round whistled in and exploded very close by, spraying dirt and debris over me. I felt some thing hot on my left arm but didn't think much of it. My main concern was that a ground attack might be imminent.

When the mortar rounds subsided I fired some rounds at where I had heard the voices.

"Chief, what are you shooting at?" Hadaway yelled.

"I heard some gook voices where the rounds came from," I hollered back. "I'm shooting in that direction." Some others fired more rounds at the tree line.

When the excitement died down we realized that our platoon had suffered a fatality. Topcat came over to where Hadaway and I were and reported that Caluchio was dead.

Hadaway told the rest of us to be alert while he went to check what happened. Caluchio's position was off to my right. While Hadaway was gone I checked my left arm and hand. I apparently had received some small shrapnel wounds. On the back of my left hand was blood from a minor wound.

We learned that Caluchio was found still in his guard position and not in his foxhole. He must have gone to sleep on guard duty and had no idea that mortars were coming in. He was killed by a round that landed between his position and mine.

I then told Hadaway that I had received some small wounds. Sergeant Jordan came over to check me out. "Let the medic look at your wound," he said.

"It's just a minor wound," I replied. "I don't think a medic is necessary."

"Suit yourself," he shrugged. "We might have to send you to Chu Lai to get a tetanus shot."

After a chopper took Caluchio's body we were put on 100 percent alert for the rest of the night. I looked into the darkness with my rifle at the ready and thought about many things. I now fully appreciated the importance of digging a foxhole every night. I also realized that my life had been spared. If that mortar round had landed another meter toward me my wound could have been more serious. I said a silent prayer of thanks to my Creator.

There was no fear in my mind. The mortar attack and losing a fellow GI only pumped me up with adrenaline. I fully expected some sort of ground attack or more mortars for the rest of the night. I was ready for Charlie. Let the bastard come, I thought. I was ready for him. He never came.

While we were getting ready for the new day, Captain Michles came toward us. He took long strides, matched by his RTO. Captain Michles asked Lieutenant Carter, "Where's the guy who received a wound?"

When Lieutenant Carter pointed me out Captain Michles came over to me and looked at my hand. When assured it was just a minor wound, he marched back to his CP group. We then prepared to continue our operation.

7. Area of Operation Awareness

AFTER SEVERAL MORE DAYS out in the field we returned to LZ Uptight. That same day replacements arrived on the resupply chopper. Two new men, Wilson and Reddy, were assigned to our platoon. I remember them standing on the chopper pad with brand-new fatigues and shiny new helmet covers. That was how we must have appeared when we first arrived some weeks back. Now we had spent enough time in-country that our helmet covers had started to fade. (Proud to be from New Mexico, somewhere along the line I had drawn the state flag on my helmet cover.)

Reddy (Stacy) was from south Chicago. He was white and appeared to have grown up in a hostile environment. He had the "I'm Ready to Fight" appearance about him. However, he became a dependable guy you could rely on in a firefight.

Wilson, also white, was from San Pedro, California. Early on he and I developed a very close relationship. He quickly became very vocal about the Vietnam War. Within a few weeks we had all felt that the United States had no business in the war. Wilson openly griped about it and wrote letters to some key congressmen. Some who responded were Senators Edward Kennedy of Massachusetts and Frank Church of Idaho. Both shared Wilson's concerns and were trying to end the U.S. involvement in the war. Although our platoon generally agreed with Wilson, we chose to keep our views to ourselves.

Wilson also wrote several songs about the Vietnam War. One song often sung by the guys was one he called "Faraway," part of which went like this:

Faraway from here is a place called home.
Faraway from here is where I like to roam.
Faraway from here is my Dad and Mom.
Far Far Faraway from Vietnam.

Wilson would often sing words to Jim Reeves's song "He'll Have to Go." I believe one reason we developed a close friendship was our mutual love of country music.

Other members of the platoon would sing their favorite songs. Some of the black GIs would sing the Otis Redding classic "Dock of the Bay." They changed the words to suit the situation. Part of their version went like this:

I'm just a sitting on a rice paddy dike, wasting time.
I'm just a sitting on a rice paddy dike, wasting time.
I left my home in Georgia, headed for Cam Rahn Bay.
I had nothing to live for. Uncle Sam done took it away.
So I'm just a sitting on a rice paddy dike, wasting time.

When we arrived back on LZ Uptight it seemed a long time since we had left. Actually it had been just a few weeks. Mail was waiting for us with some packages from home. I received very little mail, so the package waiting for me was a pleasant surprise. My brother sent me a package of goodies and a new camera. I quickly loaded a cartridge of film. I found some plastic bags to put my new camera in, to protect it from the humidity and salt. That was how I already carried my wallet and other personal items. My pocket knife already showed signs of corrosion.

After Wilson and Stacy settled into our platoon several of us sat with them. We looked out toward the South China Sea, as we always did. From LZ Uptight you could see hills meeting the ocean. Wilson asked, "How far do we have to go out there?"

None of us knew for sure. We gave him an idea of where we had been. We had seen some of the area to the north and northwest and a small portion to the south. We estimated that we had covered less than a quarter of the area we could see. The land to the east, close to the sea, was unknown to us. In our present situation it appeared we would be spending more time in this region. In time, I believed we would check all the area we could see.

"Where were you during the Tet Offensive that we heard about?" I asked Wilson.

"I was still in Chu Lai," he answered. "The whole place was damaged by a lot of 122 rockets. The airstrip was the main target."

"We heard that the whole country got hit at the same time," I added. "The gooks concentrated on the larger bases and population areas. We were on this hill when the artillery did a lot of talking that night."

"You know where the replacement center at Chu Lai is," Wilson said. "There was a large ammunition dump just over the hill that got hit. When the place exploded I thought the world ended. It scared the hell out of me. Sappers entered the perimeter on the south side. It was one hell of a night. The gooks knew exactly where the key targets were."

Fortunately, on Uptight we hadn't been hurt by any rounds or VC activities of any kind during the Tet Offensive. The Chu Lai base and Quang Ngai city were the two hardest hit in our area.

Until now we had received casualties from mines, bullets, and mortars. The main casualties resulted from mines. The land mines were dreaded. They caused much pain and misery. I still remember the screams from some unfortunate GI who encountered a mine. You prayed that it wouldn't happen to you.

One mine often used by the enemy was the Bouncing Betty. When activated it would frequently bounce to the genital area and explode. You can imagine what sort of misery the mine caused. Other mines were booby-trap grenades, antitank mines, command-detonated mines (claymore or Soviet version), or small mines designed to blow off toes or feet. The homemade versions, such as punji stakes, were hardly ever used. One of Charlie's favorite sources of mines and booby traps was our own dud artillery and mortar rounds or bombs.

Odds were in your favor if you were fired on by bullets. Charlie preferred to shoot at you from a safe distance, and so frequently missed his target. When he did shoot, you first felt something whizzing by you, then a crackling or popping sound. If the rice paddies were full of water, the water would dance around you. It resembled a sudden downpour from an abrupt storm.

The little kids became key players in the war. When they were around you felt more secure, because they were probably Charlie's own kin. You learned to be wary when the kids began to slowly move away from you. Charlie often used the kids to gain an advantage. The most deadly sort of exploitation was using them to plant mines and booby traps. They were also used as a delay tactic. The kids distracted the GIs if they spotted U.S. soldiers approaching their village. The kids would also try to distract the GIs while the enemy planted mines.

The day after Wilson and Stacy joined our platoon we made a patrol south of LZ Uptight. As usual, we left early in the morning. When we got to the bottom of the hill we followed the large trail west. When we turned south some villagers approached us from that direction. Lieutenant Carter cautioned, "Hold up and keep alert. I think the gooks want our attention."

We then sat in place on a rice paddy dike, watching as the villagers slowly made their way to Lieutenant Carter's position. The head man pointed to a makeshift stretcher used to carry a young boy. The man then motioned and made gestures to say he wanted medical attention for the boy. The villagers quickly persuaded Lieutenant Carter to call in a Medivac for the boy. When he did he motioned them to wait until a chopper arrived.

Shortly after that an elderly woman approached us. She carried a small basket that contained some sort of pastry. She gave each of us a piece of the bread. After bowing to us several times she motioned us to eat the gift. She was obviously showing her gratitude for having the boy taken to a hospital. The smell of the bread or pastry didn't appeal to us. However, we thanked the woman and pretended to take a bite of it. When she left we all hid the gift in the grass. We didn't want to appear rude, but the pastry wasn't to our liking.

On another day farther to the east a platoon was under heavy fire. We were north of them and couldn't see them. However, instead of going to their aid we were ordered to stay put. Artillery rounds from LZ Uptight were whooshing by just overhead and were exploding in the vicinity of the other platoon. Charlie suffered some casualties, including some KIA, and retreated. The platoon suffered some casualties with no KIA.

Wilson was close to a radio and later told me of listening to the conversation that went on. Apparently a sergeant had been wounded in the skirmish.

"Where are you hit, and how bad is it?" the CO inquired.

"A bullet hit me on the butt. It's not too bad," the sergeant replied.

"Hang in there, we have a Medivac on the way. You doing all right?"

"I'm doing fine. But my butt hurts like hell."

One morning, several days later, we found ourselves waiting at the large chopper area west of LZ Uptight. We had been ordered to make another combat assault, this time to the unknown area east of LZ Uptight that was close to the South China Sea. We waited in several U-shaped formations for the choppers to land simultaneously.

Willingham spotted the choppers coming in from the west. He pointed in that direction as Harlow also spotted them. I looked but couldn't make out anything.

"Don't look high above the horizon but just at the horizon," Willingham said.

After that I said, "Yeah, I see them now. They are just tiny specks and getting larger."

The choppers arrived on time, and soon we flew directly east in formation. We had the usual gunship support, the Sharks. The Sixth of the Eleventh Artillery were pounding the area we were heading into but let up as we became airborne. The "butterflies in the stomach" feeling was back.

The LZ was on the side of a large hill. It appeared as though we would be landing in clearings among hedgerows. The place was full of smoke and debris from the artillery barrage and seemed dangerous. As before, the gunships raked the area before the choppers landed in the clearings. Prior to landing we received some fire, but I didn't see any VC. The terrain was too thick with various vegetation.

After we landed we quickly ran behind a wall next to some hedgerows and shot into them and continued to advance. Our objective was the top of a nearby hill. Sergeant Williams yelled, "The place is hot.

Keep an eye out to the hedgerows in front." Just as he spoke some rounds came our way that went over our heads. Sergeant Williams shouted, "The gooks are shooting from the next hedgerow! Get a machine gunner to cover us. Hadaway, bring your fire team." He jumped onto a wall and ran forward, the rest of us following him to the safety of the next hedgerow.

Meanwhile, the gunships circled and fired rounds. They appeared to have spotted and were chasing some VC.

We eventually reached the top of the hill. By this time most of the firing had subsided. The choppers also stopped firing, though they continued to circle. The whole area was covered by a blanket of heavy smoke mixed with dust. We began checking out our surroundings more thoroughly.

Lieutenant Carter ordered us to search for and destroy any tunnel complexes in the area. This place was apparently a headquarters for a local VC battalion.

We moved out slowly, concentrating on looking for tunnels while being alert for an ambush. There were more tunnels than I anticipated. Whenever we located one, a hand grenade was tossed in if we believed it was clear. After a while we were tossing in grenades here and there, yelling "Fire in the hole!" with each one.

Some villagers, anticipating an end to the bombardment, came out of their hiding places. They were herded to a central location for their safety.

We came upon a tunnel entrance amid charred debris and heard voices coming from deep inside. Sergeant Williams told us, "If you don't get a response from the hole throw in a grenade. It's probably Charlie inside."

Someone yelled, "La dai, la dai!" into the tunnel, trying to get the occupants to come out. There was no response. Before the GI could toss in a grenade, Jordan stepped over and said, "Throw in a gas grenade instead. It might be villagers inside."

A gas grenade exploded inside the tunnel. Nothing happened. Another gas grenade was thrown in, and after a minute an elderly man appeared through the thick smoke, with his hands up in the air. He muttered something as he begged us not to shoot him. When he realized that we weren't going to hurt him, he told the others in the hole to come out. Several villagers, including some small children, emerged. How they managed to endure the burning and choking sensation of the gas grenade was beyond us. They were very lucky to be alive. I felt relieved a regular fragmentation grenade wasn't used.

That evening we set up our night defensive position in the general area. We made sure we dug a deep foxhole, because we all knew that Charlie would be very active with his mortars that night. Farther to the east were heavily wooded areas. We were most vulnerable from that direction, so several artillery marking rounds went there.

As anticipated, Charlie sent in mortar rounds that night. The difference from the previous time was that he didn't wait until midnight but chose to make an earlier call. I huddled in my foxhole as the rounds landed away from me. Only a few rounds came in—just a warning of more to come—and they didn't inflict any casualties.

Soon our artillery rounds went flying to the wooded area in an effort to discourage Charlie. Meanwhile, we waited with 50 percent alert. Around midnight the enemy sent in more rounds, this time a heavy barrage landed all around us and inflicted casualties on other platoons. Luckily, our platoon had no casualties.

After the barrage we were on full alert, ready for an attack. The artillery outpost steadily sent flare rounds to illuminate the perimeter. I felt that Charlie might try something from the east, where the rounds apparently came from.

After some time a Medivac arrived accompanied by gunships. When the chopper landed it used very bright lights to illuminate the area well. Meanwhile, the gunships concentrated on the heavily wooded area. The red tracer rounds from the choppers created a weird display of raining red bullets. After several minutes the Medivac chopper safely left with the casualties.

The gunships continued to rain red bullets well after the Medivac chopper left. This was enough to discourage Charlie, who left the area. I'm sure with all the firepower the VC must have suffered some casualties. For the rest of the night we remained at 100 percent alert.

The whole operation lasted only a few days. Its purpose apparently was to show Charlie our strength. We destroyed a large tunnel complex and confiscated rice and small arms. The gunships inflicted the most casualties. They had a commanding view of the whole area and could see the enemy trying to escape. In this short operation there were casualties on both sides. We returned to LZ Uptight.

One evening our platoon went on ambush several klicks from LZ Uptight. I was on point as we walked down the hill in the darkness. When heading across rice paddies I had a sense of immanent danger. The large mounds around us were graves. We had already spent some nights among them.

As young lads my older brother and I at times had walked home in complete darkness. Our young minds conjured up spooks waiting around the next bend as we made our way in the dark. We remembered being told that any animal we might encounter would be a ghost.

In my present situation, encountering spooks was something that other people experienced. Charlie on the other hand was very real.

8. Minefield

ONE DAY WE WERE MAKING A SWEEP when shooting erupted from the direction of another platoon. We hid behind hedgerows west of the platoon, where two hills met, and waited for Charlie to come running. The other platoon leader reported that three or more dinks were headed our way.

Shortly after that the VC appeared. They spotted us and quickly dashed into a hedgerow to the north, about a hundred meters away. After some of us gave chase into the thicket, Charlie fled straight up what appeared to be a large hill. Actually it was a large sand dune. We followed. As might be expected, running in sand was extremely difficult. We were huffing and puffing when we reached the top of the hill. Here we stayed put and waited for the rest of the platoon to catch up.

From where we stood the area to the north appeared to be mostly large sand dunes. It also had Filipino Pine trees, which resembled pine trees back in the states. The CO advised us to go ahead and check the area to the north. After that we searched the area in a large sweep to the northwest and doubled back. Realizing that Charlie was gone, we went back toward the ocean.

While we rested under some trees someone said, "The ocean looks inviting. It would be nice to take a dip."

"Why not, it'll be good for the guys," Lieutenant Carter replied. "We have a commanding view of the whole place. One squad could pull security while the rest take a dip and switch off. I don't think Charlie is nearby. He's probably on the other side of Uptight by now. There is nothing but sand. He won't have any tunnel to hide in."

This stretch of beach somewhere on the Batangan Peninsula was where I had my first taste of the sea. Half of us took off our fatigues and headed into the water. Those more familiar with the ocean went in first. The rest of us followed close behind. I was a fair swimmer and soon got the hang of the waves coming and going. The seawater felt cool.

Harlow advised us not to drink the seawater. I had to try it out for myself, however. It was very salty and tasted terrible.

While the other squad enjoyed the water I took a closer look at the beach, and a thought struck me. The coastline seemed to be a never-ending series of c shapes. Although not an expert on beaches, I believed that the ones here could rival the best, anywhere in the world.

After the quick, refreshing dip we continued checking out the area. We slowly made our way through the sand and small trees and soon rejoined the rest of the company.

One evening the resupply chopper brought more replacements. Unfortunately, they were replacements for individuals killed or hurt by mines. One replacement, a black soldier, joined our platoon. I don't recollect very much about him. But he had that look of uncertainty and tried not to show fear.

The following morning our platoon headed south. Our squad brought up the rear. We headed south toward the villages next to the large river. The other platoons were off in a different direction.

We had gone less than a klick when we heard the familiar, dreadful sound of a very large explosion, directly to our front. I immediately knew that we had multiple casualties. I shuddered as we crouched in place. Before the debris and dust settled, the frantic cry for the medic filled the air. Doc Taylor, anticipating the worst, was already on his way. We kept a lookout to the south and east as Doc and others worked on the wounded. At the request of Doc some sent their first aid packs to him. In the end we had two wounded and one dead. A Medivac chopper took away the casualties.

We learned that the point man had walked over a mine, but the new man had stepped on it. His life had ended before he was in the field a whole day.

It was a terribly common situation. Occasionally a point man would walk over a mine and someone behind him would activate it. This happened to me several times when I was on point. When it did I felt it must not have been my time to leave this world. The first time this occurred I thought of the prayers back home. By now I had accepted that prayer truly got you by on a daily basis.

I also thought of our religious ceremonies and gatherings for powwows back home. A special dance for veterans and servicemen is always part of powwows. Sometime back a friend had written to me from home and mentioned a powwow. A special dance was also held for all the young men from home that were in Vietnam.

"All the guys in Vietnam were mentioned, including you," my friend wrote. "We all think and pray for you guys."

I didn't know how, but I sometimes sensed the prayers that were conducted for me. Perhaps it was the dangerous surroundings that made me understand things I never would have otherwise. At times I could sense what was happening on the other side of the world. I knew my people and other tribes were concerned for our welfare. We were on their minds. Knowing this, I conducted myself with more confidence.

After a brief rest on LZ Uptight we were again on the north side of the artillery outpost. Lieutenant Carter was still in charge of our platoon. During this time the company had limited success with night ambushes. Charlie also limited his day activities.

One evening we received more replacements north of LZ Uptight. Strangely enough, an individual named Holmes, had arrived in the field without being issued a weapon. He was promised one in a day or so. Until then, Sergeant McCloud lent him his M-16.

Holmes was a preacher's son. I doubt, however, if that had anything to do with his coming out in the field without a weapon. One day Holmes bragged about a conquest he had made back in the World. The way he talked made us wonder if he really was a preacher's son. Hadaway said to him, "You sure don't talk like a preacher's son." Holmes just laughed and agreed. "Yeah, I know. You want to know something else? My dad had to marry my mother because he knocked her up. Isn't that terrible?"

Holmes was a squared away dude. Early in his tour of duty he found his way out of the field. His civilian occupation was working in a mortuary as an embalmer, and that's what he ended up doing in-country.

One morning after spending the night next to Vietnamese burial mounds I looked at them more closely. The mounds were of all sizes and had a small ditch or channel all around them with an opening to the east. It was wise to avoid them if you could. The reason was to show respect for the Vietnamese people's beliefs, and it was also against my traditional beliefs to be around dead bodies. We believe that once a dead person is buried, you never go back to the burial site, or even look back. Once a person is gone from this world he will work against the living.

The rainy season was several months away, but it still rained hard now and then. One night our squad went on ambush in a driving rain. We followed a large trail until we came upon a village. Here the squad leader changed plans. "The hell with it. It's raining too hard and probably won't let up. We'll just set up on this trail. Charlie's not foolish enough to be out on a night like this."

The rice paddies were full of water. The only decent place to spend the night was inside the village or on the trail. The latter was more practical but also more risky. Guards watched the trail to the north and south. I tried to find a decent spot off the trail to get some sleep. In the end I just wrapped myself with my poncho and tried to get comfortable. Late in the night the rain continued unabated, limiting visibility to a few meters.

That night we underestimated Charlie's determination. He had plans for some night activities and was using the trail we were on. Someone on guard saw Charlie when he was only a few meters in front of him. Charlie saw the guard at the same time. The guard beat a hasty retreat to avoid getting shot. This minor incident made it clear to us that Charlie operated in all types of weather conditions. Often, in fact, he intentionally chose poor conditions to carry out his campaign. I also knew that he could withstand severe hardships and bear more pain than we could.

One particular incident illustrates this point well. With the aid of a recon chopper we had gained the upper hand on some vc who were waiting to ambush us. The chopper spotted and picked off the VC and dropped a smoke grenade to mark the location. After shooting our way to the ambush site, we came across several dead VC. One, however, was still alive but terribly injured. He was badly shot up, with his guts hanging out. His right leg and left arm were dangling and useless. He was on his left knee and was swinging a large saber in his right arm. He swung at anyone who came too close. The VC remained in the same spot as we continued past him. Reaching a hedgerow, we heard shots from the rear. Someone had taken him out of his misery.

The hot weather was relentless. We drank large quantities of water and tried to stay out of the sun. Daily we continued searching for tunnels in the villages. Some were cleverly concealed. The villages seemed interconnected by a large tunnel complex. We checked out the tunnels as thoroughly as possible and destroyed them as best as we could.

During short breaks when we sat in place, we became familiar with the immediate surroundings. The country seemed to have billions of ants of all sorts—large, small, and of different colors. Flies are universal, but they weren't nearly as common as ants in Vietnam. A small brown type was called "piss ant" by GIs. They wasted no time in attacking once they crawled onto you. Their bites really stung, and for this reason they were definitely to be avoided. One day while taking a break at the crest of a small hill I noticed some strange, golden ants on an ant hill. A short distance away was the same type, only silver. I had to check them out closely to make sure I was seeing right.

There were also many snakes of different types. Most were not dangerous, although I never cared for any of them. One type, the bamboo viper, was very poisonous, and its bite could kill you within minutes. The viper was light green in color and about the size of a water snake. No one was bitten by a bamboo viper, as far as I can remember. It was rumored that if bitten by one you had ten paces before the venom killed you.

One day while on a blocking force I had an unforgettable experience with a large snake. Sitting behind a hedgerow drowsily looking out for VC, I noticed a movement to my immediate right. I froze. A large, red snake was sliding slowly by, inches from my face. It was about three inches in diameter and about fifteen or twenty feet long. I had no idea if the snake was poisonous, so I remained very still until the snake's head moved away, out of striking distance.

I softly called, "Hey, Nevins, watch out! There's a very large snake coming your way in the hedges."

Nevins had no way of knowing what was coming. He calmly answered, "Yeah, okay. I hear you." He was calm, that is, until he saw the huge snake appear next to him. Then he scrambled backward before falling down and swore, "Damn, that's the largest snake I ever saw."

After our stay in the boonies we moved to LZ Dottie for a couple days' rest. This time our bunkers were on the east end of the perimeter. The bunkers were not hotels, but they were a whole lot better than the open ground. The perimeter in this sector met rice paddies. Beyond was a heavily wooded area. Here several trails meandered through the concertina wire for day patrols and night ambushes. This was the logical place where Charlie would try to penetrate the perimeter. He could also toss in satchel charges and hand grenades.

When night arrived some of us sat and shot the breeze. Others had portable radios tuned to a U.S. Armed Forces radio station. Listening to the news on the radio enabled us to learn what was happening in the world. Other important sources were letters, magazines, and newspapers from home. We also received copies of the *Stars and Stripes,* which gave us an idea of what was happening back in the United States. Most of the time the news was dated.

The news reported on a place called Khe Sahn, farther to the north. The U.S. Marines under siege there had been the top news for the last few weeks. The Tet Offensive was considered a major blow to the enemy, although the action the VC had initiated caused major Allied damages. In the division AO, action was sporadic. The 196th LIB was in constant contact with the NVAs at Tam Ky.

When it came time for my guard, I looked out in the darkness. Everything seemed quiet. I felt confident that Charlie was somewhere else. After my watch ended I was on the verge of sleep when there was a large explosion nearby. I thought for sure mortars were coming in and waited for a barrage. Some guys began firing into the darkness. Charlie had thrown in a satchel charge. Jordan warned us to watch for sappers inside the perimeter. After a while everyone and everything settled down. There were no injuries from the satchel charge, which seemed to have been intended only to harass us. However, it was unsettling to think about Charlie getting that close to us.

Our rest at LZ Dottie was brief but essential. Once more we found ourselves waiting at the chopper pad for another combat assault. We were ordered to conduct a one-day operation and only needed our web gear with ammunition. We left our rucksacks at LZ Dottie and were flown in the direction of the South China Sea.

We landed in almost the same area where we had lost Caluchio. No one had to tell us to watch out for mines. Although other platoons had suffered more casualties here from the dreaded mines, we knew this area was the worst place around.

After organizing I was again on point, concentrating primarily on looking for mines. We had to make a sweep to the east. The ARVNs were to set up a blocking force. Another platoon ahead had already moved into some hedgerows. At that instant, Charlie opened up on us from our right front. We took cover in the rice paddies and returned fire. The firing was intense. After a while we were advised to maintain contact and wait for the Flyboys.

The firefight continued for twenty minutes or so. We suddenly heard a very large rattling sound, followed a split second later by small explosions from where Charlie was shooting at us. I looked in the direction of the sound. A Phantom Jet was making a sharp upward turn in the sky. A second jet came in silently, low above the treetops. When it, too, veered upward, the same sounds followed. The two jets worked as a team, flying in a large circle. After another pass they dropped napalm and left. The large fireballs did the trick. The shooting ended. It was strange how the jets came in silently above the treetops, faster than the speed of sound.

For the remainder of the day we continued our sweep to the east. In the afternoon we waited for choppers to pick us up, but they never arrived. When it became dark we dug in to spend the night. The place was very damp, so the foxholes were easy to dig. "I'm going to stay inside my foxhole tonight," I told Harlow.

"How are you going to keep warm without a poncho liner?" Harlow asked.

I cut off some banana leaves and put them inside the foxhole. "I'm going to use the banana leaves as a bed and cover."

He shook his head. "Good luck, Chief. I don't think that's going to work."

Although we were in the tropics the night got cold at times when it was damp. Harlow was right. The banana leaves did not keep me warm. They seemed to make matters worse.

The night was spent with a 50 percent alert. The anticipated mortar attack never came.

The next day we were airlifted north of the river closer to the ocean. The one-day operation was turning out to be longer. Later in the day our rucksacks were flown out to us. This area was still considered very dangerous because of the mines. Our fear of them never went away. On this particular day it was no different.

Our company was making a sweep up a valley heading east. It was still early in the morning. We interrogated some local villagers as we went along and passed a place where the red volcanic rock had been quarried at some time in the past. The South China Sea was close. The terrain appeared to drop to the sea, and it could have been considered a large plateau.

Shortly after our noon lunch break we followed the company heading north on a main trail. I had no idea what our objective was. Normally, the platoons went in different directions and rendezvoused in the evening. Now the whole company was in line angling up a hill. It appeared we were going over to the other side. However, once on top the company veered to the right.

Our platoon soon reached the top and took a short break. The trail continued north for a short distance before it went down. At that point another trail branched off to the east, and we followed it and the rest of the company. This trail continued down the center of some rice paddies. To the north, paralleling the trail, were hedgerows about thirty meters away. On the south side of the trail, past more rice paddies, was thin vegetation. Beyond that and over the edge of the hill was a village.

The rice paddy area of the trail was long, long enough for the whole company to string out. When it did I was the last one in line, bringing up the rear for the company. I had been in this situation before. I had the habit of turning every now and then as I walked.

I had just turned again when a very large explosion tore through the air at the far front. Immediately, I feared the worst. The whole company was out in the open. I fully expected Charlie to start shooting from the hedgerow to the north. I also scanned the area behind, anticipating something from that direction.

Cries for the medic disturbed the silence. I knew exactly what was happening up ahead. Someone was either dead or badly wounded or both. I already knew we were in a bad situation, and I didn't know what to do. The cries for the medic became more frantic.

After a few minutes there was another loud explosion. I shuddered at the sound and thought, "Oh no. Not again." My mind was racing. We were in a minefield. We had to get security for the Medivac chopper coming. Someone must have left the trail ready to do so and stepped on another mine. What were we to do?

After the second explosion, we froze in place. I knew for sure an attack was imminent from the north and waited. There was no other option. We had no place to go out in the open. The front platoon had already suffered many casualties. The situation had become very critical and tense.

It seemed like hours, but within minutes there was another explosion, this time a lot closer. The debris from the explosion rained down on us as the familiar voices of our platoon members called for the medic. Within minutes word reached us. Pops, the old man of the platoon, was dead. He had stepped on a mine, just off the trail.

At this moment Sergeant Williams decided to take matters into his own hands. He started yelling, "Get off the trail and head to the hedgerows to the north! Get off the trail!"

Nobody moved.

"We are sitting ducks here!" he barked. "We have to get to the hedgerows! Let's get moving, that's an order!"

Again nobody moved. We would rather take our chances on the trail, at least until Charlie started firing on us. After that nothing would matter.

Sergeant Williams fumed, "You guys can stay on the trail if you want. I'm going to the hedgerow."

With that he started walking cautiously across the rice paddies. We all looked at him walking with his rifle at the ready. We knew that every step might be his last. When he made it across to the hedgerow it gave us hope. Just as he entered the hedgerow, however, there was a loud explosion. Sergeant Williams never knew what hit him and died instantly. His body or what was left of it was retrieved using his footsteps to do so.

We stayed on the trail and waited for the Medivac. Eventually all the casualties were evacuated. Sadly, some of the dead had only bits and pieces of them put in a body bag. We lost quite a number of men that day. It was our worst encounter with mines.

We could no longer go forward; the only way out was back. The platoon leader beckoned to me after the Medivac left. When I reached him he said, "Chief, we have to go back where we came. You'll be on point. How do you feel about the situation?" I replied, "We have to get out of this place ASAP. I feel we will be okay until we reach the point where the trails divide. From there, Charlie probably already has set mines for us in each direction." The platoon leader recommended that we go into the village to the south and get some villagers to walk point for us. He figured that if Charlie saw one of his own he wouldn't do anything.

The CO gave us the go-ahead. I quickly went across the rice paddies without much thought of mines. I had already made up my mind how to handle the situation with mines. I knew that I might or might not step on one. I had told myself not to be afraid and strongly believed that nothing would happen to me.

When I was across, another GI followed my footsteps. From there we quickly reached the village, which appeared deserted. We went from hootch to hootch. We saw only very elderly men and a young boy. I knew the old men could not walk. I grabbed the boy.

After we returned to the platoon I told the platoon leader, "The place is deserted. This boy is the only one around. How come the company don't just follow our footsteps to the village?"

"The CO wants to go back out the same way we came in," he replied. "Bring the boy, he'll just have to do. Let's get going."

The boy was made to understand what he had to do. If he ran he would be shot. I followed the boy with doubts that the tactic would work. It seemed to me Charlie was crazy enough to expend the boy's life in order to get more of us. However, the plan was successful. We made it out of the minefield with the boy leading us.

At the end of the day we all knew we had taken a terrible beating from the mines. It could have been worse, I knew. If Charlie had had the foresight to shoot at us while we were in the open, we would have suffered many more casualties.

The anger toward our unseen enemy was at a boiling point. When we set up for the night, everyone went about it quietly, full of bitter thoughts about what had happened.

9. Pinkville

ONE DAY WE WERE WEST OF THE PLACE where the terrible incident with the mines occurred. It drizzled steadily for the better part of the day. When the day ended we set up a perimeter among some old French ruins. An old house provided decent shelter from the rain, although it had only a partial roof.

Someone built a fire in a corner using old pieces of wood. The fire soon burned strongly, revealing very large spiders on the walls. One was directly above Karaba's head. H. P. spotted it at the same time I did. Before Karaba could move I smashed the spider with the butt of my rifle. The other spiders scampered away. H. P. remarked, "Damn, they are the biggest spiders I've ever seen. They must be as big as your hand."

After a wet night we worked our way next to an inland sea. During a break I sat on the porch of an old house and lit up a cigarette. Sitting there I saw a large spider crawling out of its hiding place. It was the same type as the ones we had seen the night before. As the spider made its way across the ground a blue- and yellow-colored wasp attacked it. I watched the battle. The spider put up a game fight but soon succumbed to the quicker and smaller wasp.

All the small creatures running around here were similar to what we had back in the States, except for occasional differences in color. Back home the walking sticks, for example, resembled pine needles or smooth twigs. In Nam they resembled the vegetation. Some were twisted in odd shapes.

The following day our operation took us near LZ Uptight, which I didn't mind. We were very familiar with the area close to the ocean and on the north and south sides of the large river. The place had become notorious in Task Force Barker as a land of mines. The area south of the large river was the worst. The GIs named this place Pinkville. The reason being that it was colored pink on our maps of the place.

A few days later, while we were inside a village, Jordan said, "I don't want all of you to jump up and volunteer all at once. I need someone to walk point."

"Why, where we headed?" Karaba said.

"I guess you volunteered. We have to go in to LZ Uptight tonight. The rest of the company is already on its way."

The point element left the village. I was to be the last, so I waited at the end. While waiting I gave a small child a candy bar. After that other kids came running over.

What the hell, I thought. Give them whatever you can. You'll be at Uptight tonight. I gave the kids all of my C rations and other goodies. I knew they might be in cahoots with the VC. On the other hand, they were often unwilling pawns of a cruel adversary who used them at will. At times, out of necessity, even the GIs used the kids, as when we used the boy to lead us out of a minefield.

When I was leaving an older boy came over to thank me for the goodies. We walked side by side as he said, "You number one, VC number ten." I looked down at him. Somehow I felt that he was sincere. I asked him the same question we directed to the villagers. I said with a pointing motion, "Where VC?"

The boy pointed south across the large river. He said, "Beau coup VC, VC number ten." I believed him. That was the area called Pinkville.

At the edge of the village was a bridge spanning a large man-made channel. A boy standing at the edge of the bridge waved as the guys walked by next to him. Everyone acknowledged or ignored the boy until Hadaway came by. Hadaway walked past and gave the boy a push with his right hand. The boy went flying backward into the water, landing with a large splash, and swam like a dog to the shore. The kids watching nearby burst into laughter. I watched and doubted that the incident amused the boy. He probably ended up planting mines intended to harm GIs.

After we made it back to LZ Uptight Lieutenant Carter briefed us on his meeting with the CO. We would be heading out of our AO for a few weeks. We were told to be ready for another combat assault in the morning.

Later, I asked Hadaway where we might be going. He replied, "I don't know for sure. I think it's over there," pointing at the blue mountains out to the west.

Ever since I had arrived at LZ Uptight I had wondered about the blue mountains on the horizon. Initially, I believed that I would be spending all my time in the rice paddies. Having grown up in a mountainous terrain, the thought of going to the mountains intrigued me. It might be a good break from all of the mines and the constant wetness of the rice paddies.

Our daily patrols in the rice paddies had started affecting the bottoms of our feet. We tried to avoid getting our feet wet, but it was impossible. At times we crossed the wet rice paddies to avoid using the main trail. Whenever we could we took off our shoes and wrung out our socks. We also had to clean the white insoles that allowed air to move in our shoes. If this foot hygiene was neglected, sores and holes would appear on the bottom of our feet. Continued neglect resulted in a worse condition, jungle rot.

Early the next morning we were flown west toward the mountains. We passed LZ Dottie and all the hamlets clustered here and there. Before long we were in the foothills of the large mountains, just off to the west. We landed in the middle of rice paddies.

From there we went south until we came upon a large river, where the company stretched out westward. Lieutenant Carter announced, "We have to set up a blocking force for a few days. Squad leaders, have your men dig in well. We might encounter some NVAs."

Our platoon's position was between coconut and banana trees. We had to clear some banana trees to get a better field of fire. "I wouldn't mind being a lumberjack in a banana forest," Wilson said, as he hacked at the banana trees with a machete. All it took was one swing of a machete to fell one.

After clearing a large area, we set up claymores and trip flares at our front, gathering different types of vegetation to conceal our positions.

We used fallen trees and whatever else we could to construct mini-bunkers.

On the second evening our squad was assembled near Hadaway's position when suddenly a trip flare went off. We scrambled for our fighting positions. The machine gun sent rounds in the direction of the flare. Taking no chances, the rest of us fired off at least a magazine of ammunition.

In the morning the surrounding area was checked out. There was no sign of Charlie. For the next two days we remained concealed in that location. After that we conducted day patrols nearby. We encountered few people and many abandoned hootches. We could see more hootches on the other side of the river, which was too large to cross.

When not on patrol Wilson and I practiced knife throwing. "You're an Apache. How do you throw a knife?" Wilson asked.

"As far as I know," I replied, "as young boys we threw a knife by holding it by the tip. I have to admit I never fully mastered the art of throwing a knife."

We tried different ways of throwing. Two coconut trees spaced about thirty or forty meters apart were our targets. After a while we became good enough to hit the target most of the time. We found the best way to throw the knife was to hold it by the handle.

On one patrol we made a wide sweep to the south and back. On the outskirts of a small village was a pineapple tree growing in the wild. I cut off the fruit and took it with me. During our lunch break I shared it with some guys. It tasted like the pineapple that you bought in the supermarket.

I also discovered a grapefruit about the size of a bowling ball. It was difficult to peel, as the cover was very thick. The actual fruit inside was the size of a baseball and very bitter.

While eating lunch I saw a large snail sitting on a leaf. The size of the snails fascinated me. I had already seen them in the AO we left. They were very shy creatures and hid inside their shells, refusing to come out. Now I was looking at one as it slowly came out of its shell and stretched out on the leaf. It was about an inch wide and eight inches long. The villagers used snails as food, a delicacy to them.

After a few days we abandoned our blocking force and headed northwest. When we crossed a large rice paddy area we were at the base of the mountains. From there we followed the rest of the company on a trail sloping upward that soon was overgrown with vegetation and appeared to have been unused for a long time.

The constant discomfort of the heat became a factor as we trudged up the hill. We took frequent breaks and tried to conserve our water. By this time I carried the equivalent of a gallon of water. In the other AO we were getting water from the wells in the villages. Where we were now heading the water might not be as readily available.

When we took another break I looked down at where we had started. The rice paddies were far below. The thick wooded area was all around. I thought that the NVA had many possible hiding places in the vast area I could see. Perhaps they were watching us from among the trees. They could also be waiting for us farther up the mountain.

When we rested on the trail between the thick vegetation, Uncle Mickey nudged me and said, "Check out our platoon leader." Lieutenant Carter sat on the trail with his head drooping and eventually fell asleep. Fatigue took its toll on everyone. You tried to fight it as best as you could. Some days you went with very little sleep. You tried to get rest whenever and wherever you could.

Soon the thick vegetation gave way to more open terrain. The open area was dominated by tall grass, tall brush, and large boulders. The terrain resembled a step. It sloped at a slight angle until we encountered more thick vegetation farther up.

Here we set up a perimeter for the night. While digging in I heard a large explosion close by. An instant later a buzzing object tore my pant leg, hit a large boulder, and fell to the ground. It was a large piece of shrapnel with razor-sharp edges. Someone had set off a dud round without giving warning. Afterward, I held the piece of shrapnel in my hand. If it had been an inch closer it would have put a deep gash in my leg. I was fortunate again.

When the resupply chopper arrived it managed to land on the rocky incline. However, when it took off, its tail end brushed against the side of the mountain. The pilot lost control and crashed on the side of the mountain. Fortunately, the crew members survived the crash with minor injuries. Later, another chopper arrived to take them in.

The brief operation into the mountains lasted a couple of days. We found no evidence that the NVA used that place for a staging area. As we headed down the north side of the mountains it started to rain.

When we reached the lowlands the rain was coming down at a steady rate. The soaking rain gave me an idea. We hadn't taken a shower for a few weeks. I took out a bar of soap to clean my fatigues as best I could. I took my shirt and T-shirt off and lathered them down. Some guys thought I was crazy, but I appreciated the opportunity to clean up. It might have been strange to Charlie to see one GI cleaner than the others.

A day or so later while walking through a stream we encountered leeches. When walking through wet grass or water you had to be extra cautious, or leeches would end up on you. In the coastal area you would occasionally encounter one, but here there were many. They hung to all parts of your body. We used cigarettes to force their heads out before pulling them off. You had to be careful and get the entire leech; otherwise, the head staying in could cause infection.

We received some sniper fire when back in the lowlands, but the operation as a whole netted very little NVA activity. After that we returned to our original AO.

Around this time Lieutenant Carter went to another platoon. He was a good individual and a capable leader. Unfortunately, he lost an arm while with the other platoon.

His replacement was Lieutenant Lewis. The new lieutenant had attended college in Santa Fe, New Mexico. He knew what to expect before he arrived. "I already know where all the bad places are," he said. "They told us about a place called Pinkville being the worst." He was right.

I've already mentioned Pinkville. It was a piece of land bordered on the north by a large river, on the east by the South China Sea, and on the south and west by the ARVN AO. It was situated about five klicks south of LZ Uptight, across the river. It was actually the AO of the ARVNs, but somehow the American GIs ended up patrolling there. It was an added burden for our task force.

The GIs hated going into Pinkville. Charlie was hardly ever seen. Instead, mines and booby traps were everywhere. Although we were very careful to avoid trails, hedges with openings, and so forth, we still encountered the mines. In this area they were used to deadly perfection. It was very frustrating to be unable to do much about them. It was clear to us that the villagers knew what was happening. We continued to suspect that they took an active role in planting the mines.

After a few days in the field Lieutenant Lewis made some changes within the platoon. He reassigned us to different fire teams, so I ended up in Uncle Mickey's fire team. The lieutenant asked me to walk point for the platoon. I told him I'd give it my best shot, although I wasn't excited about the idea. I couldn't keep my mind off of Pinkville. A big factor in my decision to walk point willingly was that some of the guys were married and had families. They showed me pictures of their kids, and I noticed their faces when they did. They were so proud of the kids. I tried to put myself in their place. By now I was convinced we all had no business in Nam. For these guys it was even more so. I felt it might be better if I took more of the risk. A sense of fatalism also contributed to my decision. Earlier Winston had asked, "Hey, Chief, you don't appear afraid. How do you do it?"

"Don't let whatever fool you," I had replied. "I'm just as scared as everybody else. I just tell myself I'm going to be all right."

"How do you think to get by from day to day?"

"I don't know how others think, but I have several thoughts that I live with. One is that if your time comes you're going to go, no matter what. Another is to expect the absolute worst and hope for the best. Most importantly, I also believe in the power of prayer."

With the changes made we continued daily operations around the LZ Uptight area. By now we had lost several members of the platoon to the mines. The daily routine was the same. We investigated villages for VC activities. When we came upon an unusual amount of hidden rice or other food, we confiscated it.

On one combat assault our platoon set up a blocking force behind thick vegetation on the north side of the large river. Because the location was close to the river, it was sandy, which made it easy for us to dig in.

During the initial part of the operation we fully expected Charlie to head our way. The artillery from LZ Uptight pounded the area south of the river. The artillery rounds included white phosphorus (WP), nicknamed Willie Peter. When exploded, WP formed a white cloud that burned the skin severely.

WP rounds exploded south of the river. We saw bunches of people running away from the white cloud, fleeing east toward the Pinkville area. We assumed they were VC, because the elderly couldn't run that fast, and they looked larger than kids. When the VC reached the trees, shooting erupted. We assumed that the ARVNs were the ones doing the shooting, because their AO was across the river.

After a day or so in position we were ordered to check out the area of bombardment south of the river. This meant going across a narrow bridge about a meter wide and perhaps a hundred meters long. I was on point as we reached the bridge. At that instant we came under intense fire. We exchanged rapid fire with Charlie for several minutes.

We still had to cross the bridge. Artillery rounds began pounding the suspected source of enemy fire. When the shelling stopped Lieutenant Lewis came forward to where Hadaway and I were. He ordered me to be first across the bridge. The rest would provide cover fire.

When I heard the shots, I took off without hesitation, full of adrenaline and extra energy. This was what I trained for and was disciplined to do. Sprinting across the bridge, I felt Charlie's bullets flying past me. I thought one might hit me at any second.

As I ran across the narrow bridge I had a flashback to my youth. On September 15 of every year my tribe has a traditional relay race between our two clans. The outcome of the race determines the type of year ahead. Depending on which clan won, there would be more wild game or crops. This race gives my people an idea of how to plan their activities for the year to come.

The relay race is on a racetrack three hundred yards long and about ten yards wide. Head runners are determined at a preliminary race the day before. Before the race starts, elderly men paint the runners in an aspen kiva, conduct prayers for them, and run down the track blessing it. When they finish the race starts with the head runners running at a full sprint down the track. When they reach the end of the track another set of runners runs back. This goes back and forth until a clan gets ahead by a full length of the track. When that happens the clan in the lead wins the race. If the runners from each clan are evenly matched the race could take several hours.

I had participated in the race several times. It could be very deceptive, especially going in an easterly direction. That is because in that direction about three-fourths of the way down is a slight rise that looks like the finish line. If you are not aware of the illusion your energy is expended when you reach this point, and you have to continue on with heavy legs. Elderly men holding aspen branches give you words of encouragement and whip you on the legs with the branches for added strength. It works. You find the burst of energy needed to take you to the finish line.

I was now about three-fourths of the way across the narrow bridge. My legs were heavy from carrying my pack. I thought of the elderly men in our traditional race. In an instant, just that thought gave me the encouragement to continue. I ran off the bridge on the other side and took cover next to the trail. After catching my breath I fired toward the wood line. Out of the corner of my right eye I could see the others running the same race. Eventually, we all made it across without a casualty.

When we regrouped Lieutenant Lewis pointed to the trees and said, "We have to head for the village where the firing came from. Charlie probably left the area. But we can't think that way. If in doubt fire at anything that moves."

Backed by our firepower we quickly made our way to that village. It had been devastated by gunfire and shelling. Dead pigs, cattle, chickens, and ducks were scattered all over the place. We spent the better part of the day looking around. Charlie had fled, but we didn't chase the vc. We were already out of our AO, and we were required to stay close to the river. At the end of the day we went back across the bridge without any more incidents.

Our daily operations then moved west of LZ Uptight and toward LZ Dottie. One day while sitting under a coconut tree I observed a familiar sight. Some villagers were coming our way, carrying their burdens on each end of a flat stick. The stick, called a "dummy stick," was a common way villagers transported heavy loads. The stick was perhaps six feet long by four inches wide. It was used by balancing a load on each end at one's shoulder. The villagers would carry their burden in a weaving, rhythmic motion. Often you observed a dozen or more villagers going down a trail in unison. When one shoulder got tired the load would be transferred to the other without losing rhythm.

On this day the villagers walking toward us took a break a short distance away. As a general rule we would check what was in their wicker baskets. When they rested, Wilson, I, and two others went to investigate. They were all elderly women who knew what our intentions were. They showed us the contents of their baskets. After we were satisfied that nothing was amiss we turned to leave. At that moment Wilson mused, "Hey, I wonder how much weight the old women are carrying."

We looked speculatively at their loads, and someone said, "It shouldn't be too much, after all they're a bunch of old women. There's only one way to find out. Lift up a load and see how much it weighs."

Wilson motioned to an elderly woman to indicate he wanted to lift up the weight. The mamasan turned to her companions and said something to them. After that the women turned to us with their black betel-nut smiles. They pointed to a load.

Wilson took the dummy stick under his shoulder and attempted to lift its load. He did with some difficulty. After that we all took a turn. The load was extremely heavy. How could these old women carry such a burden? Meanwhile, the elderly women talked among themselves and laughed at us. We left them laughing in place with their big smiles. We made their day. After a few more minutes the women disappeared in rhythmic motion around a bend.

During my tour of duty I learned how rice is grown, harvested, and stored. The rice is first planted thickly in a small plot, usually in the backyard. After the rice sprouts the villagers transplant it to larger plots flooded with water. A water buffalo is used to break up the ground and make it soft for transplanting the rice.

The villagers transplant the rice in a backbreaking fashion. They tie the sprouts from the backyard plots in small bunches. They then bend down to transplant each plant in rows. These larger plots where the sprouts are transplanted become the rice paddies. They are large or small and separated by dikes. Hundreds of these paddies dot the countryside. Every available piece of land was used to grow rice.

The paddies are then kept full of water. There are various ways of doing this. The most practical way is to divert the water into the paddies by gravity. However, this isn't always possible, so the villagers used other methods. One method was to have a large bucket with long ropes attached to it. Two villagers held the ropes on each end and used a rhythmic motion to transfer the water into the paddy with the bucket. Another method was to use a paddling contraption to transfer water. At some places large water wheels accomplished this task. Whatever the method used, it was important to keep the rice paddies flooded.

When the rice started to mature it developed green pods. These, when squeezed, would emit a white milky substance, which would eventually harden to become the rice we know. At a certain stage the rice was ready for harvest. The rice paddies were then dried out. After that the villagers cut the dried plants with a sickle and tied them up in bundles.

The villagers then transported the bundles to a central location. There they separated the rice from the plants. This was called threshing, which was done by beating the plant with a stick over a large mat or by a more ingenious method. The villagers built a thresher with a bamboo frame divided into two parts. The upper part had three solid walls and an opening. A large piece of bamboo went through the center of the open space of this top section. On the bottom section a cone-shaped chute connected to the top part.

To use the thresher the villagers held the dried plants in bunches. They then would strike the bunches against the piece of bamboo in the top section. This caused the grain to separate from the dried plants and to fall down the chute into a large pan or mat. The villagers then tossed the grain in the air to separate the hull from the grain. Wind blew away the hull, leaving the rice. After that the rice was stored in large containers. There might be other ways to grow, harvest, and store rice. This was the way I remember.

We worried daily about the usual dangers—getting shot, stepping on a mine, the weather, the terrain, insects and mosquitoes. We were particularly wary of the water buffalo. These animals served as workhorses for the villagers and therefore were highly prized. Killing one made the villagers very angry.

We often saw small kids riding buffaloes or leading them effortlessly. The water buffaloes hated us, however, and would charge unprovoked, resulting in many getting killed by GIs. To avoid such situations, the small kids would keep the animals quiet when we were close, by talking to them or patting them on the nose with a stick.

One day we were on a trail heading east. There was a thick hedgerow on our left and a sharp drop on our right. I was on point. When we rounded a bend a boy was leading a water buffalo our way. My presence instantly angered the animal. It wanted to charge, so I held up with my rifle at the ready.

There was nowhere else to go. I had to go forward, but the animal wasn't about to move. The boy somehow edged it slightly off the trail. I then squeezed by the snorting beast with my rifle pointed at it. The others followed me, as the boy talked frantically to his animal. He kept patting its nose with a stick. If the buffalo charged it meant losing his prized possession. Eventually, we all squeezed by. Luckily for all of us and the animal nothing happened.

One evening while back at LZ Uptight some guys were smoking dope in a bunker when I happened upon them. By now I was familiar with the smell of marijuana. Up to this point I had gotten high only from alcohol. Brooks said, "Here, Chief, do you want a hit?" as he offered me a cigarette.

Out of curiosity I accepted his offer. I had known that sooner or later I would try the stuff. "Sure, why not. What do I do?" I said.

"Inhale in deep and try to hold it in as long as you can." I then took the cigarette, inhaled, and passed it on to the next person. The cigarette went around in a circle. When it was gone, another was lit. The marijuana smoke filled the bunker. The only one who didn't take part was a guy named Scheindler. He sat by himself in a corner.

Shortly after I inhaled the marijuana I started feeling the effects of the drug and became light-headed. The guys smoking were in a happy, laughing mood. The war went away. We laughed at anything, and everything seemed funny. With all the smoke in the air even Scheindler got stoned. He laughed with the rest from his corner.

Incredible hunger hit me next. Soon guys were asking for C rations or whatever food might be available. After eating some C rations I left the bunker. I kept my first indulgence to a minimum.

The next day the guys were joking about and kidding Scheindler. It was strange to me that there was no aftereffect like you get with alcohol. I resolved to be careful with the stuff.

During this time Harlow made friends with a mongoose. He told me about how the animal made frequent visits to his bunker. One day we put out some food for the animal and waited. After a few minutes a large weasel-like animal came through the concertina wire and nibbled at the food. It looked at us, ate the food, and left. Harlow looked at the departing animal and remarked, "At least it's not Charlie. But he could get through like the mongoose if he wanted to."

10. My Lai

AFTER SPENDING A DAY ON LZ UPTIGHT we were to make another combat assault, once again in the Pinkville area. Upon hearing the news my immediate thought was of the many mines there.

The afternoon before the assault Captain Michles went around and briefed each platoon. He told our platoon that Intelligence had reported a large VC battalion operating in Pinkville, in hamlets called My Lai. The next day Charlie Company would make the initial assault into My Lai. Our company would follow and set up a blocking force east of them, blocking the VC escape route in that direction. Other units would block escape routes in other directions.

When Captain Michles left, Hump said, "What's this place called My Lai? All I know is we call it Pinkville. Just watch, we'll end up losing more guys by mines. I don't want to go back into that damn place."

"I hear you," Wilson replied. "That place gives me the creeps. Especially if you have to walk point. Chief, be extra careful."

The guys all felt bitter toward Pinkville. Each of us was affected one way or another by that dreaded place. We had already lost many fellow GIs there, and we resented the villagers.

At times extreme measures were used to gain information from the villagers. When using such measures you thought back to when a fellow soldier got killed by a mine. In this ugly situation the animal deep inside you surfaced and took over, roughing up villagers to make them talk.

However, your conscience only allowed you to go so far. You suddenly realized that this was not the real you and caught yourself before you did something drastic. For most GIs it only went that far. For others it went further. For a few it went out of control. The resentment toward the villagers was there. You had to control your anger, however. Now we were going back into Pinkville. It would be harder to keep the animal under control.

Early the next morning we waited for choppers at the west end of LZ Uptight. The artillery started sending rounds into the Pinkville area. We knew Charlie Company was well on their way. Within minutes choppers arrived from LZ Dottie. Like Charlie Company, our company would be airlifted into the My Lai area in two lifts. This time our platoon was on the first lift. When we lifted off the pad we headed east, then turned west, toward Pinkville.

We landed in some rice paddies, meeting some small arms fire, and made our way to the hedgerows. There we set up security for the other lift and waited. After the company landed safely we regrouped.

Our objective was to quickly establish a blocking force for Charlie Company, with each platoon moving in different directions. Our platoon headed north, flanked by another platoon within sight to the east. Very shortly there was a loud explosion from the other platoon. Charlie was aware of us and had already planted some mines. There were multiple casualties, a familiar and very discouraging situation for everyone. After a chopper airlifted the wounded we continued moving toward our objective. As we advanced, some men in the other platoon ran into a second mine, suffering more casualties. Eventually we reached our objective and set up a blocking force in two-man positions behind a cover of thick vegetation. Our orders were to shoot any enemy coming our way.

When we first landed I had heard shooting to the west. I then assumed that the enemy was in the area. Soon after we set up our positions I still heard sporadic shooting. I knew the other company was close by and assumed they were in contact with Charlie. I waited, fully expecting VC to be running in our direction. We saw no sign of Charlie, however.

The shooting continued in spurts for another hour or two. Overhead, choppers circled the area and we maintained our positions for the better part of the day.

The weather this day seemed hotter than usual. I gulped down water while relaxing. Sitting under a coconut tree, I suddenly couldn't stand the heat any longer. I took off my shirt and ragged T-shirt, which I had worn for several weeks, and threw the now-useless T-shirt into the bushes. Just doing that made me feel much better.

When the sun started to set in late afternoon I saw movement about two hundred meters to my front. I alerted Brooks.

A GI slowly came into view. He was the point man and kept coming our way unaware of us. As he did I just sat under the coconut tree waiting for him. When he was about fifty meters away he became aware of our presence and hesitated. Before he could do anything drastic we waved at him. He immediately recognized us and held up.

We learned that the point man was from Charlie Company. While he stood waiting for further orders we asked him, "What was all the shooting about? For a while we thought you guys might send Charlie our way." The point man received his order to continue and left us without saying another word.

I sat under the tree as the rest of Charlie Company walked by and asked several of them the same question.

"How did you guys do? With all the shooting, did you kick some ass?" None of them seemed willing to share any information.

All one said was, "We shot a bunch of them," and then moved on. Eventually, the whole company passed by. After that our platoon broke up the blocking force. We followed the company to the night bivouac area. I believe that both companies spent the night together. The other company was C First of the Twentieth.

Our operation continued in the same area the next day. Believing that it was a total VC-controlled area, we checked out hootches close to the beach and set fire to them. Later someone mentioned that some gooks were captured when trying to escape a flaming hootch.

While heading north we held up at a concrete bridge. The platoon on point said they had received sniper fire from the other side of the bridge. We crossed the bridge without incident, however.

Somewhere in this area, Taylor, from the First Platoon, stepped on a mine. Winston, who witnessed the incident, said, "You know, the human body can take more than we realize."

"What do you mean?" I asked.

"I saw Taylor after he stepped on the mine. His foot seemed all right but his M-16 was a mangled mess. It was all twisted out of shape."

Just north of the bridge we set up a position for the night. That night we received some mortar rounds but no casualties. In the morning we continued north along a beach area, eventually reaching a small peninsula where the ocean halted our progress. This area had more people.

Here, for whatever reason, our operation changed. We were ordered to bring the whole population to a central point by the beach. We spent the rest of the day doing that. After a few hours there was a continuous line of villagers heading to the staging area. There must have been hundreds. The villagers didn't know what to expect. They grabbed whatever possessions they could carry and hurried along. When the villagers were assembled on the beach a Medivac chopper arrived, and medics tended to the people's needs. This went on until the medical team left at dark. Charlie Company airlifted out, leaving our company to deal with the situation.

Our night defensive position was north of where the villagers were congregated. We were in sand and small vegetation, which provided little cover, and were too close to the heavy vegetation to our north. This area deeply concerned me. I told Wilson that there should be an ambush or LP sent out to the north because Charlie could easily walk in mortars on us from there.

When the day ended and night fell we were all well dug in. I felt very uneasy when it became dark. I still had a strong feeling something was going to happen from the north, mainly because of what had happened the past few days. If I were Charlie I would have been mighty upset about my villages being burned to the ground.

We had also heard rumors of villagers and livestock being killed by GIs, mostly by Charlie Company. I thought about this. Innocent people and livestock sometimes got into the line of fire, all part of the horrible reality of war. However, some said the killings were deliberate. I had seen no such killings up to that point while in-country. I felt it was not possible to do that. Especially as a unit.

Around midnight while on guard I kept my attention to the north. The night was one of almost total darkness. Visibility was very limited. I relied on my sense of hearing, which was affected by a strong ocean breeze. The darkness often played with your senses. You would find yourself seeing or hearing things that weren't there. I thought of how Charlie turned claymores around on you.

I heard the familiar thud. Mortar rounds went off from the woods to the north. Immediately, shouts of "incoming, incoming," sounded throughout the perimeter. I took cover in my foxhole. Within a minute many mortar rounds came whistling into our perimeter. A few landed very close, the explosions flinging sand down on us. I hoped that the guys all made it into their foxholes.

Charlie was at his best with mortars that night. He landed about a dozen rounds inside our perimeter on the first volley. He didn't walk them in as he usually did. Our platoon had no casualties, but the other platoons did. One guy died that night as a mortar round exploded next to his foxhole. It took a long time for the Medivac to take out the dead and wounded.

Immediately following the mortar attack, we turned our attention to the north, convinced that a ground attack would follow from there. We sent a large volley of fire in that direction to deter any such event. Soon gunships came around and shot up the suspected area with rockets and minicannons.

What followed was bizarre and totally unexpected. An aircraft that literally rained bullets arrived. Some referred to it as Puff the Magic Dragon. It was a dramatic sight to witness. The tracer rounds coming from the aircraft literally sent down showers of red bullets. The unexpected firepower was more than enough for Charlie. He remained silent for the rest of the night.

In the morning we located Charlie's mortar site but not him. Our platoon then was airlifted to LZ Dottie, ending another operation in the Pinkville area. Again we hadn't fared too well with the mines.

When thinking back to the My Lai operation I believe that the enemy already knew of our plans. The intelligence reports of a large VC unit in the area were correct. However, when Charlie Company landed, the unit had left, except for those left behind to harass us and plant mines.

I believe that Charlie must have known our exact landing area that day. Previously when we had been in the area we ran into mines only if

Charlie knew of our general direction. He then would guess which direction we might go when leaving a village. On the day of the My Lai operation, however, our company had run into mines immediately after we started moving.

In July of 1969 while stationed at Ft. Bragg, North Carolina, I heard news of an incident called My Lai. I listened with interest to stories of a possible massacre cover-up in March of 1968. During the many months of investigation into the My Lai operation, the main inquiry focused on what happened during the C First of the Twentieth assault into My Lai. Other units involved in the operation, including mine, B Fourth of the Third, were also included in the inquiry.

Many individuals were called in to testify. The conclusion of the Peers Inquiry was that there were civilians killed in large numbers, at least 175 and perhaps more than 400. A later combat report was exaggerated, especially the body count. There had been a major cover-up among the top-ranking officers. Lieutenant William L. Calley Jr. was the only individual convicted regarding the massacre and later was acquitted. His commanding officer, Captain Ernest Medina, and others were also charged but were acquitted.

I can say that I did not witness any civilians killed that day. We had different orders. I do not condone the killings. However, having spent much time in the Pinkville area, I can understand why it happened. On the day of the My Lai Massacre the situation was ripe for the animal to emerge. Unfortunately, at My Lai it appears that the animal completely took over not just one individual, but a whole unit. When it did, the men were unable to stop it until it was too late.

When in the Task Force Barker AO, you saw places where there were many craters, evidence of B-52 air strikes. One can only imagine how many civilians were killed by the bombs. I'm sure there were more than what happened at My Lai. These deaths are, however, brushed off as an unfortunate happening of war.

The finger is pointed at the grunts, but we were merely pawns of the grand scheme of things. The local villagers, top U.S. military brass, and politicians back home had a major responsibility. The grunts were dying in an effort to free the country from communist domination. We wanted the local villagers' assistance in destroying the VC for them.

Early on in the war we realized this was never going to happen, but we couldn't convince the top military brass and politicians of this. During the first stages of the war, during the critical time, no one listened to the grunts. As a result the war escalated.

The My Lai Massacre reflects negatively not only on the Americal Division but on the U.S. military as a whole. I'm sure every major unit had a My Lai on a large or small scale. It is worth mentioning that we pronounced "My Lai" just as it looks—"My Lie" rather than "Me Lie". It's ironic when you think about the news media's pronunciation. You could go further and call it the Me Lie Massacre. Me Lie about reports, Me Lie about a cover-up, and Me Lie about body counts. Perhaps because of the massacre the military subsequently made more accurate reports. I have no way of knowing for sure. I do know that in the Americal Division the cards were laid out on the table.

11. Close Call

THE COMPANY'S NEXT DESTINATION was an area west of LZ Dottie along Highway One. Here we did pacification-type activities, including spending leisurely time with villagers. During the day we set up shades with our poncho liners. The villagers soon became aware of us and came around to sell us souvenirs, Cokes, beer, marijuana, and so forth. The young kids took an active part, which included selling pictures. One little girl said to Shriner, "GI, you want buy phuck phisures?"

Shriner checked out the pictures and remarked, "I don't know about this place. You are supposed to be fighting for these people. They don't help you. When it comes to taking advantage of you, they are all into it. They want your money. Even the little girls sell dirty pictures. There's something wrong here. I gotta get out of here."

A chunky girl in her early twenties came by with others to sell souvenirs. Someone jokingly told her, "You boom boom GI for free."

"Never happen, you pay beau coup money," she retorted.

The guys had no intentions of doing anything with her but led her on. When the kidding continued the girl became serious about selling herself. The guys told one another to take her on. No one did, so H. P. half-seriously made a deal with the girl and led her off into some bushes.

When through he went to Whitaker and said, "Hey bro, I got what I wanted, and I didn't have to pay for it."

The villagers quickly became aware of this incident. The following day we asked some boys, "What happen to girl GI took in bushes?"

The leader of the group said, "She beau coup mad at GIs. Mamasan want money. Mamasan beau coup mad at girl."

During this time more replacements joined our platoon. One was a very likeable fellow named Vic, who was white, from Utah, and raised a Mormon. Vic and I quickly became friends. We were both from the western part of the United States.

One day Vic, myself, and some others sat under the shade of a coconut tree. Out in a clearing a short distance away were some cattle grazing peacefully. Usually we never bothered these animals as they roamed all over the place. On this day Vic looked at one and said, "You know the cattle look like the Brahma bulls used in the rodeos back home."

Not knowing what he was up to, I replied, "I know what you mean. They are smaller, but I see no bulls out there with the cattle. I wonder what they do with the animals. The people don't appear to use beef in their diets."

Vic continued, looking at the cattle, "Chief, you think we can make one of them animals buck?"

Some kids helped us catch a larger animal. We put a homemade rope around the animal's midsection. Vic then jumped on and held onto the rope with one hand, simulating riding in a rodeo.

Instead of bucking, the animal ran away as fast as it could. Vic immediately slipped sideways and hung on for dear life. The frightened animal ran straight across the clearing to a canal, where Vic fell into the water with a big splash. When he came out dripping wet, the kids were roaring with laughter.

That same day word reached us of an operation involving several companies, including ours. It was well known that Charlie had a large force close to the ocean east of LZ Uptight. We would try again to flush him out and, we hoped, fight him in a major battle.

And so we made another combat assault into the area. When we landed our platoon was farthest to the east. Here we engaged Charlie before he began to retreat toward a small pass. We started toward the pass, going fire teams abreast. The rest of the company was behind us.

When we reached the pass we held up and waited. The grenadiers fired rounds into suspected places, and we continued forward. After another few meters Charlie opened up again. We found cover behind rice paddy dikes. None of our guys was hurt. After an hour we reestablished control of the situation and continued pursuing the VC toward the south.

I was on the right flank as we crossed a large clearing. Reaching hedgerows, we encountered a small trail. Here the platoon held up next to very thick terrain.

The platoon leader said, " The CO advises that we use caution and follow Charlie south on this trail. He feels that there are more VC in the immediate area. Another unit is somewhere further to the south. The rest of the platoons are behind us and will be making a sweep to the east and come back by the beach area. Chief, you will be on point. I don't have to remind you that Charlie is still close by."

I already knew that Charlie might be leading us into a trap or setting mines for us. By now I had a sixth sense about when danger was imminent, and I was leery of possible ambush sites. Of course, you could not locate mines with any degree of proficiency. You just used your best judgment. I felt it best to continue at a rapid pace, leaving Charlie no time to set mines. You took your chances that he wouldn't fire at you from close range.

After about twenty minutes on the trail I approached a long clearing through the thick vegetation. I knew something might be amiss, so I held up before I was in the clearing. When Lieutenant Lewis came forward he asked, "What's up, Chief?"

I looked ahead. "There's a long stretch of paddies ahead. It's very thick on our left. From where we are standing I can't see across the paddies. Charlie could be waiting in the thickness across the clearing. It just seems like a good ambush site to me. We might go a little further and fire some grenades into the coconut grove at the other side of the clearing."

When a grenadier came forward the platoon leader said, "We'll need to fire some rounds across the clearing. Wait until Chief goes further and checks out the area better."

I advanced to get a better view of the coconut grove. I thought Charlie might open up. Then again, I felt that he wouldn't waste the effort to eliminate one GI. Reaching the point where I could see across, I thought I saw movement. Instantly I crouched down, expecting the worst. When I cautiously looked across again there was more movement. This time I spotted GIs waiting. They were covering the trail we were on. I took a chance and came into view, waving at them as I stood out in the open. Luckily for me they recognized me and waved back.

When we reached their position I noticed they were loaded down with ammunition. We took a break alongside them. "What outfit are you guys with?" Hadaway asked.

"We're with the 123rd Aviation Battalion out of Chu Lai," a sergeant replied. "We're the opposite of the LRRPs [Long Range Reconnaissance Patrol]. We go on a mission to make contact. We go to places in the Americal AO where heavy contact is expected."

"So that's why you guys are loaded to the max with ammunition," Jordan said. "You see any sign of Charlie? He held us in place for about an hour and headed this way."

The sergeant shook his head. "He didn't come this way. The bastard could smell you out. He has a thousand different ways to go."

After a few minutes we bade them farewell and continued west. From there we went around a large hill and ended up at the mouth of a wide river. Out in the distance were strange contraptions in the water. I asked Harlow about them. He thought that the villagers used them to separate the salt from the water.

While waiting for the other platoons we checked out a village. We soon discovered several hootches filled to the top with salt. After looking at the hootches, Captain Michles, our company commander, told us, "There's too much salt for the villagers. Battalion advises that the salt is for the VC and should be confiscated. A chopper will bring sandbags. We'll set up a perimeter around the salt. I estimate the chore of filling sandbags with salt will take a couple of days."

When the sandbags arrived we had the village kids do the work. One platoon had the kids fill sandbags, while the others provided security. The salt was to be bagged as quickly as possible. The laborers were given entrenching tools and put to work. We soon had a good system going, but a problem cropped up. Our laborers' bare feet were burning from the salt. To resolve the problem we wrapped them with sandbags. When bagged, other kids took the salt to a temporary chopper landing pad. The salt was to be distributed to friendly villages in the province.

We spent about three days in the village, next to the sea. Because I was raised in an entirely different environment, the sea life fascinated me.

While taking a break I observed some green and orange crabs creeping out of the water. They didn't see me as they came across an open court-yard to a hootch. I tried to hit one with the butt of my rifle. When they saw me they made a mad scramble back into the water. Another time, Harlow and I decided to check the sea life next to a long causeway. Harlow took a fish in his hand, said, "watch this," and he squeezed the fish several times in rapid succession. The fish ballooned to a much larger size. Harlow told me it was a puffer fish.

When the salt was hauled away, Captain Michles came by our platoon sector and said, "You guys did a good job with the salt. We have to hurt Charlie anyway we can."

When he started away again he spotted a scrawny, sickly looking kitten. He ordered, "Put that sick animal in a sandbag, and toss it out into the ocean. You might put some sort of weight into the sandbag." Someone did as the captain ordered.

That same day Uncle Mickey's fire team and another from a different platoon were to investigate an area. I went with them. Our team went west across the causeway with the other team already ahead of us. Both teams made it across and into a small village without incident, and then spread out to look around. Although other villages continued west on the north side of the river, our force was too small to go much further. We remained close to the causeway.

Soon the small kids came over and hung around us in the usual manner. As always, I felt secure with them around us. However, at some point I noticed that the kids were becoming scarce. I told Uncle Mickey that I didn't like the looks of things. I thought something might be up. Maybe Charlie had wanted us to go further west to ambush us. Since we weren't going to do that, maybe he was planning something else.

Uncle Mickey agreed with me. He advised the other team to be on the lookout. After we made a good search of the area, Uncle Mickey called on the radio for instructions. The CO advised us to come back across, saying that they would make a sweep in the morning.

By now all the kids had left. We knew something was up. We had to be ready for anything. Two of us stayed at a good vantage point while the others started across the causeway. Members of the other fire team were already going back across.

Meanwhile, the two of us who stayed behind kept our weapons pointed at suspected places. We waited until our fire team was well on their way before we followed. We thought we were the last to leave until we spotted some members of the other fire team nearby. We then headed back across the causeway. I looked back several times until the others finally came into view. We were now about halfway across the causeway. Just as I looked back again I heard the crackling of small arms fire. A GI fell to the ground. The familiar screams of someone in great pain followed. Another GI went to the fallen companion as the rest fired into the village. Two returned fire from a crouched position.

We were halfway across the causeway, but we raced back as fast as we could. When we were close to the fallen GI another volley of fire erupted from a different direction, striking a second GI in the chest and spinning him to the ground. By now our fire team took over. We fired into anything and everything as rapidly as possible.

I raced forward into the village, fully expecting to be cut down. However, I made it to the trees at the edge of the village. I jumped into a canal and ran along its length to the end of the small village. Meanwhile, the rest continued to fire and advance to the edge of the village. I cautiously peered out of the canal, hoping to catch Charlie from behind. There was no sign of him. I then rapidly fired several magazines into places where I assumed Charlie to be. Soon after that the rest of the guys came around. Charlie was gone.

Soon after a Medivac chopper arrived to take in the wounded. We stayed put until the rest of the company came across. I believed this should have been done in the first place. Later I learned that one of the GIs died.

"I knew that the guy who had the chest wound didn't have a chance," I told Uncle Mickey. "The one wounded before him seemed to have a leg wound, though, and I thought he had a chance."

"The one with the chest wound made it," Uncle Mickey replied. "The one with the leg wound died of shock."

After the incident the company searched the area thoroughly. Some felt that burning the place down was warranted. Besides a few weapons found buried in animal pens, there was nothing else. The villagers would only say, "No bic, no BC."

It took a few days to get back to LZ Uptight. After we arrived we heard on the radio what was happening outside of our world. The marines at Khe Sahn had survived the NVA onslaught. I was aware from my brother that our cousin Marvin was with the marines around the DMZ. I had a feeling he might have been at Khe Sahn and survived the ordeal. Other news was D 4th of the 3rd had found a very large weapons and food cache somewhere in the mountains. The 198th had successfully repelled the NVA from Chu Lai during the Tet Offensive. The 196th had seen a lot of action around Tam Ky.

During this time we received the Americal newsletter called the *Southern Cross* and the Armed Forces newsletter, the *Stars and Stripes*. The *Stars and Stripes* gave us an idea of how other units were faring throughout the country. While it may not have been a good idea, we read the KIA section to see if a buddy had been killed. One day as I scanned through the KIA section a name caught my attention. It was my friend Leon-Guererro from basic training whose parents I met in Oakland. This made me sad. I thought of what his parents must be going through. During the rest of my tour of duty I would see more familiar names in the KIA section.

When we were at LZ Uptight there was an individual who often hooked up a water container for the chopper to take in. The water container was either a tank on wheels or a gigantic rubber ball. When it was empty a Chinook chopper brought in a full container and took the empty one. The chopper never landed. It hovered above the container as it created a very strong wind. I still picture Tregarten standing on top of the water container, unhooking the new container and hooking up the empty one.

The guys in the weapons platoon called him Tree. He was white and stocky and had a handlebar moustache. He was very interested in my native culture and often asked questions about it. One day Tree and I sat by the water container. We talked as we looked out toward the ocean. Tree said, "How was it with you growing up? I'm sure it must have been a lot different from the rest of us."

"You're right," I replied. "Would you believe I lived in a canvas tent until I was five years old before I went to boarding school? Even after that I still lived in a tent during vacation from school."

"Do you know how to speak your native language?" Tree asked. "I understand that you are Apache."

"I spoke very little English before I went to school," I told him. "My older brothers and sisters taught me what they could before I did. In my youth all the kids entering school spoke our native language. We had to learn English as we began attending school."

Tree then wanted to know how I felt about being the only Indian in the group.

It wasn't a difficult question. "It doesn't bother me. I'm treated first as an American soldier and then as an Indian."

He changed the subject. "It seems that your platoon depends a lot on you, especially walking point. Sometimes I wonder about you walking in front of the company taking most of the risks. I'm just glad that you are there. You seem to have a lot of confidence about you."

I downplayed his praise. "It's not as it seems. I do the best I can, besides others also walk point."

"That's true," he conceded, "but not as much as you seem to."

Sitting there I went on and explained to Tree some of my growing up experiences. Tree was built like a giant oak tree, as his nicknamed implied. He was a squared away dude.

One day we were again on the north side of lz Uptight, in a village we had checked earlier. On a routine search through the place someone found a hidden tunnel. A volunteer exploring the tunnel soon came out with a vc prisoner. This was an unexpected surprise. Usually there was no one in the tunnels. The tunnel rat reported a large tunnel complex under the village. Believing there might be more gooks underground, we herded all the villagers to the central part of the village.

Lieutenant Lewis called for volunteers to check out as much of the tunnels as possible. Karaba was one who volunteered. Before the guys went underground, Lieutenant Lewis cautioned, "Be careful. Don't become too involved with the tunnel. Don't go too far."

Surprisingly, more prisoners were soon brought out of the tunnels. As additional prisoners were brought out the villagers began murmuring. Some were crying. The way they carried on it was obvious the prisoners were their kin. With all the excitement going on with the prisoners, no one missed Karaba.

A tunnel rat coming out said, "The tunnel complex is very large. It still goes a long ways in all directions. I think we've covered only a small portion of it."

Lieutenant Lewis decided to leave the tunnels to the demolition people. He then asked, "Is everyone out of the tunnel and accounted for?" It was then that we realized Karaba was missing. He hadn't come out since the guys first went in. We feared for the worst. Karaba might have run into foul play. The villagers and prisoners huddled together while we searched in vain for him. As the minutes turned to hours, the worst scenario weighed heavily on our minds.

Suddenly someone shouted from the edge of the village, "It's Karaba, way out here. He's bringing in a prisoner."

Everyone was relieved as Karaba proudly walked in with his prisoner. The distance from which Karaba came indicated that the tunnel complex was very large. Lieutenant Lewis then advised the CO to have demolition experts destroy the tunnel complex.

In all about a dozen prisoners were brought out of the tunnels. After they were flown into Chu Lai for interrogation a demolition team arrived with all types of explosives. The whole demolition operation took about two days. Much of the tunnel complex remained, however, because it was so extensive.

After that we were heading southwest when a small chopper came into view. The chopper was hovering over a village when shooting erupted. We found cover behind rice paddy dikes and waited, focusing our attention on the village where the shooting occurred. Suddenly, a lone figure wearing a cone-shaped hat and black attire darted across the rice paddies. Harlow and I opened up on it. The figure fell to the ground. The way the figure had evaded us, Harlow and I thought we had shot a VC.

The chopper continued flying in circles. We advanced until we reached the place where the figure had fallen. To our surprise a young boy lay on the ground with a leg wound. Harlow and I looked at each other, knowing one of us had shot the boy. Doc Taylor attended to the boy's wound before a Medivac chopper took him to Chu Lai.

A day later at midday we headed north on a main trail. A lone chopper flew in circles directly in front of us. The chopper surprised some VC waiting in ambush, and it chased them into the hedgerows. We were soon inside the hedgerows, following instructions from the chopper. Every now and then the chopper would fire into the thickness in front of us. At a small clearing the chopper landed while the door gunner jumped off. He quickly retrieved a rifle from a dead VC, and the chopper quickly took off again.

We worked as a team, with the chopper chasing some VC into the open as we all opened fire on them. During this time we couldn't see the VC. We just fired into the suspected hedgerows. The chopper eliminated about half a dozen VC in this manner.

After the incident we were ordered to check out the village where the VC had originated. The villagers knew what had happened and were very cold toward us. We also knew that the dead VC were related to them. This knowledge kept us in a high state of alert, knowing there were still some VC in the area.

When the sun started to set we left the village and headed south on a trail. I was the last one to leave. As I left, I had a strong feeling Charlie might try something. Brooks was ahead of me. I warned him to watch out for something from behind.

Brooks muttered, "Don't scare me like that, Chief. You seem to know things at times."

I kept turning around until we passed a grove of banana trees. From there the terrain opened into a large rice paddy area. The banana trees continued west and gave way to thick groves of coconut trees. The large open area was about four hundred meters long with a rice paddy trail down the middle. With the platoon strung out in the open area, I still anticipated an attack from behind us. I said to Brooks again, "I still don't trust the rear. Keep a lookout in that direction."

We were now all in the open. Suddenly something whizzed past my ears, followed by the popping sound. I dove behind whatever rice paddy cover was available. Once again we were under intense fire. Lucky for us the rice paddies were dry, although they provided very little cover. The rice paddy dike Brooks and I dove behind was about a foot high.

Meanwhile, Charlie continued firing at us. It was a mixture of small arms and automatic rifle fire along with grenade launchers. I was on my side and tried to return fire as best as I could. When I did Charlie answered with an intense volley of bullets and grenade rounds.

The rounds hit the paddy dike, and the grenades exploded close by. They seemed to be just barely missing me as I brought my body as close to the dike as possible. I fired my rifle again by holding it above me with one hand and pointing it in the general direction of fire. I didn't feel safe behind the small dike, but that was all that was available.

I looked at Brooks and shouted, "Brooks, how come you're not shooting back? We have to get some fire power back at Charlie."

"I can't," he yelled back. "Charlie's shooting at me. Every time I move the bullets fly by. There's not much cover."

I fired off another magazine as best as I could and waited for some instructions. The machine gun position to the far front was in a much better position than the rest of us. The team was effectively returning fire but had run low on machine gun ammunition.

Lieutenant Lewis shouted, "We have to take some machine gun ammo to Watts. He's in the best position to return fire. The rest of us will have to somehow move further up to his position. How's everyone? What about you, Chief?"

"Brooks and I are in a bind," I hollered. "We hardly have any cover. I agree we have to get in a better position. If we don't, Charlie will outflank us and shoot us from the blind side."

"Chief, do you think you can take some machine gun ammo to Watts?"

"At the moment I can't. I can hardly move a muscle. Every time I do Charlie shoots my way."

"Can you crawl over here?"

"I probably can if I take off my pack."

Charlie continued to fire at us. This was one time he definitely had the upper hand. With my pack off I grabbed my machine gun ammo and started crawling forward. The bullets flew as I took machine gun ammo from each individual I came across. By the time I reached the platoon leader I had seven belts. I told Lieutenant Lewis I was ready to go forward.

Lieutenant Lewis had already called in for gunship support. But we had no time to wait for them. Half the platoon members were badly pinned down behind the shallow rice paddy dikes. Most returned fire as I was doing. I was mainly concerned about Charlie going around and shooting at us from behind. I wondered why he hadn't done that. He had the upper hand. However, we realized that if we stayed put this was exactly what would eventually happen. Then we would truly be in a bind.

When I was ready Lieutenant Lewis yelled, "Get ready to cover Chief, but watch your fire. He'll be coming down the trail in your line of fire."

I knew that the moment I got up intense fire would follow. With the order given I got on the trail and ran as fast as my legs could carry me. I felt rounds flying by, some going through my fatigues. The combined weight of the machine gun ammo wasn't light. After what seemed like an eternity I reached Watts's position and threw the belts of machine gun ammo to his assistant.

Lieutenant Lewis shouted, "Watts, give us some cover fire so the rest of us can get a better position."

Watts and I fired at the far wood line, where I had seen the main enemy fire coming from. That must have been Charlie's position, because the return volley wasn't as intense after that.

With the guys in better positions we continued to direct our fire at the wood line. After that we quickly advanced and overtook the area. Charlie had vanished, leaving behind drops of blood. It was a blessing to have been able to locate his exact position. Charlie would have had an excellent opportunity to inflict a lot of casualties on us if he hadn't remained in place. Fortunately, we received no major casualties.

The sun was setting by the time we regained control of the situation. It would soon become dark. We had to move quickly to the company night position. To do so we walked another klick to the south and moved behind several layers of hedgerows. When the resupply chopper came it brought ammunition to replace what we had expended earlier.

When it became dark Lieutenant Lewis came around and said, "Don't bother digging in tonight. We have to go out on ambush to the area where we were pinned downed today."

This type of situation was not unexpected, but we weren't excited about the change of plans. Soon I was on point as we headed north in the darkness. Lieutenant Lewis ordered us to keep on the main trail until we passed the first village. After that we would go across the paddies. When we reached the village I held up until the platoon leader came forward.

When he did I said, "The villagers are still active. You can see them through the hedges. I hope they don't detect us going by. Maybe we should go into the paddies and swing around."

Lieutenant Lewis replied, "Let's just continue and hope we don't get detected."

"We have to be extra careful when we reach the large opening into the village," I cautioned him. "When we get there we have to go across quickly one at a time."

"Do whatever," he told me, "and we'll follow your lead."

When I reached the opening I stood in the darkness and looked into the village. I also looked at where the main trail went across open rice paddies from this village to another one about two hundred meters away. When the coast was clear I quickly crossed the opening and went to my left into the paddies. The others followed until we all passed undetected. It was getting dark, and the stars were out.

Lieutenant Lewis told us to go further into the paddies, but stay close to the main trail. When we were in the middle of the paddies we were to check our bearings before crossing them.

As instructed, I waited for the platoon leader to come over to where I was. The rest of the platoon members bunched closer due to the darkness and silently sat in place.

Before we could talk strategy someone whispered a message to us. "There's some gooks coming down the trail. Be ready."

With that Jordan whispered, "Everyone spread out, and be ready to fire."

We quickly spread out in the rice paddies and waited, ready to fire. Meanwhile, the figures slowly came down the trail. First there was one, then two, then three, and more. We couldn't distinguish them in the darkness, but we assumed them to be VC on the move. There was no reason to think otherwise. The villagers usually remained inside their villages when it became dark. This was especially true when GIs were in the area.

I had my rifle on automatic and braced myself to fire short bursts. From earlier experience I had learned how to fire the weapon on automatic.

The figures were now in our kill zone. We waited for our leader to fire his weapon. Before that happened one of the figures spoke. It sounded like an elderly woman.

Jordan whispered, "Everyone hold your fire. They sound like women and kids." After that more voices verified that Jordan was correct. I put my rifle back on safety and thought of what might have happened.

More than a dozen women and kids were walking in the darkness. They never knew we were out in the paddies and how close they came to getting killed. If one hadn't made a sound, I know we would have wiped them out.

12. Blessing in Disguise

AFTER THAT NEAR DISASTER we sat in place for a few minutes. We then started north across the dry rice paddies. I was on point with a good idea of where to go in the dark. Within a few minutes I could vaguely make out trees ahead. Beyond the trees was the village where the chopper had eliminated the VC. Off to the left was the wood line where the VC had pinned us down.

Our plan was to set up a couple of ambushes. We hoped Charlie might be active. We went about another two hundred meters before Lieutenant Lewis sent word to hold up. He had a radio message from the CO. I got down on one knee and waited, pointing my rifle toward the front.

A few minutes later the lieutenant whispered, "Our plans have changed. The CO wants our platoon back inside the company perimeter. Chief, you will still be on point. Let's get moving quickly."

After we arrived inside the perimeter, Lieutenant Lewis conferred with the CO. After that he told us the company was on alert status and we might go to Pleiku in the morning. The Fourth Division was having major problems with the NVA and might need our help.

We turned in for the night with that thought in mind. When my turn for guard came around I had next to me a Starlight Scope. This was a recent invention that gave the GIs a night vision advantage. The scope used the light of the stars to allow you to see at night. How clearly you could see depended on how many stars were in the sky. The scope worked best on a clear, star-studded night. If the night was overcast it was impossible to see with the scope. The scope also featured a greenish light in the viewing area. You had to be very careful to avoid being detected by the light. The Starlight Scope was bulky and heavy and was used only when the conditions were right. Therefore, no one cared to lug the extra weight around. However, out of curiosity new members of the platoon often did carry one.

On this night a partial moon rose, making the Starlight Scope that much more useful. When I looked into the scope I could see clearly. We were behind a hedgerow as I checked out the open area to the next row of hedges. I was sure Charlie would not be foolish enough to be sneaking around on a night like this. If he were I could easily spot him with the scope.

In the morning we continued our operation, knowing we might be airlifted to Pleiku shortly. Nothing happened. We then headed farther to the west of LZ Uptight.

One night our platoon was moving south. On point, I used the now-familiar constellation the Southern Cross as a guide. After a while I noticed a village directly in front of us.

Several meters before the main entrance I hesitated. The villagers did not seem to be aware of us. Lieutenant Lewis ordered me to scout ahead.

I put my rifle on automatic and slowly crept through the entrance to the village. Using the hedgerows as concealment, I moved toward the places where fires were burning. Nothing appeared out of the ordinary. Some villagers were sitting next to fires, jabbering away. My attention was on a hootch where a large number of villagers had gathered. I crept closer and could hear them talking. At this point I reached to my side to make sure a hand grenade was readily available.

I crouched behind a hedgerow observing elderly men and women sitting around a fire. Some villagers were going in and out of a hootch, pointing in different directions as they talked. Maybe they were saying where the VC had gone that night. I sensed that the VC were in the area and soon would come out in the open. I waited as long as I could, then silently made my way back to the platoon.

Arriving back, I realized I had been gone longer than anticipated. The platoon members were just outside the village, awaiting my return. After I told Lieutenant Lewis what I had seen, he ordered us to set up an ambush beyond the village.

We then continued for another klick and set up an ambush where two trails met. Nothing happened that night.

In the morning we made contact with Charlie toward the west. One or two VC were shot trying to escape into the thick hills. We were still in the area when the day ended. We set up a night defensive position on a hillside. From our location, two large hills hid LZ Uptight from view and a chain of hills prevented us from seeing LZ Dottie

As always, we welcomed the end of a day. We could shed out heavy, sweat-soaked rucksacks. Weary bodies found instant relief from the burden. The air that hit your wet fatigues felt good. However, the wetness caused by sweat often caused another discomfort. When Hayes discarded his rucksack he complained about pins in his back again. The sensation he referred to was known as "prickly heat." It felt like hundreds of tiny pins were sticking you in the back.

When we got comfortable we sat down to our meal of C rations. By now I didn't care what type of C ration meal I had.

Night was approaching when Lieutenant Lewis called me over and said, "Our platoon will be on ambush tonight. Don't look directly, but do you see the wooded area across the rice paddies?"

"Do you mean the one about two or three klicks away?" I asked.

He nodded. "Yes, that's the place. Can you make out a river and a bridge?"

I looked out of the corner of my eye. "Yeah, I can barely make out a bridge."

"That's the place we head when it gets dark," he said. "We'll set up an ambush past the bridge. The CO tells me that a large VC unit is operating in the area directly south of the bridge. Do you think you can find the place?"

"It should be no problem."

Before it became dark our platoon headed out from the perimeter. We went down the hill, avoiding main trails. From the bottom of the hill we walked across dry paddies, eventually coming upon a small trail heading southeast. The first stars appeared in the clear night sky. We moved as quickly as possible while keeping quiet.

We soon reached a larger trail going southeast. Lieutenant Lewis said quietly to me, "Chief, I don't trust trails, but we have to get to our objective as soon as we can. We'll just have to go on this trail to make faster time."

With that we continued on the trail, heading southeast. I recalled from the map that this trail met up with a trail going southwest, and after a while we did reach that juncture. We were in a large open rice paddy area and began heading southwest. A strong breeze was blowing from the east. Out in the distance was the faint sound of water flowing. I knew when we crossed the open area we would be moving through different vegetation and would be very close to the river. I had my rifle ready as I cautiously made my way across the rice paddies.

After we reached the denser growth the sound of the river became loud. Here another trail headed toward the west, parallel to the river, so we followed it. I became much more cautious, as we were very close to some villages. I hoped that dogs would not sense us and start barking. We slowly crept by, undetected, as the sound of the river became even louder. I knew a bridge would be coming up shortly.

We left the villages and continued forward, with thick vegetation flanking our left and rice paddies to our right. Shortly after, another trail appeared, winding toward the river and, presumably, toward the bridge.

Following that trail, we reached the river and the bridge within a short time. By now the sound of the river was very loud. I held up until the platoon leader came forward and said, "Chief, we have to cross the bridge. We'll have to maintain good spacing as we do." The bridge had large poles tied end to end to walk on and waist-high guide rails for balance. I put my rifle in my right hand and used my left hand for balance. H. P. aimed his machine gun across the river as I started across. I deliberately took small steps and used the guide rails.

It quickly became apparent that crossing the bridge would not be easy. It was dark, so you had to watch your step closely and hang on to the guard rail. Down below you could still see faint reflections of the rapidly flowing water. You had to be careful not to be hypnotized by it, as it caused an illusion of the bridge moving. I was in a precarious position but had to keep moving. Charlie might detect our position.

When I was about halfway across I had second thoughts. Was this the right bridge? It seemed that the bridge I had observed earlier would have been easier to cross. When I reached the other side I knew I had made a mistake and crossed the wrong bridge. Fortunately, the bridge was very sturdy and allowed several of us on it simultaneously.

The trail on the other side wasn't used much. Ahead there was a strong smell of human waste. The local villagers apparently used that spot to relieve themselves.

When Lieutenant Lewis crossed I told him, "I think I made a mistake. This is the wrong bridge. I think the one we wanted is further to the west."

Lieutenant Lewis replied, "That's okay, the platoon crossed safely. Just continue to the west." He stopped and sniffed. "What's that smell?"

With the platoon reoriented I led them west across the rice paddies, using a cluster of bamboo for a bearing. It was barely visible against the night sky. The sound of the river was still loud. When I arrived at the bamboo cluster the rice paddy dike next to it was waist high. We were next to a small trail that appeared to lead to the bridge we wanted. Here I held up and waited until Lieutenant Lewis gave me the go-ahead to follow the new trail.

I then climbed on the trail and slowly headed into the darkness. When I reached the bamboo cluster I froze. I thought I saw movement farther up the trail.

I whispered to the person behind me, "Something is up ahead. Pass the word back to be ready."

In the next instant I heard a gook voice, so I remained silently in place, concealed by the bamboo cluster. A shadowy figure headed my way and appeared to be alone. At that moment different ideas of what to do crossed my mind. My first thought was to blow the guy away with a burst of fire. However, there might be others. It was best to remain silent. I then reached for my survival knife and grasped it. Again I reconsidered. It was best to take prisoners alive, because of the possibility of obtaining valuable information from them.

Meanwhile, the person was getting very close and appeared unaware of me. When he was close I gave him a horizontal butt stroke with my rifle. The darkness threw me off and my blow wasn't accurate. However, it stunned him enough to disable him momentarily. I then jumped into the rice paddies and clamped my hand over his mouth. The guy was very light, so it took very little effort to subdue him and throw him over the dike.

What happened during the scuffle often comes back to me. Harlow was close behind me that night. He later told me that the gook I captured was part of a large VC unit. When I was scuffling with him, Harlow saw shadowy figures scurrying away against the night sky. He couldn't say for sure, but he estimated that there had been more than a dozen.

The bridge we were supposed to have crossed was only a short distance away. It appeared that Charlie had been waiting for us at the bridge, but fate got in his way. Had we been on the bridge as planned we would have taken heavy casualties. That night was the first and only time I missed my objective. As it turned out it was truly a blessing.

Our plans changed after the incident. We headed south with the prisoner toward some hills, crossing rice paddies to reach them. We climbed a hill in total darkness, going through several rows of hedges. After reaching the summit we set up a perimeter. We dug in well and set up a 50 percent alert for the night. We knew there were more VC in the area.

When we settled into our night watch Harlow and I whispered to each other. "I have a bad feeling about this whole thing," he murmured. "There were a lot of gooks going by in the darkness. I know they are still out there waiting for us to make the wrong move."

"As long as we have artillery support from Uptight we should be okay," I whispered.

"That's only as good as whoever is reading the map and getting grid coordinates."

We talked quietly for a while longer. "Let's hope the lieutenant knows our exact location," I said. "You know this is the stuff that boyhood dreams are made of."

"I know what you mean," he replied. "I dreamed of this as a boy myself. The only problem is when it's the real stuff the situation is a lot different."

"One of these days when we get back to the world we'll remember this night. Hopefully we can all get together."

I had just fallen asleep when I was awakened and told to get ready to move out. The prisoner had escaped and we needed to move our position.

We quickly brought in our claymores and trip flares and moved out. In the darkness we made our way down the hill and headed southwest. When we reached a main trail we went to the middle of the dry paddies. The rice paddies were high enough to conceal us well, so we spent the night there. In the morning Lieutenant Lewis came over to where I was. He apologized for his CP group allowing the prisoner to escape.

"Are you sure the guy was a VC?" I asked.

"I have no doubt he was," he replied. "Chief, you never make mistakes when on point, but I'm glad you did last night. I'm convinced Charlie was waiting for us on the right bridge. I hate to think of what might have happened."

He paused and added casually, "By the way, I'm putting you in for a Bronze Star."

I was mildly surprised and could only say, "What for? I didn't do anything."

13. Landing Zone Bronco

AFTER A RESTLESS NIGHT we prepared for another tough day. Using the tall rice paddies for concealment, we made our way to a tree line before it became light. Here Lieutenant Lewis told us, "Our objective this morning is to check out villages to the south. This place is supposed to be the ARVN's AO. We'll look around anyway. The other platoons will also be in the area. I don't know how long we'll be here. Take nothing for granted. We might make a sweep to the southeast when the other platoons arrive. If Charlie knows there is a company of GIs he'll surely head there."

The company was to search only the villages close to the river. Around noon our platoon was in a large village when we were told of a change of plans. That afternoon we joined up with the rest of the company and headed north, back across the river.

Within a short time we were next to a bridge spanning a large river. It was the same bridge where we had nearly run into disaster the previous night. When I crossed the bridge I again had a strange feeling of how fate had stepped in our way. I felt fortunate for our platoon. We had dodged a large bullet.

After crossing the bridge we continued north into large open rice paddies. From there the company strung out, with dry rice paddies on each side of us. When well into the open area we passed a guy, who turned out to be a fellow named Jones from another platoon, squatting next to the trail. Apparently he had diarrhea and had to go, no matter what.

When Whitaker reached Jones he said, "What's happening bro? It looks like you have the GIs."

"I sure do," he grunted, "and I think it's the damn water from a well."

"The well has nothing to do with it," Whitaker replied. "That's what you get for not using your iodine tablets bro."

Jones remained squatting and shrugged. "It's too late to worry. You know how it is. When you gots to go, you gots to go."

"Don't spend too much time in place," Whitaker warned. "Charlie might get a good bead on you."

After crossing the rice paddies we headed southeast along a large trail until we reached a hill. From there we went north straight up the hill. The hill appeared small, but it was higher and steeper than it appeared. The hot sun baked us as we slowly ascended. I was glad to have enough water, and every now and then I swallowed a mouthful. With sweat pouring down my face, I climbed and looked out over the countryside. Out in the distance in a hazy mist was Pinkville. I knew we were better off on this side of the river.

By now some guys were wearing flak jackets, although they made the hot weather more intolerable. We weren't required to wear them. They were worn under the rucksack and were useful for stopping shrapnel and small-caliber bullets. Their added weight and bulkiness were the main reasons some GIs chose not to wear them. I never wore one, feeling more confident when I was as mobile as possible. Of course, when your tour of duty was winding down and you became a short timer, you could put up with the extra weight.

A guy named Shriner was a short timer and took no chances. He wore a flak jacket religiously, even as we climbed the hill on that hot day. He had arrived in-country with the Eleventh Brigade. Earlier, Shriner told me that he had tried to avoid coming to Nam. He continued, "It's just my luck to join the Eleventh Brigade just before they departed for Nam from Hawaii. At the time I had five months left in the army. Before I knew what was happening I found myself in Nam and in the infantry." When Shriner finally made it to the top of the hill the combination of heat and extra weight had left him frustrated and irritable. Hayes, already at the top, asked Shriner what time it was. Shriner threw his soaked rucksack and flak jacket to the ground. He looked at his watch and snapped, "It's four fucking thirty. I'm glad I have only a few more weeks to put up with this crap." Shriner eventually did make it back to the States.

When the entire company reached the top of the hill the CO chose a large clearing as a perimeter. The remainder of the day was relatively leisurely. Some guys wrote letters; others formed groups and chatted away. I laid back under a shade tree and continued reading a paperback I had picked up along the way.

The following day our platoon went east down the hill for a day operation. There I recognized a village—the same one we had searched my first day in the field. Returning there made me realize how much time had elapsed since I had arrived in the field. I had become a lot more sure of myself. I felt good about walking point and being able to lead the guys. I was more aware of what was expected of me and knew that it was more than luck that had gotten us through some close calls.

That afternoon the company met back at the same hilltop spot as the night before. The resupply chopper brought fresh supplies and mail. After eating we anticipated getting orders to go out on ambush, and so we waited.

Before it became dark Lieutenant Lewis and I spoke with Captain Michles. The captain advised us that there might be VC activity in an area closer to the sea and showed us a map of where he believed the VC might be intercepted in the early morning hours. The area was about five klicks away according to the map.

Pointing to the map, Captain Michles asked, "Do you think we can get to this spot after it gets dark?"

Lieutenant Lewis looked at me. "What do you think, Chief?"

It looked doable. "I'm sure I can get there" I answered. "We have to cross the hills to the east. All the trails go around them. To avoid detection we are better off going cross-country through the hills. The going will be very slow, and it will take some time."

Captain Michles nodded. "As long as we are in position before midnight. Let's do it."

When it was dark we left the hill on a trail and skirted the north side of a village. I had learned that it was best to avoid trails whenever possible, though the trails the villagers used a lot were very safe. Upon reach-

North of Chu Lai. *Foreground*,
TeCube; *background* (facing
camera), McCloud (Smokey),
unknown, Nevins.

(*Above left*) TeCube (*foreground*) and Geary, getting ready for combat air assault, LZ Uptight.

(*Bottom left*) Inside a bunker, LZ Uptight. *Left to right*: unknown, Hadaway, Uncle Mickey, Topcat.

(*Above*) TeCube (*left*) and Espinosa (Tex) next to a bunker, LZ Uptight.

Villagers selling wares, west of LZ
Dottie. *Left to right*: Wilson, Fields,
Geary (with beret), Hayes, Ladd,
Jordan (leaning on tree).

(*Above right*) Entertainment by a
Filipino musical group, LZ Dottie.

(*Bottom right*) Vietnamese kids,
west of LZ Dottie.

Chopper pad, LZ Dottie

Duc Pho. *Left to right*: Kent, Anderson, Karaba, TeCube.

ing the rice paddies we headed cross-country. Walking in the darkness, we had to keep the pace slow, which I felt better about. By now the darkness was completely upon us, intensified by a slightly overcast sky.

We entered hilly terrain. The hills were small, but hedgerows and the darkness forced us to go slowly when crossing them. Now and then our platoon had to halt to allow the rest of the company to catch up. After crossing the hills we held up in the rice paddies and again waited for the rest of the company. When they did we all rested at the edge of the paddies. We had been moving about two hours at this point. Within a few minutes our company commander came over to our platoon.

"How are we doing?" Captain Michles whispered.

"From here the terrain is rice paddies," Lieutenant Lewis answered. "We should be at the right place before long. Our objective is about two klicks."

About half an hour later we were moving slowly through the rice paddies. I knew that ahead lay a main trail that ran from north to south and swung around to the east. That was my objective as we plodded forward.

I came upon that trail and followed it south and then east toward a populated area. I was certain Charlie was not aware of our presence. After reaching the villages I moved, as ordered, in a northerly direction to skirt them. However, I kept encountering hootches on both sides. Eventually we set up a long blocking force on the north side of the hootches.

Charlie didn't show this time. Only a couple of VC were captured by another platoon. Our tactic, however, had been successful at other times. On an earlier occasion Guthrie had nabbed a VC while we waited in some paddies. The VC were usually captured in small numbers, since they were smart enough not to move in large groups unless absolutely necessary.

For the next few days we continued operating in the area. The platoons spread out in different directions, checking as many villages as possible. One afternoon I was on point, leading the platoon northeast. Suddenly small-caliber rifle fire erupted, and then machine gun rounds flew over our heads. Some of us returned fire immediately. The rest jumped into the dry rice paddies and raced to cover behind the far paddy dikes, from where we also returned fire. A moment later more machine gun fire came at us. This time we could see the red tracer rounds.

Lieutenant Lewis yelled at us to cease fire when he noticed the tracer rounds. After a radio check we realized that another platoon had been firing at us. Charlie had either planned or accidentally caused two platoons to fire at each other. I learned later that a GI in the other platoon who carried a machine gun had just fired from the hip when rounds came at him.

When we regrouped the captain advised the platoons to make a large sweep to try to outflank Charlie. If he were still in the area we might run into him. We then went north across rice paddies to avoid mines that Charlie would set if our path was obvious. After we went a klick or two we doubled back, again avoiding trails, in order to meet up with the company.

In doing so we took a chance and followed a main trail. Walking point, with rice paddies to my left and hedgerows to my right, I rounded a bend. I spotted someone squatting next to the trail doing something. He looked up at me in complete surprise with large, open eyes. We looked at each other for a split second before he bolted into the hedgerows. I knew the guy was planting a mine.

I quickly fired my rifle into the hedgerow and raced after him. He ran across a small clearing, heading toward a grove of coconut trees. I fired one round after another as he entered the grove of trees. My rifle was on semiautomatic. To my surprise a coconut tree a foot in diameter fell down. The VC disappeared into the thick vegetation.

When the excitement ended Uncle Mickey, who was behind me, said, "It surprised the hell out of me to see that coconut tree fall down. I saw your bullets hit the trees and bushes the gook ran behind. It must be his lucky day."

A cautious check of the place where I'd first seen the VC confirmed he had indeed been setting a mine for us. In another minute or so our platoon would have suffered at least one more casualty. The odds were high that it might have been me. Once again I had dodged a bullet.

A day later we headed west toward LZ Uptight, following the main trail that ran just south of the outpost. The place looked deserted, which wasn't surprising, given that it would be foolish for anyone to be out in the heat of the day. I saw the point element meandering up the large hill and felt a sense of relief. We would be inside the perimeter with some daylight to spare.

That evening a large number of VC were suspected to be nearby. We were alerted to a possible attack. In times like this no ambushes were conducted. Instead, listening and observation (LP, OP) posts covered the possible avenues of enemy approach. In my view, the posts weren't sufficient to cover all avenues from the west. The hill was too large. I never feared Charlie coming up the steep slopes on the north, east, and south sides of the perimeter, where the slopes were heavily mined.

Many of us were still awake around midnight, anticipating that something might happen. Just before midnight shooting erupted on the west end of the perimeter. It continued for a few minutes. After that the artillery fired illumination rounds into the air. I wanted to see better and so grabbed a hand flare nearby, even though I wasn't too familiar with it. I only knew you hit it sharply on the bottom. I pointed the flare into the air and gave it a sharp thrust on the bottom. The flare shot up into the air and within seconds it glowed bright red. This wasn't the type of illumination I had expected. I watched the flare slowly descend to the ground. Within minutes Lieutenant Lewis and others came huffing and puffing to where I was.

The platoon leader demanded, "What the hell is going on? Who fired off the red flare?"

Standing next to him, I admitted to the deed.

The lieutenant drew himself up and looked at me. "You aren't supposed to fire a red flare unless you are under heavy attack."

I apologized and was told to forget it. I wouldn't repeat that mistake.

We learned that something had tripped some flares, causing those on guard duty to fire. The lieutenant assumed that sappers might have tried to probe the perimeter or deliberately set off the flares from some distance. The CO ordered us on a 50 percent alert for the rest of the night. I still believed that Charlie would have a hard time penetrating the perimeter on the side we defended. Yet our rule was not to take chances.

No more shooting disturbed us that night. The only sounds of gunfire I heard were far to the north. I thought that perhaps the 198th Light Infantry Brigade stationed in that direction might be heavily engaged with Charlie.

During this brief rest on LZ Uptight we had a slight change of diet. Until that time we had eaten C rations three times a day. To our delight, the Sixth of the Eleventh Artillery had just started providing hot meals. A large tent served as a kitchen. Outside the tent someone made a sign that read "Greasy Spoon." The hot chow from the Greasy Spoon was a welcomed change. We even had breakfast. The artillery personnel also had TV reception good enough that one night Nevins, Guthrie, and I watched *Gunsmoke.* While out in the field we often relied on the artillery personnel to get us out of a jam. Now they gave us hot meals and entertainment to boot.

Although LZ Uptight had a small perimeter, there was an area in the center large enough to play basketball. A basketball goal had already been erected there by earlier units. Here the platoons would compete against each other, or a game would develop among anyone who was present. The weapons platoon was a favorite challenge for our platoon. Their leader was a tall, black soldier who happened to be quite talented at round ball. Our star player was Watts, another black. Watts teamed up with his favorite buddy, who was white and whose name I can't recall (but I do remember that his favorite expression was "My damn self.") Anyway, he and Watts gave the weapons platoon a run for their money.

The USO sent young ladies, called Donut Dollies, to remote places like LZ Uptight to entertain the troops. I remember seeing them on a couple occasions. Their main mission was to boost GI morale, so the Donut Dollies spent as much time with the troops as possible. They were a good source of information on what was happening back in the world. They got the infantry and artillery to compete against each other in trivial games, which proved to be great fun for everyone involved.

On one visit the young ladies shared a meal with us, compliments of the chef from the Greasy Spoon. The north side of the hill, where the Greasy Spoon sat, was steep. One had to be careful walking in the area. Nevins and I were sitting together eating our meal when a young lady came our way. She nearly lost her balance and fell down the steep slope. We quickly came to her aid. After spending a few hours and lifting our spirits, the young ladies were flown back to Chu Lai. Only later would I realize just how much of a chance they took to come to places like LZ Uptight. They flew over the same territory where Charlie often fired at choppers. Thank God for the Donut Dollies.

Once when our platoon was going out on ambush we intentionally left while it was still light, heading south out of the perimeter. Lieutenant Lewis had hoped to fool Charlie about our destination. When it got darker we planned to change direction and continue west around the hill toward our position. After night fell, we made good time in the darkness. I felt comfortable with the strong breeze muffling our movement. I could see the faint outline of the large hill off to the right. From there I knew that much of the terrain would be rice paddies. I had my rifle at the ready and walked slowly to allow the rest to keep up. Coming over a slight rise, I knew we were close to our position. From there we moved forward another three hundred meters or so until we were close to two villages. We set up an ambush to cover the mail trail between the two villages and set in for the night in tall, dry rice paddies. Nothing happened that night, however.

At daybreak we spotted some VC, who came out of the hedgerows and quickly made their way toward the village off to the left. They were outside of claymore range so, just before they reached the village, we fired at them with a machine gun and several M-16 rifles. A large hail of bullets hit some and followed the rest as they raced for cover in the village.

We quickly scrambled through the brush to the village entrance, where we found two VC downed and followed blood trails further inside the village. The villagers denied that the VC were there. Instead, they brought to us a small boy who had been shot in the leg. They pleaded with Lieutenant Lewis to call in a chopper for the boy. The lieutenant told them he'd do so if the villagers would show us where the VC were hiding. The villagers continued to deny the VC were there, so the lieutenant refused to call the chopper. The boy was instead carried by his relatives or neighbors in a homemade stretcher toward LZ Uptight. When we returned to LZ Uptight later that day, we learned that the boy had been flown to Chu Lai.

Early the next morning our company left the hill, and after reaching the main trail, we headed west. We continued at a steady pace. Some villagers were already using the trail that day. About two or three klicks farther were hills. The main trail that we were following wound through the hills from Highway One all the way to the South China Sea. We were unsure where we were going. LZ Dottie? Maybe even LZ Bronco? We certainly wouldn't mind leaving this AO. We had had enough of mines and booby traps.

We passed the hills safely and then entered more open terrain. After going another klick, we "took five" on the trail. I leaned on my rucksack next to Whitaker and Doc Taylor. "Hey Doc, how can you hump all that lead around?" Whitaker said

"I have to make sure I don't fall short if a bunch of guys get wounded," Doc Taylor replied. "I can handle the weight."

"I know what you mean, but it looks like you carry twice as much as the rest of us."

"That's nothing. When I was with the 196th I carried a heavier load, farther."

By that evening we had journeyed about twelve klicks and had reached LZ Dottie. We learned that in the morning we would be going to LZ Bronco by truck convoy. Some guys were familiar with the place, but I looked forward to seeing it for the first time.

In the morning we loaded onto deuce and a half (two-and-a-half-ton) trucks by platoons. Soon we headed south on Highway One with an armed escort. The ride was a new experience for us. We weren't as concerned about getting shot at as we were about hitting a mine. Our tension eased as the civilian traffic increased.

All kinds of people were on the road. A common sight along Highway One was the three-wheeled Lambretta vehicle. When you saw one, you thought it large enough to carry only three or four passengers. However, the Vietnamese used this vehicle to its limit and beyond. Sometimes you saw it carrying up to a dozen passengers as it sped along the highway. Some passengers would be clinging to the sides; others would be holding live chickens and pigs. The vehicle would sway back and forth like it was about to tip over, but the passengers didn't seem the least bit concerned. Other civilians rode bicycles or motorcycles or walked, some carrying their wares with the dummy sticks.

The landscape rolled rapidly by yet remaining unchanged—nothing but rice paddies and hills. As we were driven down the dusty road I thought back to my youth on the reservation. I remembered how we often rode in back of a pickup truck as we sped down a similarly dusty road. My cousins and I enjoyed throwing rocks at bottles as we sped along. I also thought of my uncle and how he took the time to teach me how to drive.

There were a million things I wanted to do when I got home.

Eventually we reached a fairly large settlement, Quang Ngai city, the largest town in Quang Ngai province. It was bigger, but the place wasn't modern by any stretch of the imagination. The same hootches that we found everywhere were here too, but so was a Shell station, which seemed strangely out of place.

The convoy stopped briefly in the center of the city. Here we all stood in place, stretched our muscles, and looked around. The brief stop gave the local vendors time to rush to the vehicles, hawking the usual wares. I bought a soda pop from one of them.

While we waited in the trucks the kids gathered around to talk to us. Most of the kids appeared happy to see us, because we meant money to them. However, an older boy became offended at some writing on a GI's helmet. "How come you put Fuck Vietnam on hat? If you no like Vietnam, how come you come Vietnam?" he asked the soldier.

The GI glared at the boy and cursed. "Hey, fuck you. You little son of a bitch. I had no fucking choice. If I had my way I would blow this whole damn place to hell."

The boy became even more offended. As the convoy pulled away, he shouted, "Hope VC kakadao you!"

The GI gave the kid the finger and said to us, "Fucking VC anyway."

We continued south from Quang Ngai city, and within an hour we were within sight of LZ Bronco. From a distance the large hill rising from the center of the base camp stood out like a giant Vietnamese grave. The terrain around the base camp was the familiar mixture of hills and rice paddies. The smaller hills gave way to larger mountains to the west. The mountains met the sea around LZ bronco, and rice paddies lay in between.

When we neared the base camp I realized that the place was larger than I had imagined. More villagers and military vehicles were coming and going. The base camp had bunkers all around the large hill. On the north side were choppers and fixed-wing aircraft.

A small Vietnamese settlement, Duc Pho, was just outside the base camp. LZ Bronco sat to the east of the village, a short distance off Highway One. Our dusty convoy turned just north of Duc Pho and went east toward the main gate of the base camp. Before the main gate was a large laundry where GI fatigues swayed on a clothesline. Our convoy left a large cloud of dust on them.

Inside the main gate the convoy turned right and continued to the south side of the perimeter. This was the Fourth of the Third Battalion sector. The other battalions, the Third of the First and First of the Twentieth, were farther to the east. From there other units completed the large perimeter.

LZ Bronco was the main base camp of the Eleventh Light Infantry Brigade (LIB). Originally the main base camp was farther to the east. It was called LZ Carentan. The Eleventh Brigade soldiers were nicknamed "Jungle Warriors." They conducted operations mainly south of Chu Lai. The My Lai Massacre gave them a bad reputation, but it must be admitted that they held their own against the VC and NVA in their AO. They had to conduct an effective campaign against a seasoned enemy with very little in-country experience.

In the fall of 1967 there was a call for additional U.S. military troops for Vietnam. The Eleventh Brigade was part of the buildup. However, it was badly undertrained in Hawaii. Many replacements were assigned to the brigade just before it left for Nam. This overall lack of experience contributed much to the early mistakes that the unit made in Nam. Like all main units, however, the Eleventh Brigade soon became battle wise and an effective fighting force. This part of the brigade's history is overlooked by military historians. I'm sure the other units were all too glad to leave the responsibility for the area around Pinkville to the Eleventh Brigade.

The convoy passed a holding area with vc prisoners or suspects. Inside the pen the prisoners squatted the way the Vietnamese did. I wondered what their fate might be. A Chieu Hoi program urged the vc to give themselves up. Around lz Uptight an airplane often circled high in the air, urging the vc to surrender. The message was broadcast through loudspeakers and by dropping hundreds of leaflets. These were called Chieu Hoi leaflets. There were several types, and they measured about four by six inches. I can still picture the leaflets turning and fluttering as they drifted down from the sky. Over time they would scatter throughout the countryside. I don't know what the words said, but the pictures on the leaflets told the whole story.

The truck convoy stopped next to the battalion area. Here we got off and got into formation. The co advised that we would be here for a few days and that we shouldn't expect hot showers. We didn't care whether the water was warm. The luxury of a bath or shower was almost nonexistent in the field. After a good cold shower we changed clothes, then selected cots in one of the large tents erected for us. It felt good to be able to relax with clean attire.

The tents had large ditches around them to divert water during the rainy season. The ditches also served as refuge in case of a mortar or rocket attack. To the west of the tents were pallets of sodas and beer; to the east was the battalion headquarters. The mess hall was located to the north, and the perimeter to the south. There was a large open area between the battalion headquarters and the mess hall.

The hot meal was a welcomed change from C rations. While eating I noticed one of the cooks was the same Puerto Rican I had filled sandbags with at Chu Lai. After eating I grabbed a couple cans of beer and went back to my cot. Again it sure felt good to relax.

Until then I had received mail occasionally. Receiving mail was the thing that boosted your morale the most. Getting any news from home made your day. Of course, as a precautionary measure we were warned not to carry letters and to burn them after reading them. If Charlie got a hold of your letter, he might send a booby-trapped package or whatever to your home address.

On this day I received a package from home. It was from a ladies' church organization and contained nonperishable goodies. The package also contained a modern version of the Bible called *Good News for Modern Man*. This I put in a plastic bag, next to my heart. I kept it there for the rest of my tour of duty.

When you received a package of goodies others shared it. That night I, Nevins, Vic, and some others feasted on the goodies. A few days later I sent a letter to the organization and the local paper thanking the group for their act of kindness. It was a simple gift, but it made you realize that there were people supporting us, despite those who were protesting the war.

14. Back to Chu Lai

WHILE AT LZ BRONCO almost everyone in our company received a Combat Infantryman's Badge (CIB). One morning the company held a formation, which was unusual. We were used to getting information through a chain of command. Now we stood at attention in our weathered attire. Captain Michles explained the significance of the CIB and how we qualified to receive one. Then the CIB was issued to us one by one. We had met the criteria and then some. When I received mine I held it in my hand and looked at it. The badge had a blue background with a wreath around a rifle.

I had received various awards through the years and took them in stride, but I felt differently about this one. A great sense of pride and accomplishment, not for the suffering and ugliness of combat but for being able to deal with the hardship, washed over me. The badge meant that I had successfully met the enemy in the extremely hostile environment of his own backyard.

Other medals were awarded at that time. Captain Michles also gave us a general idea of how the brigade, the division, and the U.S. military were faring against the enemy. As a whole, according to the captain, the war seemed to be going in our favor. What we had experienced in the past months, however, seemed to indicate otherwise. I thought back to all the trails walked and villages searched. It's true that Charlie had been eliminated in many instances. He still controlled the countryside, however.

After the awards were issued we had some free time. We went to the village of Duc Pho in small groups with several bandoleers of ammunition. Although small, the village had quite a few shops. At one I saw displayed many GI military items that seemed brand new. I wondered how they had ended up here. I remembered requesting some of those same items on resupply, including a new survival knife, but I couldn't get them.

This was the first of my many experiences with the black market. I asked Nevins, "I wonder how all that stuff ended up in the gooks' hands?"

"It's a racket, corruption, or whatever you want to call it," Nevins snorted. "The REMF [Rear Echelon Mother Fuckers] sell them to the gooks."

"I heard this is a common practice throughout the country, mostly at the grunt's expense," Vic added.

In Nam I believed most of the rear area personnel did have a genuine concern for the grunts. Many of them had already spent time out in the field before they found assignments in the rear. For every grunt out in the field there were five noninfantry personnel to support him. There were rear personnel who looked down on the grunts and often took advantage of them, however. These were the ones called REMFs by the grunts.

One evening a group from Australia, including a live band and go-go girls, entertained the troops. To make the show livelier, beer flowed freely. As the show went on the GIs hooted and hollered. We were in a party mood.

One of the songs they played was by the rock group the Animals, a song that I believe best identified how the GIs felt about the war. As the song started, the words "My little girl you're so young and pretty" quickly caught our attention. By then everyone seated, standing, or within hearing distance was listening. Some who could follow or halfway follow the words were singing along. When the chorus began, singing ability didn't matter: drunk or sober, everyone joined in as loud as he could:

We gotta get out of this place.
If it's the last thing we ever do.
We gotta get out of this place.
Girl there's a better life for me and you.

Our short rest ended all too quickly, but it was good while it lasted.

We returned to the Task Force Barker area, ready to go back out in the field. Our company first headed east of LZ Dottie. Parts of this area were hills dense with trees and vegetation. This was the type of terrain where a machete came in handy. The guys took turns whacking a path until we reached more open country. Our progress was better, but we also afforded a better target for Charlie. I recognized this area as the place where a member of our platoon had been killed earlier. We felt uneasy.

We continued searching villages that day. At an abandoned one Hadaway found a hidden crossbow that he took as a souvenir. I knew that Charlie had an array of weapons, but somehow his using a crossbow never crossed my mind. During the war many GIs took souvenirs off a dead enemy to send home. Most of the time it was a rifle. According to my tradition, taking a dead person's belongings was taboo, so I refrained from doing this.

After leaving the abandoned village we were crossing open rice paddies when we came under intense automatic weapon fire. We huddled behind the paddy dikes. Some returned fire by holding their rifles above the paddy dikes and firing short bursts. I tried the same with my rifle, but it wouldn't fire. What was wrong? I quickly chambered another round and put in another magazine. Still it wouldn't fire. I felt utterly helpless but tried not to panic.

Meanwhile the firefight continued, and we remained pinned down. "Does anyone know where the gooks are shooting from?" Jordan hollered.

"I think they are coming at us from two directions!" someone yelled back.

Jordan looked over at me, puzzled, "What's the matter, Chief?"

"My rifle is jammed. I'm trying my best to get it working. I could feel more shooting coming from our right."

Lying on my back behind a foot of cover, I took my rifle apart. I poured LSA (special oil) over the working mechanism and worked it back and forth. I could hear Jordan shouting for H. P. to bring his machine gun over to him. I tried everything, without success. I repeated what I had already tried. After a few more minutes I pushed all the moving parts with a finger and quickly reassembled my weapon. I then held it above the paddy dike with one hand and was relieved when it fired.

After pummeling the paddy dike with bullets, we raked the wood line to the right. We continued shooting a few more minutes and then Sergeant Jordan shouted, "We have to get moving! We can't stay here forever. Is everyone ready? What about you, Chief? Is your rifle working?"

"It is, and I'm ready."

As H. P. concentrated heavy fire at the far wood line the rest of us moved out. As I ran to the next paddy dike, I prayed that my rifle would continue to work. It did, and I felt a great sense of relief. We eventually managed to overtake Charlie's position with our firepower and artillery support.

Until that fight I believed I took good care of my rifle. We all carried rifle cleaning kits, which we used often. From that moment on, I assumed nothing about my weapon—it was always better to double-check. On the other hand, one of Murphy's Laws of Combat might have come into play. That is, "Never forget that your weapon is made by the lowest bidder."

One day we were west of the large hill in the lz Uptight area. Our platoon had captured several vc suspects. They were held off to the side as we rested on a main trail. To escape the heat we rested under a grove of coconut trees where two main trails met. We waited for a chopper to transport the prisoners into Chu Lai.

While we waited, Hadaway and some others interrogated the prisoners. I knew from past experience that it would be impossible to get useful information from them. I rested in the shade.

After a few more minutes the chopper arrived and took away the vc suspects. When it left Winston said, "Hadaway and some others worked them over real bad."

"Did they get any information out of them?" I replied.

"No," he grimaced, "you know you can cut off their ears, but they still won't talk."

"We only made better vc out of them," I speculated. "Maybe they will accidentally fall out of the chopper."

Winston took me seriously. "You know, we have never seen that sort of thing, but I have a feeling that it does happen. I heard that in some units vc suspects are interrogated in flight. If they choose not to talk, one will be pushed off. If the others do the same they receive a similar fate."

"If that's true," I remarked, "I'm sure the prisoners talk. It seems like an effective method to me."

After the chopper left, instead of heading south we remained in place. As we waited I observed a spotter plane circling high above. This type of plane scouted for and observed VC movements. They appeared more frequently during combat assaults, but to my knowledge there were no combat assaults in our area. I wondered if we were due for one.

The plane circled farther to the south around the ARVN AO. Perhaps the ARVNs were making a combat assault? The notion seemed remote and absurd. I had been in-country long enough to know that the ARVN units were very reluctant to conduct combat operations. Of course, there might have been some good ARVN units, but the majority seemed reluctant to fight. Instead, U.S. military units made the initial combat assaults, and it wasn't until an area had been secured that the ARVNs would move in. Between this type of ARVN conduct and the persistence of the VC, you wondered how South Vietnam could endure.

After another hour we headed south toward a village across the rice paddies. Along the way, we came across a dud artillery round lying off the trail. We carefully checked the round for a booby trap. After determining that it hadn't been tampered with, we had to blow it up in place to prevent Charlie from using it against us. This was how all dud rounds found in the boonies were handled. It was very important to do so.

The explosive C4 was most often used to explode dud rounds in place. TNT was sometimes used, but C4 was the preferred explosive. It was white, looked like dough, could be kneaded into any size, and was very handy to use. To blow up a dud round a chunk of C4 was placed around it. After a blasting cap was inserted into the C4, a fuse was set and lit. The demo man knew how much fuse to cut to get away from the explosion safely. Every platoon had an individual who volunteered to do this dangerous task. He usually carried the C4 in rectangular canisters.

A popular and unauthorized use of C4 was to heat up C rations. The standard way to heat C rations was by using heat tablets. These came in a foil package similar to an alka seltzer pouch. An empty C ration can served as a stove. Holes were cut around the top and bottom of the empty can with a can opener (the old-fashioned type, before pull tabs). A heat tablet was placed inside the can and lit. The meal was then placed on top of the "stove" and would heat up within a few minutes. A small chunk of C4, however, would heat the meal evenly within seconds. When lit with a match the C4 burned quickly and very hot. Although the C4 had to be obtained illegally, many GIs were using it. Some didn't, reluctant to carry an explosive with them.

On this day we had no demo man, so one from another platoon came over to blow the dud round. I was familiar with this person. He had been with the company for the past few months and didn't look or act particularly bright. Hump, who was quite vocal at times, used the word *doofus* to describe the guy. Well, the demo man seemed to know what he was doing in this case. He quickly had the explosive ready and told us, "I set the explosive for about three minutes. I advise you guys to get farther away."

When the demo man left, children from the nearby village came running toward the area. Anticipating a disaster, we yelled at the kids from the coconut trees. They froze in place and just stared at us. They had no idea that an explosion was going to take place and that they were well within the kill zone. To get our point across, someone fired over their heads, scattering the kids toward the village. The dud round exploded noisily. Satisfied that everything was all right, we quickly caught up with the rest of the company.

Meanwhile, the company had continued west on a trail into the hills. On top of the hills a village was nestled among the thick jungle growth vegetation and trees. It was a typical village with one exception—on a slope stood a large building that appeared to be a temple. We had gone through this village before but hadn't checked it out thoroughly enough. We entered the temple and were confronted by a very large statue of the Buddha. The ten-foot high statue had a forbidden appearance, and was arranged in the usual sitting position. It seemed to be made of gold the way it shone, but I assume it wasn't. All around the statue and large interior room were other religious objects. This quiet place made a deep impression on me and reminded me about the many diversity of religious beliefs around the world. Out of respect, we were very careful not to do anything inappropriate.

After leaving the village we continued toward LZ Dottie, arriving at the main gate when the sun was still above the horizon. After getting settled, I decided to get my long hair cut, to make it easier to manage. I walked to a tent that had a barber pole outside, where I was greeted by a heavyset soldier who wore a military uniform and was flashing a big smile.

The cheerful dude said, "How you doing, soldier? I gather that you want a haircut?"

Glancing around, I answered, "Yeah, but I'm not too sure what type. I haven't had a haircut in quite a while." I gestured toward my hair. "All I know is it's getting too long to manage. Why don't you just cut it short with a flat top."

"No problem," he said, and proceeded to cut off my long hair. After the barber was through, we chatted for a few minutes before I left.

When I entered my bunker the only one inside was Scheindler. He just stared at me but said nothing. When we did talk he appeared hesitant and puzzled by my presence in the bunker.

After a few minutes we went to the mess hall. Scheindler went along, still looking perplexed. We got trays of food and sat with several platoon members. Everyone treated me as a total stranger. Vic asked, "Who's the new guy with you, Scheindler?"

Scheindler shrugged. "I don't know. He came into my bunker and seems to know me."

Vic peered at me and said slowly, "Is that you, Chief?"

"Yeah it's me," I said, looking around at the guys. "What do you guys think?"

Scheindler spoke first. He looked at me and said, "Chief, I didn't even know it was you. I wondered how some stranger seemed to know me."

Vic and Nevins didn't like the haircut and felt I should have left it long.

During this time I was promoted to the rank of Specialist Fourth Class, or Spec Four. This rank was almost equivalent to that of being a corporal. In Nam everyone coming up the ranks made Spec Four after Private First Class. I understood that I was one of two who received the promotion. I had not expected it, and it gave me a great sense of pride. I also knew the new rank would bring responsibility. So far I had taken orders and was comfortable doing so. Karaba came over to me several times to comment about my promotion. He couldn't believe it or didn't want to believe it.

I've mentioned Karaba in passing before. He was an individual you never forgot. He was white, about six feet tall, and on the lanky side. He didn't seem to have had a decent education and had difficulty reading and writing. Sometimes when Karaba received a letter he would ask me to read it to him. I obliged and also wrote several letters for him. I still remember him holding his knees together as he sat on the ground. While he leaned on his knees he would ask me to repeat a sentence that had caught his attention. Eventually I knew as much about happenings in his hometown as in mine.

One incident in particular comes to mind. One day Karaba was writing on his camouflage helmet cover. He asked Wilson, "How do you spell 'War is Hell'?"

Wilson spelled it, repeating himself until he felt Karaba understood. After a few minutes Wilson noticed that Karaba had written WAY IS HELL on his helmet cover. "Karaba, you spelled it wrong," Wilson chided. "You put WAY IS HELL. It should be WAR IS HELL."

"It doesn't matter," Karaba replied good-naturedly. "Any way you look at it, it is hell."

Wilson laughed and agreed.

One day Lieutenant Lewis decided to send guys to Chu Lai on a regular basis, just to give as many of us as possible a chance to get away from the field.

I would be the first to go. I had no problem with this and got my gear ready—no matter where you went, you always took all of your gear. When the resupply chopper came I climbed aboard and soon was being flown toward Chu Lai as the lone passenger. The South China Sea was a blue haze to my right. I looked at the terrain below and recalled the first time I flew over it. Then I had had a lot of questions. Now I knew what was down there.

I relaxed, feeling good about making a dent in my tour of duty. About halfway to Chu Lai the chopper came under automatic rifle fire. A round hit the side. The door gunner immediately swung his machine gun downward and fired off about two hundred rounds of ammunition.

When we neared Chu Lai I recognized the large complex, sprawled from the foot of the mountains to the sea. The battalion area had changed, and now was located closer to the airstrip. After the chopper landed I reported to the battalion personnel. I was to spend a couple of days in Chu Lai and hoped to get out of guard duty. I soon learned, however, that every available body had to pull guard. I ended up in a bunker with guys from different companies.

When it became dark six of us were in one bunker. All of us were grunts from different companies, in Chu Lai for various reasons. We talked and exchanged information about what we had done. Most of our operations were identical. We were all chasing Charlie throughout the countryside. We felt we had no business in Nam. For whatever reasons, however, we had to continue the offensive.

Soon the conversation changed. Someone remarked, "I heard that Korean entertainers will be here tomorrow. It might be worth staying another day."

When it got dark a rumbling began in the large mountains to the west. This time Charlie had nothing to do with the noise. Instead, mother nature put on a show for us. There was lightning and thunder at the top of the mountains. It was a striking sight. The top of the mountains was the only place where there were clouds. The lightning would burst into a ball of light inside the clouds. The thunder wasn't very loud.

We were to pull one guard shift for the night. I had the first watch. Later, while we were shooting the breeze, someone brought out some dinky dow. Everyone had a turn, and so I did too. After a couple of hits I had drifted into my own world. The rest of the guys were laughing next to me, but they seemed far away. I had completely erased the war. My thoughts were back at home. Well into the evening hours, the guys called it a night.

In the morning I caught a bus to the northeast part of the base, about two miles away from the battalion sector. The bus driver was a Vietnamese who was very unfriendly. I asked him where the bus went. He snapped, "Bus go to beach and PX on hill." I found a seat close to two marines. They acknowledged me by waving their hands. Infantry personnel usually recognized each other.

When we neared the beach, a GI waved the bus down. He asked the bus driver, "Is this bus going to the replacement center?"

"No," the bus driver said abruptly, and slammed the door in the soldier's face.

One marine muttered, "I know what I would do with that bastard if I caught him out in the field."

This incident exemplified the attitude many Vietnamese had toward us. They were rude and believed that the GIs were in Nam to do their bidding. If this type of behavior occurred at the peasant level, one could imagine how it was at the top. It's no wonder that our government met the demands of high-ranking Vietnamese officials to escalate the war.

I got off the bus at the main PX. The last time I had been there was with my buddy Wilcox. I hoped I wouldn't see his name in the KIA section of *Stars and Stripes*.

For a change, I didn't have to be anywhere and was in no hurry. I walked around the PX, looking at and into everything. I spotted some small suitcases in a pile and, on the spur of the moment, bought myself one. I also bought other items for the guys back in the field.

I then headed to the beach area, where I had walked when I was a replacement. The beach area was down an incline from the PX. It looked the same as it had when we were new replacements. To the south, as before, trucks transported replacements to the processing center.

The USO was my main destination. I had hoped to get a cheeseburger and fries there, but the place served only cold sandwiches and chips. It also had magazines to read and records to listen to. The atmosphere gave us a temporary escape from the war. I bought a sandwich and sat down to do some reading. All the popular magazines and major newspapers were available. Reading the periodicals, I realized there was much opposition to the war. Nam was big news for people back in the world.

A few hours later I arrived back at the battalion. I met up with Sergeant Harris from the weapons platoon, a guy I was aware of. He also knew of me, as the Indian who walked point a lot.

I knew that some members of the platoon thought of Sergeant Harris as a lifer, one who went strictly and harshly by the books. When I sat next to him at the mess hall I wondered if that might be true. It is my way to give someone a chance to show his true self. As we talked, Sergeant Harris turned out to be different from his image. I got along with him and actually enjoyed his company. He had a good sense of humor.

That evening Koreans entertained the battalion personnel. Sergeant Harris and I sat at a table as we watched the show. I took a close look at the Koreans. To me, they had certain features that distinguished them from other Asians. The evening's entertainment was what we needed. We ended up in a good frame of mind.

The resupply chopper was scheduled to leave the next afternoon. This gave me another day to do whatever I wanted. Another soldier and I went to a village close to the perimeter. It was no different from the ones next to Highway One, boasting the usual souvenir shops selling the usual black market items. The only difference was that there were more bars and prostitutes here. As usual the establishments' primary concern was to make the GIs part with their money. It was no different from any city next to any military installation anywhere in the world.

In the evening I rejoined the platoon at LZ Uptight. Wilson asked, "Well, how was it like in Chu Lai? I know it is probably still the same, but is there anything different?"

I thought about this question for a moment. "To be honest, there hasn't been much change. Only that our battalion sector is away from the mountains. I really enjoyed the free time. I had a chance to talk with others to get an idea of what is happening in the division. According to what I heard, other units are conducting the same types of operations. I think another battalion will be joining the Eleventh Brigade. It's the Fourth of the Twenty-first and will be coming from Hawaii."

In the morning we were back in the field, conducting another routine search and destroy operation. During this time there was a lull in VC activity. Our operations in the Pinkville area were temporarily on hold, which no one minded. Charlie seemed to have melted into the surroundings.

Sometimes our morale would get very low, and we would think of the days crawling by. Our clothes were torn and often had gaping holes. The once shiny helmet covers and the messages on them had faded.

The faces and attitudes of the guys had changed. We had all experienced what the animal inside could make us do. Our real selves were dying, being replaced by individuals molded by the dangerous world we lived in. Any way you looked at it you would never again be the same person you once had been.

We all counted down the days until we would be leaving. Harlow got approval for early discharge to go back to college. He was now a short timer. Shriner was leaving soon. Most of us had less than six months to go. The business of conducting a war had to continue, however. You still lived each day thinking that it might be your last. That thought was on your mind every time you left a perimeter.

What separated the infantry personnel from the others was that it didn't matter if you made contact. Just living with this constant danger was enough to make your tour of duty a lifetime.

15. Observation Post Black

IN EARLY JUNE OUR COMPANY was transported to Chu Lai by truck convoy. We spent the night at the northeast sector of the perimeter, where the rocky cliffs met the ocean. The following morning a ferry took us across a channel to the north. The terrain there was thick jungle and rocky shoreline.

From the shore we climbed a steep incline to reach an outpost called Lamsite. Once inside the perimeter, a marine sergeant gave us instructions about what to expect. Marines normally manned the place; in this instance we were to relieve them for a few days.

An area reserved for cleaning weapons was off to the side. It was the only place of this type that I encountered in Nam. It contained a large reservoir of cleaning solvent, much like auto mechanics use to clean parts, which we used generously.

The food served at the mess hall was better than most we'd had. The whole environment so far suggested that this would be a good place to spend some time.

Lamsite was located next to the sea. At the bottom of the hill was a village nestled in the thick jungle. The section of the perimeter closest to the sea consisted of steep rocky cliffs. The layout of the perimeter gave you a great sense of security. However, Charlie was still in the area and had to be kept in check. By day we conducted operations as we had at LZ Uptight. One platoon manned the bunkers while the others went on patrols. The sea surrounded most of the perimeter, so all the day patrols went to the west, encountering a dense mixture of coconut trees and jungle growth.

In the nearby village vendors sold the usual souvenirs or black market items. The people were friendly toward us when we searched the place. At one shop two young ladies were very friendly and spoke good English. The presence of able adults was something new and strange. At all the other villages we had checked previously we had seen only the elderly or the very young.

One young lady in particular caught my eye. She was very attractive, although she had a bad burn on her chin and neck. One afternoon as we chatted with them, Guth, a new GI, wandered off by himself. The rest of us sat in a hootch and drank cans of soda. The young lady kept glancing around and appeared uneasy. Finally she said, "What happened to the new GI?"

"Don't worry about him," Uncle Mickey reassured her. "He's just checking out the place. Like we should be doing."

Meanwhile, she continued to look around nervously. Uncle Mickey took us aside and said, "The girl is acting strangely. Maybe she knows something we don't."

"She's trying to tell us something," I said. "I think Charlie is closer than we suspect. We'd better be on guard and look around for Guth."

At that moment Guth returned. He looked agitated. "I thought this place was safe, but I became uneasy when I realized I was by myself. I felt like someone was watching me."

I knew that feeling and told him that's exactly how you feel once you become familiar with your surroundings. I warned him that that type of feeling should not be taken lightly. Charlie was undoubtedly not far away and was just waiting for the right moment. We warned the others to keep alert.

While not on patrol some guys went to the Ole Swimming Hole. The problem was getting there—you had descend a steep cliff. Ropes were used to reach the ocean next to the cliffs, which were pounded by large waves. Only individuals who knew how to swim well could go down the cliff. I was just an average swimmer, but one day I decided to take a chance and climbed down with some others.

Once I reached the swimming hole I had second thoughts. The sea was one giant rolling swell, sending waves crashing onto the ledge I stood on. I wanted to back out, but instead I jumped into the treacherous water with the others. The constant motion of the sea made it very difficult to swim. I was lucky enough to grab a rope nearby and pull myself out with it. I left the rough sea to those who could handle it.

At Lamsite was an Enlisted Men's (EM) club of sorts. However, both EMs and NCOs mingled inside. At the first opportunity I went with a group to check out the place. Once inside we talked to some marines seated in a corner. We found out they were also temporarily out of the field and were operating just south of Da Nang. One marine insinuated that he had been at Khe Sahn during the siege. We sat with the marines and exchanged information for about an hour.

Later that evening, at an outdoor setup, I had just sat down to watch a movie when a sergeant came over. He said, "Chief, there's no one at your bunker. Someone has to be on guard."

"Fenstermaker is supposed to be on guard," I said, not taking my eyes off the movie. "Check with him."

The sergeant didn't go away. "I don't know where he is. All I know is someone has to be on guard and you're it."

This was my first chance to enjoy a movie, and I argued as best as I could. Finally the sergeant ordered me to get to the bunker. I lost my cool, told the sergeant I hoped he got zapped, and stalked over to the bunker. Later I apologized to the sergeant. He, being a professional, understood and left it at that. During the year these types of outbursts often happened in the heat of the moment.

We spent a week or so at Lamsite. The day before we left, Wilson, I, and several others out on patrol stopped at the village. On a spur of the moment we all bought bush hats from a vendor. When we arrived back inside the perimeter, Lieutenant Lewis laughed as we paraded around with our new headgear.

I was on guard duty our last night there. I didn't go to the EM club with some others, but I heard later that our guys got into a scrap with some marines. One guy at the scene told me a marine, probably the one who claimed to have been at Khe Sahn, provoked H. P. into an argument. H. P., who was very stout and heavily muscled, wasn't the type to be messed with. When the argument heated up, H. P. sent the marine flying across the floor, which started a ruckus. No one was seriously hurt, however. Incidents such as this involving different units were quite common in Nam.

Early the next morning we boarded swift boats and headed farther north. We passed through large channels before wading ashore at a very shallow landing area. The unfamiliar area appeared secure.

We stayed in the area for a few days before making a combat assault farther north. We eventually ended up next to a large road that we knew had to be Highway One. While we humped along the highway I had the feeling we were headed to a base camp. After walking for a few klicks we did just that, entering a base camp next to the highway.

I called to the man who always seemed to know things, "Hey, Whitaker, where we at?"

"I heard this place is Hill 54," he shot back.

"What outfit's AO is this? I know it's not the 11th Brigade's."

"I'm not sure, but I think it's the 198th Light Infantry Brigade's."

Once again Whitaker was right, Hill 54 was in the 198th's AO. The 198th LIB was nicknamed the Brave and Bold. Their assignment was the defense of Chu Lai, and they had base camps all around the perimeter. It was a tough assignment, as they engaged both the VC and the NVA, to keep them from inflicting heavy damage on the important base.

Across the highway from Hill 54 was an OP atop a small hill. Our company was to secure the perimeter of Hill 54 and the OP as well as to guard a bridge farther south.

I learned that VC sappers were active here. They had tried several times to infiltrate the perimeter but had failed every time. On some mornings their bodies dangled on the concertina wire. Charlie also actively mortared the base camp. He would walk the mortars into the perimeter after it became dark, firing a few rounds and quickly leaving. Ambushes went out, but Charlie remained elusive.

One night our platoon went out on ambush south of Hill 54. Around midnight we heard and felt the familiar thumping of mortars close by.

The sound appeared to come from a thick grove of trees. We knew Charlie would soon be gone, so we had to do something fast and quickly got on line. We sent a large volley of fire along with artillery rounds at Charlie's suspected position.

At daybreak we checked out Charlie's location. There was evidence he had received heavy casualties. His mortar tube was nearby, along with blood trails here and there. After that incident we received no more mortar rounds.

Fortunately I was left out of the bridge security detail. Hadaway had to take a squad to spend several days guarding the bridge. Word was Charlie wanted to destroy the bridge, and he had almost succeeded several weeks earlier. After a couple of days at the bridge, Hadaway came down with malaria and was evacuated by chopper. He had a very high fever followed by chills.

Those who came down with malaria did so by failing to take their daily malaria pills. I understood that the critical problem was the fever, which could cause body temperature to rise to 106 degrees. The temperature had to be lowered immediately. To accomplish this, the afflicted individual would be placed in a bed of ice. You could just imagine what it must be like when you had the chills.

One day the company set up a perimeter next to Highway One. An ARVN soldier took advantage of the situation and brought a Vietnamese prostitute to where we rested. The soldier said, "She good boom boom. Only twenty dollars."

"Too much," someone replied. "She's too scrawny looking. I'll give you five dollars."

The ARVN soldier became irritated. "She no too scrawny. She number one. I take ten dollars."

At this point a young Kit Carson scout with us intervened. He cautioned, "No boom boom. She no good. She same girl who give GIs clap. I know, she also give me VD."

When the ARVN heard the interpreter, he insinuated that the scout was lying. Most of the guys listened to the Kit Carson scout. However, some took their chances and took the girl behind the bushes for five dollars.

While operating west of Hill 54 one day we received sniper fire from a village directly below a large hill. The village appeared to wrap around the hill to the right. We slowly approached the village and then were ordered to get to the top of the hill. The sniper fire came from the right, so we swung around to the left in the rice paddies.

Soon we reached a trail that went around the large hill to the left. Here I went on point and continued forward, trying to locate a possible way up the hill. The slope was covered with dense and tangled growth.

Going up that hill was easier said than done. I used a machete to try to hack my way through the thick vegetation. The going was painfully slow, and the intense heat was no help. I hacked and hacked and hacked and still came to a point where I had to crawl on the ground. That's what we all ended up doing. It wasn't easy crawling up a hill with the heavy pack, particularly with limbs, leaves, and branches reaching out and grabbing you.

We inched our way up the hill, soaking with perspiration. About three-fourths of the way up I saw daylight ahead and became even more cautious. Eventually I reached an open area with tall grass, which extended about a hundred meters farther north. After catching my breath, I continued moving to the end of the open area. Brooks and H. P. were right behind me with the machine gun, and the rest of the guys were still making their way up the hill.

When I reached the summit, I realized that it was more open on the other side. The hill dropped away sharply and offered a broad panorama. I stood and watched a trail directly below the hill. It led north through rice paddies to more thick vegetation.

At that instant my mind went back to a crisp October day back home, when I had been out hunting with my uncle and cousins. I had stood at the top of a place called Honolulu Mesa. When you stood on top of a rocky layer, above the surrounding trees, you could see a large area below. That day a herd of deer had kept just ahead of me. From my rocky vantage point I checked out the piñon trees and rocks below. Suddenly, I heard the thumping sound of the elusive deer. I turned and saw the herd. The bucks were making their way down a ridge. When they were in the open I fired my rifle. One fell to the ground.

As I stood on a distant hill in Nam, reminiscing of better times, I heard a commotion below. I looked down to see some VC coming out of the jungle to my right. The leader waved his hands, urging the others to hurry. At the same instant I motioned with my hand to H. P. and Brooks to do the same. When they reached me I pointed to the VC, who by now were on the trail headed toward an open area. Without any hesitation we opened fire. Some fell and the rest scattered. We continued firing at them until they disappeared again into the thick bush.

When the shooting stopped Lieutenant Lewis came huffing and puffing over to us, demanding to know what the hell was going on. After we filled him in, the lieutenant told us to continue forward. He warned us, "Remember, Charlie plays dead at times. If you see bodies, watch out. There might be a live hand grenade."

I made my way down the hill to the trail the VC had taken. A body was lying in the middle of a rice paddy. We soon found more after a quick look around. The VC had documents on them, and they also wore a belt of rice around the waist. The belt consisted of a long cloth with several compartments of rice and evaporated milk. This, a hammock, ammunition, and weapons were all each VC soldier usually carried. He also wore sandals made out of old truck tires. Those he often discarded when he had to get out of an area quickly.

We also discovered heavy blood trails leading into the thick jungle. We began to follow these, but we were soon ordered to abandon the search.

Our platoon received orders to continue north and intercept VC headed our way. As we moved out, choppers appeared ahead of us, a scene I was familiar with. Charlie was caught out in the open by the choppers, and the whole operation netted some VC.

Shortly after this operation we went back south of Chu Lai to a location somewhere north of the Task Force Barker area. Earlier while in this area, we had encountered mines, which again became a major concern for us.

During this time I continued walking point. I recall that once we were trekking cross-country to avoid the mines. Most of the time this strategy worked. Not this time. Just as I reached the top of a small hill I heard an explosion behind me. Miraculously, no one was badly hurt. Only Guthrie, the GI from my home state, sustained a wound, which the medic quickly tended to. The wound was minor, but as a precautionary measure Guthrie was flown to Chu Lai.

Guthrie had stepped on a booby-trapped hand grenade. Normally this type of booby trap inflicted a severe wound or caused a fatality. In his case the booby trap must have had a heavy cover or something like that. When the explosion went off it sent him flying in the air with something preventing the main blast. The men closest to him were startled by the blast and nothing else. This incident made us even more wary of the area. No matter how much caution we used, however, we still encountered mines.

One day I was leading the platoon toward a coconut grove to the south. As we approached the trees I sensed something wrong. I held up, telling Lieutenant Lewis, "I don't trust the place. There are no villagers around. Normally, you see them standing out in the paddies."

Lieutenant Lewis respected my judgment, but we had orders. We needed to rendezvous with the company ASAP. I was told to proceed with caution.

Before I reached the coconut trees a large explosion rocked the ground behind me. Screams of pain and cries for a medic filled the air. I anticipated rifle fire from my left and crouched behind a rice paddy dike. I fired some shots into the trees to my left. Our right was exposed, but there was a long, open stretch of paddies on that side. I just hoped Charlie wasn't there. Not receiving fire, the point element advanced to the trees to provide better security.

Meanwhile the medic and some others frantically worked on the wounded. Word was relayed to us that Lieutenant Lewis and Larry, his RTO, were both badly hurt. Those nearer to the wounded passed their first aid packs to the medic. Every now and then I glanced back at what was happening about fifty yards behind me. After a while someone said, "The lieutenant is gone. We have to try to save Larry."

Larry had a sucking chest wound. A piece of shrapnel had punctured his right lung, and it was in danger of collapsing. The medic yelled, asking if someone had a piece of plastic. Jordan thought of the plastic that covered the spare battery. The medic used that plastic to cover the hole in Larry's lung, allowing him to breathe. Larry and the lieutenant were evacuated to Chu Lai. We were relieved to find out later that Larry survived.

One of the GIs who had tried to save Lieutenant Lewis told me about his last minutes. When they realized that the lieutenant had both legs blown off at the knees, they had tried their best to stop the bleeding. In fact, they had succeeded. The lieutenant was awake and appeared very strong. He could have made it, but he read someone's face. He knew then that both his legs were gone. After that he went very quickly. He didn't want to live with both legs gone.

Our platoon leader was gone. Sergeant Jordan assumed temporary command.

Shortly afterward we ended up at a small outpost called OP Black, which was close to the South China Sea and at the mouth of a large river. The OP was inside a village with concertina wire around it. On a rise above the village was another small outpost. That place was on sandy terrain and had a small perimeter with several bunkers. It wasn't very secure, protected by only one strand of concertina wire. However, it did give us a good view of the surrounding area. We were to spend a few days here providing security for the villagers. We settled into bunkers and mingled with the villagers in small groups. One fire team secured OP Black in the center of the village.

The village was generally the same as others except for one interesting difference. The villagers were more friendly. Kids adopted GIs, tagging along and waiting on us in order to gain our favor. They mostly wanted C rations. There was a small boy who would hang around me. I told him my nickname. He tried to say Chief, but it came out as Sip. The little guy did whatever he could. I usually gave him a can of C rations.

Another friend I made was a small girl named Ow Wee. She was about ten or eleven years old and quite smart. She was more fluent than most in English and could carry on a good conversation. One day she showed me a gold necklace around her neck. I asked her if it was real gold. She handed it to me and commented on the weight. The necklace was heavy, like lead. It appeared to be pure gold.

"How much you want for the necklace?" I asked her.

"I bought necklace for thirty-five dollars," she replied. "I give you necklace for thirty-five dollars."

She then produced a receipt for the necklace, but I didn't buy it. Years later when the price of gold skyrocketed, I regretted that decision.

Another friend was a young girl about fifteen or sixteen years old, but I don't recall her name. She knew I was different and took a special interest in me. She understood about American Indians and often asked me questions about them.

A young man about fifteen or sixteen years of age gained the favor of all the GIs. His name was Mike, and he was very bright and likeable. Mike had picked up a lot of English and was very good at speaking it. He enjoyed our company, and we all felt comfortable with him.

I also became well acquainted with a barber. I struck up a friendship with him after he visited our compound to cut hair. He was very good at his trade, using only a hand clipper.

Until our time at OP Black, I thought no place existed in Nam where you could strike up genuine friendships. Yes, there was no place that was truly peaceful, but this village came the closest.

One day the reality we knew best again intruded. Brooks and I were sitting next to a bunker when we came under heavy sniper fire from a far wood line. Bullets flew and hit all around us. One bounced off the bunker and missed Brooks by inches before falling into some empty ammunition crates. Another tore a hole in his fatigues. Brooks later retrieved the bullets and kept them as souvenirs.

Our location seemed remote, but other units were nearby. Once a squad of marines visited while on a routine patrol. They had come from an outpost farther to the east. One soldier said, "You guys have nothing to worry about around here. All the action is taking place up north along the DMZ. We would rather be up there but are stuck here."

Ladd, my soft-spoken friend from Michigan, replied, "As for me, I would just as soon be here."

"I know we will be going back to the bad places soon," Tex admitted in a resigned tone. "I hope we don't go back to the place where all the mines are. I'd rather be up north than put up with mines."

A night or two later we heard a lot of shooting from the marine outpost. The marines must have been getting it bad. We wanted to go to their aid, but we had to stay put. Charlie's intention was for us to leave our perimeter so that he could take advantage of the situation. Another unit close by did help the marines, but they arrived too late. Most of the marines had been killed.

I do have some good memories about OP Black. One fine day we thought a dip in the ocean would do us some good. Those who wanted to swim toted their air mattresses toward the beach. The village kids knew what we were up to and came running. My little buddy and the other kids blew up our air mattresses, which they then carried to the beach.

The beach rimmed a large cove. The waves were very small, and the setting seemed like a south-sea paradise. As always, we set up guard positions for security. The rest, including the kids, jumped into the water with the air mattresses. This water felt better than the turbulent ocean I had tried to swim in the last time.

Stacy, Nevins, and I floated and kicked farther out to sea than the others. We went out as far as we could safely. We dove into the water and noticed that the deeper we went, the colder it became.

When we made it back to shore, the kids came over to us, bearing a slimy ball the size of a grapefruit. I was surprised to see that it was an octopus. Until then, I had thought they were all very large sea creatures.

Another memorable occasion was when the village barber invited me to his home, which was toward the back of the village. When we arrived there he introduced me to family members and friends. I understood very little of the conversation, but I enjoyed their friendship and hospitality.

An elderly man took out a board game and played with the barber. After a while the man invited me to play, while the barber went to get a bottle of liquor and some Cokes. He mixed the liquor and Coke in two glasses and gave me one. I motioned to inquire what was in the bottle of liquor. The barber said, "Is rice," meaning rice whiskey.

Meanwhile the game continued, with several men playing. An elderly man said something and held up a glass. The barber said, "Papasan want make toast to you. He say you look like Vietnamese."

"Tell papasan I drink to that."

The barber said something to the group and patted me on the back. The group of men and women standing to the side had large smiles on their faces. They laughed at a remark the barber made.

Soon everyone was into the board game, every now and then yelling out or laughing aloud. There was a great deal of laughter, and somehow I didn't feel like a stranger.

The atmosphere at the barber's house reminded me of my own people back home. They also laugh and joke a lot. When a group gets together there is always laughter. A lot of good-natured joking goes on among certain relatives. It is all in good fun. The person who is the butt of a joke is not supposed to get angry, no matter what. If he does, it only makes matters worse for him.

Histories of my people usually tell how they survived through many hardships. However, nothing is ever mentioned about their ability to laugh during times of distress. Personally, I believe that this trait is what pulled them through the times of despair.

I miscalculated my ability to handle the mixed drink. I had not realized how potent it was. I had always felt that I could handle my liquor well. Not this time. As the game progressed I became woozy. Everything started spinning. The villagers were amused, but the barber realized that I should be back at the bunker area. He led me back up the hill. I don't remember much about the rest of the night but I do recall dropping my rifle in the sand and some guys settling me in a bunker. I was vaguely aware of two new replacements, who I later learned were Hastings and Brittenham. That night I didn't pull guard duty.

I woke up the next morning with a headache. I didn't get up immediately; instead, I remained in place and tried to recollect what had happened. I knew that I was on top of a bunker. There was movement inside the other bunkers, which indicated that someone was still on guard duty. After a while, I lifted my head slightly. No one else was on top of the bunker or any of the other ones. My mouth was dry, so I looked around for a water canteen. When I couldn't find one, I got up with the intention of going down to look for one.

At that instant a hail of bullets flew past me, followed by a popping sound. I forgot my headache. It seemed to me that I was Charlie's only target. He appeared to be shooting from a wooded area to the south. Next to me was an M-60 machine gun. Determined to return fire, I grabbed the gun, got on one knee, and directed fire to the wooded area. I used the tracer rounds to guide me. After I fired off a belt of ammunition I leaned down to put another one in the machine gun. It was then Charlie's turn, as he retaliated with another volley. The bullets came close, hitting the sandbags that concealed me. When the shooting subsided somewhat, I fired off another hundred rounds. Our duel continued back and forth until the GIs began firing.

"Chief, is that you?" someone said.

"Yeah, it's me. It's time to get up."

"Forget the wisecrack. Where's Charlie shooting from?"

"It's from the wooded area directly south. Just shoot in that direction, he'll get the message."

As always, when too many bullets came his way, Charlie stopped shooting and fled the area. A patrol later in the morning found drops of blood, but Charlie was long gone.

The same day E Company Fourth of the Third, the recon company for our battalion, walked into the perimeter. The recon company was more like a platoon and had about thirty men. They unloaded their gear in the center of the perimeter. I recognized one of the guys coming toward me. He said, "Is that you, TeCube?"

"Yeah, it's good to see you, Hanson. How you doing?"

"I'm okay—just counting the days like everybody else. By the way, we also have an Indian in our platoon."

Hanson called the guy over. To this day I can't recall the guy's name, but I do remember that he was from San Juan Pueblo, which is close to my hometown. We talked for about half an hour, until a large chopper arrived. The chopper took E Company toward the west.

The perimeter at the outpost wasn't very secure. During the day, little kids often walked through the concertina wire to talk to us. The kids came to do different chores or just to be nosy. Once when I was sitting writing a letter, a small girl came over to where I was and tried to talk as best as she could. After a while my little buddy joined her. Uncle Mickey and I sat talking to them for a while. As always, their objective was to get something out of us. When we gave each a can of C rations they left. Alone again, I continued writing a letter home.

That was when Tex yelled, "Hey, Chief, your girlfriend is calling for you."

"What girlfriend?" I asked, puzzled.

Tex grinned and pointed to the far end of the small perimeter. There stood my teenage friend, wearing a cone-shaped straw hat. I walked over to her and saw that she was dressed in her best attire.

She said she was going to Bing Son and had come over to let me know. She was taking a shopping trip to the larger city. Here, though, the river served as the main means of transportation.

We talked for a few minutes and strolled to where a large open boat full of villagers was waiting. On the spur of the moment, I handed her a ten-dollar bill. I told her to buy herself something nice. She smiled big and joined the villagers in the boat. Propelled by an outboard motor, the boat moved off around a bend toward the west.

A few hours later I happened to be in the vicinity when the boat returned with the villagers. My friend was delighted to have spent the day at the larger settlement. This young lady liked me and showed a great deal of interest in me.

All too soon we left this small part of Nam. It was a rare place, one rich with opportunities to observe and get to know local people. Their livelihood seemed independent of the Vietcong's. These people seemed to be in control of their own affairs.

16. Hiep Duc Valley

WE BEGAN THE MONTH OF JULY in the Task Force Barker AO. A huge blow to our morale was the loss of Captain Michles and Colonel Barker, who were killed in a chopper crash. Captain Michles was a leader who cared about his men, although some thought he pushed us too hard at times. A platoon leader assumed temporary command of the company.

We began hearing rumors that we might be going farther north of Chu Lai. The hot days continued to crawl by, and some guys were going home. Shriner had completed his tour of duty and left. Harlow would be leaving toward the end of the month to pursue his education. Orders were eventually received for the company to go to Chu Lai. We left LZ Dottie by truck convoy. As we passed the village next to LZ Dottie the villagers waved to us. A young lady ran out from the back. Someone recognized her and teased, "Hey, H. P., your girlfriend is chasing after you."

Whitaker had to add something. "H. P., why don't you bring her along? She can take care of that puppy of yours." During this time H. P. had become attached to a puppy and carried it with him.

The trip to Chu Lai seemed short, and we were soon inside the sprawling Chu Lai compound. The dusty convoy stopped at the 4th of the 3rd Battalion. We jumped off the trucks and left our gear to the side. The CO advised the company to be ready to move out but said we would be spending the night. We washed up and put on clean fatigues. There was cold beer and soda pop on ice.

For whatever reason, Willingham had arrived the day before on a chopper. When he joined us it was obvious that he had already helped himself to the cold beer. He stumbled around in a drunken manner, but no one paid attention to him.

Tents with cots were our accommodations for the night. We tried to relax, although it was hot. Hot chow would be served shortly.

In the evening we sat in groups and speculated about our next move. An act from the Philippines was to entertain us that night. By nightfall the guys were in a proper festive mood from the beer. Other companies joined us to form a large, receptive audience of GIs. There were about two or three hundred additional men at the compound. We sat in a wide semicircle to hear the music and watch the dancing girls. A rock band played some popular music from the states. The guys sang along with songs they knew. The entertainment went on into the night.

It caught my attention when the MC introduced a female singer with a surname of Gonzales.

I said to Wilson, "It strikes me as strange for Asians to have Spanish surnames."

"I hear you," Wilson replied, "but I happen to know that most Filipinos have names like from your part of the country."

I stood corrected. "I guess it shouldn't be too strange," I responded. "My own people have Gonzales and other Spanish surnames."

As we talked, the singer was well into her performance, which included a striptease of sorts. All the guys, being in the mood, kept yelling, "Take it off!" The act continued until the alcohol got the best of Brittenham. He jumped on the stage and danced with the girl. This was a cue for the person in charge to end the show.

In the morning Whitaker announced, "I understand we'll be joining the 196th Light Infantry Brigade up north at LZ Baldy, their main base camp. We'll be operating under their control for a few weeks."

Hump shook his head and asked, "How come you know all these things?"

"I can't tell you," Whitaker replied mysteriously. "Just trust me."

What Whitaker told us was (again) true. Chargers was the nickname for the 196th Light Infantry Brigade, which operated north of Chu Lai. Their main adversary was the 2nd NVA Division. When the 196th arrived in Nam, they were part of the 25th Infantry Division around Tay

Nihn. In the fall of 1967 they deployed to Chu Lai to become part of Task Force Oregon. The task force later became the Americal Division. A segment of the 196th LIB was the last American combat unit in the Vietnam War.

We realized that we'd be dealing primarily with the NVA. I already knew that the 196th had made heavy contact at times with the 2nd NVA Division. The NVA were more organized as a fighting unit and better equipped and trained than the VC.

When ready we waited at the Chu Lai airport in the hot sun. Willingham sat off to the side, miserable and trying to get some relief from the heat and hangover. I had refrained from drinking the night before, and I was now glad of it, after seeing the look on Willingham's face. I approached him and asked, "How you feeling?"

"Chief, the heat is bad enough," he groaned. "A hangover on top of that is pure hell. I hope I have enough water. I keep drinking it. I just have to get through the day somehow."

I tried to be reassuring. "Hang in there, Willingham. You might sweat it all out sooner than you realize."

Finally a transport plane called a Caribou arrived. The plane was a smaller version of the C-130, which you loaded from the back. The flight was brief, and we soon landed on a very short landing strip. The Caribou could do that by reversing thrust as soon as the tires hit the strip. The landing was even worse than that we had experienced on the C-130. After we rounded up our gear we waited close to the landing strip.

From LZ Baldy a Chinook chopper took us west into the mountains. We ended up at FSB West, or LZ West. The FSB perched was on top of a large mountain chain. To the west was a valley, beyond which were more mountains covered with thick trees and vegetation. Far below in the narrow valley among densely covered terrain were rice paddies wherever space was available. I heard that we were stationed at the west end of Hiep Duc Valley. We arrived in the afternoon and would spend the night at the firebase.

After we settled into assigned bunkers we noticed another unit nearby getting ready to move out. Some guys told us they were Company B 4th of the 31st. The 4th of the 31st was a battalion of the 196th LIB and was nicknamed the Polar Bears. We talked with them for a few minutes before they slowly started to descend the steep slope. Within a short time they disappeared over the edge.

In the morning we would follow them. For now we sat around our bunkers and checked out our surroundings. Somewhere beyond the mountains to the west was Laos. The thick terrain in that direction was the type preferred by the NVA. It was triple canopy jungle and could hide a whole division.

That day happened to be the Fourth of July. When it got dark the artillery unit located on LZ West sent flare rounds soaring into the night. Shortly afterward somewhere to the west more flare rounds went up. Within a matter of minutes flares went up from nearly everywhere around us. Clearly, other units must be nearby. Some guys at the bunkers even sent off hand flares. The whole scenario lasted for about half an hour. The firepower display was intended to celebrate the Fourth of July and to show our strength. During the celebration, I realized that no flares had appeared to the far west, where the jungle appeared nearly impenetrable.

In the morning we checked our gear and ammunition and were ready to move out. The day before I noticed that B Fourth of the Thirty-first all wore flak jackets. It made me wonder if I should wear one during this operation. Our platoon followed another as we left the perimeter and headed down the steep slope. In the Task Force Barker area we had climbed large hills, but not as steep as these.

We slowly went down the hill. I already knew it was hard to descend a hill with a heavy pack. The vertical drop here was sharper than all those we had climbed so far. As I trudged along, I kept feeling like I would topple forward at any moment. I had to work very hard to maintain my balance. Years later I developed knee problems that I blame largely on this type of operation.

We finally arrived at the valley floor, which was covered with rice paddies and thick jungle growth. There were villages here and there, although the area seemed lightly populated. We commenced the usual search and destroy operation.

Daily we headed deeper into the narrowing depths of the valley, fully aware of large, ominous craters pocketing the hillside. Some places were littered with the remains of many choppers. It was clear to us that a fierce battle had taken place here. It made us wonder if the NVA were watching and waiting for the right moment to attack. No one needed to tell us that we were inside NVA territory.

We eventually came upon some crumbling French ruins where the NVA had written on the walls. One message warned, "10,000 French Expeditionary Forces died here, don't follow their footsteps." We looked at the messages and pressed onward. I double-checked my rifle as I passed the ruins. At this point the valley narrowed further and continued west.

Meanwhile, the weather became extremely hot and humid. There was very little breeze in the narrow valley. Reports said the temperature was around 120 degrees or more. At least it felt that hot. There were no clouds in the sky, and the blazing sun beat down on us. We guzzled canteens of water. Luckily for us water was readily available. When we reached a stream we would all drop to our knees in the water and use our helmets to douse ourselves. We didn't care about leeches. Temporary relief from the heat was the priority.

We contended with the hot weather while trying to stay alert. We knew we couldn't risk letting our guards down. The hot weather also made tempers flare. In one instance, an argument ensued between Watts and Hump. In the middle of the argument Hump took out his .45 caliber pistol and threatened to use it. Hadaway then jumped into the argument and broke them up. A few minutes later both cooled down. Hump put his .45 away, shook Watts's hand, and said, "Sorry bro, it's just the hot weather that's getting us on edge."

I watched the incident from a distance. I'm sure Hump now remembers it and has a good laugh.

When I passed a small stream our new company commander, Captain Davis, waved me over. He and his CP group were resting under a bamboo thicket. When I reached him he asked, "I heard the guys call you Chief. What tribe are you?"

I sat down to the captain and replied, "I'm Jicarilla Apache from New Mexico." He mentioned that he was part Indian. When I looked at him I could tell he was right.

"What do you think of our situation?" Captain Davis asked.

I looked around and thought a moment before answering. "We are in very thick terrain. I would be very careful while out in the clearings and fire rounds into suspected positions. If the NVA chooses to make contact he'll have to be in complete control. Also, in the other AO, Charlie shot at us from a safe distance and usually missed. Here a firefight would be at very close range, and we could sustain heavy casualties in a short time."

The deeper we went the less population we encountered. Whoever tended the large fields of rice and corn hid from us. There was much more corn in this area than in the other places we had searched. In all probability, the rice and corn was for the NVA.

One night four of us went out on a listening post (LP) about four hundred meters from the company. We set up next to an abandoned hootch under a partly cloudy sky. Although we were concealed in a thick jungle canopy, I could still make out the clouds overhead. The lone guard directed his attention toward the main trail. It appeared to be the only avenue of enemy approach. Those not on guard quickly went into a light sleep. Sometime in the middle of the night Whitaker woke us all up. He said softly, "Be very quiet, and be ready for anything."

"What's up?" I whispered to Whitaker.

"The guard saw some enemy soldiers coming our way, but they retreated back into the bushes."

"How many?"

"Don't know. About five or six."

We then moved back into the bushes toward the company and waited. Whitaker called the CO, who advised us to get back into the perimeter. We did, and the company was kept on alert for the remainder of the night. Charlie remained quiet and hidden.

We seemed to be venturing into a no-man's-land, a place where soldiers never went and were not welcome. In Nam the soldiers called it Indian Territory.

In my tour of duty, I sometimes heard references to the Indian wars of a century ago. It didn't offend me. Every now and then, I would compare my present situation with how my ancestors had fought against the United States. Of course, that had happened about a hundred years before. Now the circumstances were different. We now fought on the side of the U.S. government. If you could visualize the latter part of the nineteenth century, immigrants were pouring into the western United States by the thousands. For every white man killed there were a hundred ready to take his place. On the other hand, there were few Indians to replace those killed. Overwhelming odds beat the Indians. Ironically, in Nam the situation was reversed. For every VC or NVA killed it seemed that there were many more ready to take his place. And although the terrain was different, the enemy practiced a guerrilla-type warfare, as my ancestors had.

I was an Indian, but the enemy couldn't have cared less what color I was. All he knew was that I wore a U.S. military uniform. Charlie wouldn't hesitate to blow me away. I might have been in an isolated outfit, but I never felt that I was singled out in a negative way for being Indian. We all referred to each other's race in a friendly way. There was a lot of kidding.

Once at base camp a group of us were drinking beer and in a kidding mood.

"Chief, where did the Indians come from?" Geary asked.

"In the United States there are over a hundred different tribes," I told him. "Each has their own version of where they originated from."

A guy from the weapons platoon remarked, "I read somewhere that the Indians came from Asia. If that's true, the gooks out there are probably your distant cousins."

"Perhaps you are right," I replied. "Since you know so much about history, I'll bet you don't know what type of shirt General Custer wore at Little Bighorn."

He thought about that awhile and then guessed. "As far as I know he wore a buckskin shirt of some sort."

"No he didn't, you dummy. He wore an Arrow shirt."

I nudged another GI and motioned like I was using a bow and arrow (at the time the Arrow brand of shirt was a popular one). After a few seconds he burst out laughing. When the guy from the weapons platoon got the joke, he smiled big and pointed his finger at me.

We traveled as far as we could without going into Laos before eventually turning back. German shepherd dogs and their handlers were flown in to help locate enemy activities. When they arrived, we deliberately took our time and let them do their work. Anything suspicious looking was destroyed, including tunnels and food supplies. We concentrated more on food supplies, because it was obvious that only the NVA used the food in the area. The dogs also sniffed out suspected VC or NVA, who were then airlifted out for further interrogation. I personally felt the NVA were very close, waiting on the other side of a large river nearby.

During this time there was another dog with our company. It belonged to the Chieu Hoi who interpreted for us. (A Chieu Hoi was a former enemy soldier who had defected to the South Vietnamese cause.) The former enemy was a middle-aged man, and his dog was the size of the German shepherd and yellow in color. The dog and his master were very close, and both were quite friendly.

During a lunch break the interpreter invited me over to him. When I came over, he motioned me to sit next to him. As I did I wiped my forehead and said, "Beau coup hot."

"Yeah, too beau coup. You same same Vietnam."

"I know that's what you all say, but let's talk about you." The interpreter knew enough English to understand what I meant. I sat under his temporary shade as he prepared a meal for himself and his dog. I watched as he poured hot water into a packet that resembled an LRRP ration. An LRRP ration was a meal in a pouch. All you did was add water to it and eat. To the GIs LRRP rations were much better than C rations.

As he prepared his meal I asked, "Where VC, NVA?" pointing in all directions.

"VC ti ti, NVA beau coup." The interpreter implied that the NVA left just before we arrived and he thought they were across the large river.

"Where your mamasan, babysan?"

The interpreter just shook his head and said, "No mamasan, no babysan. VC no good." He had a faraway look. I knew then he was alone in the world and didn't have much hope for the future. At least he had his faithful dog, which panted nearby.

After the interpreter fixed his meal, he offered me some. In exchange I gave him some C ration. His meal was very spicy, just how the Vietnamese liked their meals. Before I came to Vietnam I could handle some hot chili peppers from the southwest. They were supposed to be some of the hottest chili peppers anywhere. When I went to the boonies I came upon some local peppers that were long and stringy. These, I soon found out, were hotter than the hottest chili peppers back home. I could eat them, but only in smaller portions.

I ate a small portion of my friend's meal. He smiled, knowing I could handle his spicy food while most others couldn't.

A few days later we found ourselves trudging up the large hill that protected LZ West. The hot sun blazed down on us. This was the worst heat and humidity we had experienced yet. In this situation one took extra precautions to avoid heat exhaustion or heat stroke. We took frequent breaks and were glad to come across small streams along the way. These we used to replenish our water supply and douse ourselves. About halfway up the hill the German shepherds gave up, refusing to go any farther. Their handlers put them under a shade tree and doused them with water. The handlers ended up carrying the dogs up the hill on their shoulders. An RTO in the company command group had to be evacuated. He had stopped perspiring and was on the verge of a heat stroke.

I stood up to catch my breath and could see some soldiers far ahead and above us, who had already made it over the steep part of the hill. "I wish I was up there," someone remarked wistfully.

Hayes, standing nearby, grunted, "Just keep going, your wish will come true."

Although it seemed to take an eternity, we finally did make it back inside LZ West. Later that day, after chow, Wilson said, "I know where we might be able to get a telephone call through to the world." He pointed to a place where large antennas had been set up. Ham radio operators throughout the world were relaying messages. Every now and then some lucky GI got through to family or friends back in the world.

We walked over to a small bunker where many others waited and gave telephone numbers to a GI. He told us we might have to wait for hours. Wilson went back to the bunker while I waited there with many others, all of us sitting on the floor. I hoped I might get a call through to my brother-in-law's service station. I soon realized, though, that very few calls were getting through. I looked at the number of guys waiting, decided it would take forever, and left.

There was still some daylight as I walked back to my bunker. The air was a lot cooler up here than in the valley far below. Looking around, I saw guys taking it easy and listening to portable radios. One group was taking turns flipping a quarter in the air. I was six months in-country and had become used to paper money. Now, here was actually a quarter.

When I joined their circle, someone tossed me the quarter. I automatically flipped it in the air. I did this a couple of times before passing it to the artillery forward observer. The Chicano soldier exclaimed, "Boy, a real quarter!" as he turned it in his hand and flipped it in the air.

We all passed the quarter around and made positive comments about it. I never knew what an effect a small, trivial object like a quarter could have on one's morale. To this day I can still picture the GI flipping the quarter in the air marveling over it.

After a day at LZ West we went back down into the valley, once again testing our knees by carrying heavy packs over steep slopes. When we reached the valley floor we began searching the immediate vicinity. Over the past months other units had conducted operations in this part of the valley, and we were ordered to keep up the routine. There were more villagers here, all of whom had the same distrustful look on their faces.

On this day I again saw evidence of what the war would eventually do to you. I knew Wilson usually kept his cool with the villagers. That day, I saw him become very frustrated trying to get information out of some of them. He was about to strike a villager when one of us intervened. Wilson backed off and cooled down. Later he admitted to me, "Chief, I think this place is getting to me. It scares me."

While humping on a trail later that day, we took a short break, always welcomed. For short breaks, we usually sat in place and leaned back on our rucksacks with our weapons at the ready. I did just that. As I leaned back on my rucksack I encountered no resistance, continuing backward until I landed inside a pit. The pit had some old punji stakes inside. The rucksack and some books I carried kept the stakes from penetrating farther into me. I yelled for help. Within a few seconds Wilson appeared at the edge of the hole, chuckling. "What's the matter, Chief? You seem to be in a bind."

I glared at him. "Just help me out of here."

Someone else helped him pull me out. I was relieved that I hadn't stepped into the pit. The punji stakes did have some sort of poison on them, and they could have caused a severe wound. I had dodged another part of Charlie's arsenal of destruction. It was the only pit I ever encountered in-country.

While operating in the valley, we were often reminded by the enemy that they were around. We received sniper fire that was mainly for harassment and didn't cause any injuries. It kept us in a high state of alert, however. In one instance we received more fire as we neared a small village. It came from an area of dense growth to the northwest. After artillery rounds were directed there, we were ready to advance. However, in a sudden change of plans, we pulled out and moved east to rendezvous with the other platoons.

When we reached the rendezvous site, the other platoons were already settling in for the night. After being briefed about our platoon receiving heavy fire, the CO thought it might be worthwhile for us to go back for an ambush. According to intelligence reports NVA were in the area. It was common knowledge that the NVA chose to move under the cover of darkness. We needed to be very careful and avoid walking into an ambush ourselves, where we would be badly outnumbered.

We rested for an hour, waiting for darkness to set in. When the time was right, we headed toward our earlier location, about two klicks from the company perimeter. I was on point as we moved carefully through the thick vegetation before crossing open rice paddies. We slowly and cautiously made our way toward our objective.

Once we reached a stream I knew that we were close to the site. I stopped and waited for the platoon leader to come over. When he did I whispered, "When we cross the stream and get past the bushes, we should come upon a trail. As I remember, the trail goes through rice paddies for a ways before reaching more heavy vegetation. Farther past that is where we received all the fire today."

The platoon leader and I sat silently in place. In the darkness I could make out the trees across the stream. To reach them you had to go down an embankment, cross the stream, and climb up on the other side. Finally the platoon leader reached a decision. "Chief, go ahead and cross the stream. Check out the other side. We'll wait for you here."

I moved out. The stream was off to the side of the trail, and I believed that if the NVA were in the area, they would concentrate on the trails. We had arrived by coming cross-country, and with luck we were undetected. I crossed the stream and advanced farther into the trees, then waited and listened. Deciding the place was safe, I crept forward until I came upon a trail. After that I returned and advised the platoon leader.

We all moved forward and eventually made our way through the trees. When we came upon the trail, we stopped and waited. Farther up the trail was an open rice paddy area. The platoon leader decided to set up the ambush area where we were.

We never had a chance to set up. At that moment, we heard distinct sounds coming from the trail. Only half the platoon members were close to the trail; the others were still in the jungle behind us. Everyone kept still and waited.

The noise coming from the trail became louder. It was sort of a rustling sound. I first thought that villagers were foolishly moving at night. Within a few minutes, we saw figures in the darkness, slowly coming our way. When they were close enough for us to determine that they weren't villagers, someone opened fire on them. Then we all joined in. Some in front fell down. The flashes of light from bullets and tracers revealed bodies on the trail and many more figures farther up the trail. The platoon leader quickly determined that we had encountered a large NVA force on the move.

We wanted to retrieve weapons, but we also knew that the enemy would instantly figure out the size of our own force. We quickly retreated back into the trees and crossed the stream. The CO heard all the rifle fire and grenades going off and called to ask what had happened. We were ordered back to the company perimeter ASAP. Our platoon leader gave grid coordinates so that artillery rounds could be lobbed at Charlie.

I wasn't on point during the initial part of the withdrawal; instead, my fire team provided rear security. The last one in line, I hunched behind a coconut tree, expecting an RPG, a favorite weapon of the NVA, to come slamming in at us. We began our retreat in the darkness. In another instant, word reached me that the platoon leader wanted me on point immediately. I quickly made my way to the front of the platoon. Our leader quickly summarized the situation. "The guys have no idea where to go. The night is black as coal. Can you get us back to the company?"

It was pitch-black, but I had an idea of where to go. We had passed this way earlier, and the night visibility then had been good. Now, though it was a lot darker, I already had a good sense of where we came from. As I made my way in the darkness I encountered certain terrain features that I remembered passing. All the time I had spent in the woods and darkness during my youth was paying off.

This time I wasn't concerned about anything in front. The danger was behind us. We heard explosions that weren't artillery rounds coming from the area we had just left. The NVA were on the offensive.

We weren't out of danger and had to continue. Eventually we reached more dense cover, which limited visibility even more. From there I just followed a hedgerow. Meanwhile, the company was on alert status and waited for our return. When we got close to the perimeter we radioed our position and moved quickly back inside. Finding my way in the dark had been second nature. The rest of the platoon had a great feeling of gratitude.

In all probability the NVA were on the move with a definite purpose in mind, possibly to infiltrate a smaller firebase in the area or even our company position. Our platoon appeared to have messed up their plans.

In the morning the company headed back into the valley. We fanned out and made a slow sweep across. People were already using the trail when we arrived at the approximate sight of the previous night's incident. From there we checked suspected areas of concealment and ambush sites. Our objective was locating the enemy if he were still in the area.

After making the sweep and coming out empty-handed our plans changed. We went west and slowly started climbing the mountain range, using the denser vegetation as concealment while we continued upward. As sometimes happened, no one seemed to know what the objective was. There wasn't any trail to follow. No large NVA unit could be hiding here. We were forced to put up with the awful heat and the pulling, tearing bushes. It was extremely frustrating, but we had to refrain from making loud noises.

We continued steadily upward for the better part of the afternoon, as the valley floor became smaller behind us. We had a good view of it from breaks in the jungle canopy. About two-thirds of the way up the mountains we stopped at a small knoll, where we set up a perimeter in the thickness to avoid detection. From our vantage point we could see the surrounding area quite well. Out in the distance was a large river we had yet to cross.

Our CO ordered us to remain in place for a few days. During this time no ambushes were sent out. LPs went to possible avenues of approach, and daily small patrols checked for signs of the enemy.

After the second day we were running out of water. By now the NVA knew of our presence, because we were being resupplied by chopper. Our squad had to go farther west to locate a source of water. We traveled light, carrying only weapons, ammunition, and web gear. When we came out of the jungle-type terrain, a stretch of elephant grass provided concealment until we reached denser cover. We then followed a small ravine, eventually reaching an area dominated by large trees. There was no sign of the enemy.

I soon heard the familiar sound of running water. It reminded me of rushing mountain streams common to the Rockies. As we approached the stream it became louder, and soon we stood next to it. At that moment, the heat strangely seemed to disappear. It was really cool next to the clear running water. The stream made its way among and around large boulders as it formed a large pool.

We were all captivated by the beauty of the moment as we took a cool drink. A large area within the vicinity of the pool was secured. When we were satisfied that no enemy was around, half the guys pulled security while the others took a cool dip. We had located an excellent source of water and an unexpected place to beat the heat. Soon we all had taken turns swimming.

In the boonies it was essential to dig a cat hole when relieving yourself and, like a cat, to bury the stuff. On the third day it became apparent that some of us weren't doing this, because the smell was getting intolerable, especially when the hot breeze shifted in our direction or the air stood still.

On an earlier occasion someone had said, "One way you know you're near an NVA base camp is by the smell. There is a heavy odor of crap in the air." Now I understood what the GI had meant. Before the smell became even worse, we moved back down the side of the mountain. When we reached the valley floor, we set up a perimeter in a large clearing.

Across the clearing I spotted Sergeant McCloud standing next to a steel tank. I recalled when he was with our platoon and the guys called him Smokey. He still had a rebel flag taped on his rifle butt. After a while he walked over with the tank and spoke with our platoon leader. The leader then turned to us and said, "I don't want everyone jumping up all at once, but I need a couple of volunteers." No one did, so Tannacore and I were volunteered. Tannacore was white and overweight. When he arrived with Fenstermaker, I thought he had no business in the field and that he would end up with heatstroke. He had a lot of body hair, and for that reason he was quickly nicknamed Bear. However, as big and hefty as Bear was, he could hump like the rest of us. This certainly surprised everyone.

We soon learned that we would be making a combat assault across the river in the morning.

Sergeant McCloud turned to Tannacore and I and asked, "You guys know what I have here?"

"I believe it's a flame thrower," Tannacore said.

"That's correct. And do you guys know how to use one?"

Neither one of us did, so the sergeant gave us a ten-minute lesson. After that we both experimented with it. It seemed to weigh a ton.

"Use the weapon sparingly," Sergeant McCloud cautioned. "Take quick shots. It has about ten seconds before it's gone. That might not seem like long enough, but if you use it wisely, it will be."

To be honest, I didn't care to lug the heavy thing, especially on a combat assault. I always felt safer with an M-16 rifle in my hands. Bear and I went through the motions with the thing before it became dark. We agreed that I would be the one to carry the weapon on the initial assault. Bear would port my rucksack. Any way you looked at it we were burdened with a lot of extra weight.

When it got dark, everything quieted down except for the crickets. Later in the night a lone airplane flew by with a flashing light, taking infrared pictures. It flew over the site where we were to make our assault in the morning. When I saw the plane, I became convinced that we would be making contact with the NVA—a bad time to be using an unfamiliar weapon. I looked up to the heavens and prayed to my Creator that everything would be all right the next day.

The choppers arrived early in the morning. Before long we were airborne and speeding toward the area across the river. The artillery from LZ West and O'Conner were sending preparation fire. Gunships were also at our sides. When we crossed the river, the choppers wasted no time in landing at the base of the mountains.

Jumping off the chopper with a heavy weapon, I should have fallen over, but somehow I managed to keep my balance. We were coming under fire and returning it. The platoon leader ordered us to advance up a nearby hill as quickly as possible.

I followed the lead squad, ready to use the flame thrower. My adrenaline surged, allowing me to keep pace with the others going up the hill. We met light resistance. Coming across a suspected bunker, I tried out the weapon. As instructed, I took a short burst and directed a large flame at the bunker.

As we continued, I handed the flame thrower to Bear. He then repeated my actions, using it on anything suspicious. I followed behind, toting his heavy rucksack. The combined weight was almost as heavy as the flame thrower and just as bulky. Nevertheless, inconvenient or not, you did what you had to when real danger was present.

Before noon the whole area was secured. Intelligence had reported that a large force was present. As we advanced, however, it became apparent that the NVA had largely left. A large bunker complex had been occupied, but the occupants left in a hurry. Bear used the flame thrower to destroy part of the complex before he ran out of fuel. We then spent the rest of the day destroying the complex. We didn't meet the enemy on a large scale, but we destroyed items such as food supplies. I didn't blame the NVA for leaving. Nobody in his right mind would fight in this heat. Instead, the enemy retreated farther into the mountains. There would be another day.

Before the day ended, we again approached the river. Crossing the strong current would be very dangerous. Teams of soldiers strung a rope across the river and inflated a small rubber raft, a handy means of ferrying us to the other side. When we were all across, we continued to the west.

Not too far from this point was another LZ on a small rise. It was nowhere near the same elevation as LZ West and the other firebases. This place was called LZ Karen. It had been built to provide temporary artillery support for units farther to the west.

The big guns at LZ Karen were larger than the others we were familiar with. Until now we had been accustomed to 105s or 155s, but here there were 155s, 175s, and 8-inch guns. The noise generated this close to the big guns threatened to burst your eardrums. When they were fired, the air and ground shook. I had lost my earplugs, so I had to be careful to cover my ears when the rounds went off. Sometimes I couldn't, and my eardrums suffered as a result. The rounds seemed to go on all night long. I put up with the loud noise, knowing some unit somewhere out in the field needed support.

Whitaker told us that the night before the infrared flight cameras had taken pictures of the NVA retreating. They were in groups of thirty and carried what they could. Word had apparently leaked out to them of our planned combat assault. Whitaker added that the NVA were making plans to attack some base camps in the Hiep Duc Valley. I had no reason to doubt him. I wondered what would have happened if we had made contact with the full force, instead of the few left behind to harass us.

We left LZ Karen after a couple of days and continued operations in the valley, before again heading up the steep hill on our way to LZ West. This time we followed a well-used trail. When we reached the halfway point, it was every man for himself. There was no order by platoons, so we started mixing and bunching up. It was midday, and we figured the enemy was nowhere near. All we cared about was reaching our objective, LZ West.

Everyone had his own method of getting up the hill. I took off, went as far as I could, and looked back into the valley as I caught my breath. A guy from another platoon made his way up the hill slowly, one step at a time, without stopping. Every now and then he caught up with me.

After a while I was with the group that was out in front. When I stopped to look back again, Bear was a short distance behind and drenched with perspiration like the rest of us. Other than that he didn't seem the worse for wear. I yelled, "Way to go, Bear. Hang in there!"

Bear didn't say anything. He just flashed a wide, toothy smile. We were at the point where the hill became less steep. We could see LZ West farther up the hill.

After we reached LZ West and rested up, the platoon leader advised that we might be going somewhere else in the morning. We still had to go on ambush and LP that night. Wilson, Brooks, Winston, and I were ordered to go on LP. We had been hoping to get some rest, but we didn't have a choice.

When darkness fell we left the perimeter, traveling light. We informed the last bunker where we would be and that we would be coming in before daybreak. My thought was of the last time we had been on the hill, when a platoon set off an ambush. As secure as LZ West seemed, the enemy still probed the place.

With this fact on our minds we quietly left the perimeter and silently made our way down the hill. Our destination was the part of the hill that became steeper, about a klick from the perimeter. As we followed a small trail, no one spoke aloud, only whispering occasionally.

When we found the place, we wasted no time in setting claymores and flares. The LP was a permanent site and was slightly off the trail. You had to look over bushes to see the trail, but you could see a long way. Not taking any chances, we put pieces of branches on our helmets for better concealment. LPs weren't to be taken lightly. We had heard stories of GIs getting their throats cut while on LP or OP. Avoiding this was a lot easier said than done. We had just gone through several exhausting weeks of constant humping and followed by a long climb up a large hill, and fatigue was a constant problem.

Those not on guard, including me, quickly went to sleep. When it was my turn for guard duty the sky was partly cloudy. Through openings in the clouds a half moon slightly illuminated the area. I put the claymore detonator next to me, put on my helmet, and looked down the slope. It seemed impossible for the enemy to be climbing the hill with this much light. I thought if he were, he would surely use places with better cover. Then again, the LP site was chosen because it was the best avenue of approach. The enemy had to come near, and I imagined that if he did approach I would hear a rustling sound.

I sat in place and glanced over at my companions sleeping nearby. We had gone through a lot in our six months together, but we had managed to stay in one piece. I prayed to our Creator to continue watching over us and allow all of us to make it back to the world. One soldier started to snore, so I rolled him over on his side. After I finished my watch I went back to sleep.

17. Tracks

OUR OPERATION IN THE HIEP DUC VALLEY concluded, and the company was airlifted to Hill 54, back in the 198th LIB AO.

One day I ended up on KP duty at Hill 54, with the unpleasant task of scrubbing pots and pans. I hated KP duty with a passion, and now I toiled under the hot sun with several others. We bitched a lot as we went about our work.

Earlier I had observed a skirmish developing to the west. It began small but it was rapidly escalating. The artillery pounded the area well, and soon fighter jets arrived, raking the area with 20-millimeter cannons and dropping heavy artillery. We continued with KP, watching and fully aware of what was happening. Within an hour, members of the First Platoon passed by, loaded with full combat gear.

"What's happening?" I asked. "Where you guys headed?"

"To where all the action is," Jenkins replied, "to the west. Get your stuff. You can come with us."

"I'm tempted to do just that."

I looked again to the west. Tanks and armored personnel carriers (APCs) were in the thick of the skirmish, and some were heading in our direction. Within minutes our platoon leader came around and said, "The company is ordered into the fight to the west. It seems like nothing major. If you guys want to stay and pull KP, you can do that. If you want to come along, I advise that you get your gear ASAP."

Without hesitation I dropped the pan I was scrubbing and threw down my apron. No way was I staying there and doing that crap. One or two soldiers stayed behind, but the rest of use raced to get our gear. Within a matter of minutes I was ready to move out.

Upon reaching a small rise, we saw APCs and tanks heading toward us. Behind them the skirmish had grown into a full-scale battle. Gunships were busy flying around, firing rockets and bullets.

The APCs and tanks had come to take us toward the skirmish. The APCs and tanks, or tracks, was a troop from the First of the First Cavalry Regiment. The mechanized unit was part of the American Division and had arrived in the fall of 1967 from Ft. Hood, Texas, providing armored support anywhere in the American AO. They were heavily armed but were good targets for enemy RPGs, rockets, and antitank mines.

We rode toward the fighting, traveling through hedgerows and rice paddies with ease. We held up when we got close to the battle. From there we went on the right flank, intending to block the enemy's escape route. Our immediate objective was a village to our right, from where we received some rifle fire. As we advanced slowly the firing stopped, before we reached the village. We continued past, moving north.

Meanwhile, heavy fighting continued to our left. I heard someone mention that a heavily fortified NVA position was the main objective. Farther to the southwest, some tracks also came under heavy fire, so we headed back toward them.

The large NVA force under attack subsequently retreated into the mountains. Our new objective was to follow and keep the pressure on them. We met up with the tracks again and moved with them toward the west. At times we mounted them in order to move more quickly. We kept up this tactic for several days, going through hedgerows and rice paddies with relative ease until we stopped at a large gully. It seemed impossible for the vehicles to get across, and going in another direction would take too long.

Accompanying the tanks and APCs was a strange vehicle that seemed to have no purpose. It just went along folded in half. At the gully the vehicle was moved to the front and parked next to the gully. The vehicle then unfolded itself and made a bridge across the gully, allowing the other vehicles to cross. After they all reached the other side, the vehicle folded itself in half on the other side.

When we neared the mountains we had every reason to believe heavy contact with the NVA was imminent. The area was sparsely populated, with large bomb craters everywhere. The craters were filled with water, which we used to clean up.

As we continued west heavy fighting erupted again, this time farther south. Again some tracks had been caught in an ambush and had to fight their way out of it. We maintained our position on the right flank as more air support arrived. Phantom Jets concentrated their attacks on the mountains just ahead.

Late in the day, we rounded the crest of a hill. A steep valley fell away below. Beyond that were more mountains. A large mountain rose across from us and dominated the terrain. We set up a night defensive position in the elephant grass.

When we had settled in for the night, H. P. put up Old Glory on top of a tree. By now most of us were past the halfway point of our tour of duty. The flag flapping in the breeze was a reminder that another place awaited our return. We had to keep up the faith.

That evening I chatted with some of the guys. We talked about our hometowns and what we would be doing if we were back there right now. H. P. was from South Carolina. He talked about sitting on a curb and pigging out on clams.

"What about you, Chief?" Brooks asked. "What would you be doing?"

"I don't know, maybe cruising the countryside with some buddies."

"What is your country like?"

"My people are lucky. We have a nice piece of land that offers a little of everything."

The conversation became more philosophical. Winston asked, "Chief, what do you think life is all about?"

"This is my own personal philosophy. To me life is in four stages. You are born, you make memories, you live on your memories, and then you die."

Winston was one who understood this type of thinking. He replied reflectively, "I think I know what you mean. If you don't make many memories, you don't have much to talk about in your old age."

"That's right," I agreed, "but you also have to make good memories to feel good about yourself. What we do here will one day come back at us. I hope we can cope with the memories we make here."

"I hear you, Chief. Like you said a while back, hope for the best."

When we set up for the night we knew the NVA were near. For the past few days we had made a strong push to the west, hoping to get them out in the open. The squadron we were operating with was moving right along.

We soon became familiar with some of the squadron's crew members. Their CO was on the heavy side. I wondered how effective he would be if he had to hump for a few hours. The members of the crew took turns driving the vehicles on a daily basis.

In the morning we parted with the tracks and headed down into the valley. Upon reaching the valley floor we kept a sharp lookout for possible NVA ambush sites. A favorite type was the horseshoe-shaped ambush. Without the tracks next to us, I felt insecure and vulnerable. I had become dependent on their superior firepower.

I knew we would meet up with the NVA as we moved through heavy vegetation and a few rice paddies. The dense growth continued up the opposite hill. A radio report told us that some of the tracks had run into mines farther to our left.

After continuing north for another klick we swung to the west and soon approached a large clearing with thick woods all around. Walking point, I held up at the edge of the clearing. Before we could advance, the platoon leader said, "We'll wait here. We'll send some grenade rounds across before we continue."

Our orders changed before a round could be fired. Our initial objective had been to reach the base of the hill and continue upward. Now we were told to go south, and as a result we didn't enter the open area ahead of us.

We switched directions along the edge of the clearing. I ended up at the rear and lagged about thirty meters behind the platoon. I looked back every now and then. When I was still in the open, bullets flew by me. It appeared that I was the only target.

I spun around and fired a short burst into the wood line behind me, where we had been headed before we changed directions. Then I ran and caught up with the rest of the platoon, who were crouched behind some rice paddy dikes and out of Charlie's effective range.

I made my way up to where Sergeant Jordan was and said to Doc Walker, "Doc, the gooks are shooting at me."

"Where is the shooting coming from?" Jordan asked.

"It's coming from the thick area we were headed toward. If we go there we have to be careful of an ambush. Maybe that is what the shooting is all about. To entice us into the opening."

Before we went any farther Jordan was on the radio with the CO. He said, "We request permission to check out the sniper fire."

The CO replied, "That's a complete negative. We have orders to get out of the area ASAP. Forget the fire and continue moving back up the hill."

I often wondered what might have happened had we kept going toward the thick wood line. Had we chosen to check out the sniper fire, I believe the NVA would have been waiting for us. We would have been out in the open without any cover. Perhaps fate intervened on our behalf again.

For another hour we steadily went back up the hill we had just come down. Phantom Jets pounded the area immediately behind us and the large hill to the west. They blasted the area with all types of bombs, including napalm, which exploded in giant fireballs. When we reached the top the jets continued bombing the valley and hillside.

Across the valley, on top of the large hill, was another unit. The NVA we were pursuing were trapped in the valley and hillside. I never knew the outcome of that battle. I understood the NVA received many casualties, mostly from the napalm.

Our operation with the First of the First Cavalry ended after that. We were airlifted to another location and ended up at LZ Bowman. The place seemed to have a larger perimeter than LZ West. Most of the bunkers were large culverts cut in half, with sandbags built around them.

There were ARVNs here, unlike at other firebases. Out of curiosity, I walked to a flat area at a high point, where older Vietnamese men in military uniforms were seated under a canvas shade and on one side of several tables. I gathered they were top military brass for an ARVN unit. A few meters in front, Vietnamese civilians cooked a meal over an open fire. I noticed one person preparing a chicken. Not wanting to act foolish and stare, I continued over the hill, to where Bear, Fenstermaker, and others in our platoon had bunkers.

That evening we received mortar rounds at the west side of the perimeter. This was the section manned by the ARVN. After the rounds landed, the ARVNs shot up a storm into the darkness.

When not on day patrol we filled sandbags to replace the hardened ones. This was a necessary task done periodically. If the hardened sandbags weren't replaced, they did more harm than good, as an exploding round hitting one could send hard fragments everywhere. At all base camps or fire bases sandbags were replaced every few months.

One day I was part of a sandbag detail. We filled the bags at a place close to where the ARVN top brass were. It appeared that there was a general with them. I wondered what they were doing here. Soon they sat down to eat at tables with all kinds of food. We were just a short distance away, but the ARVNs didn't acknowledge our presence.

We took our time filling the sandbags. Every now and then we sat in the shade of a bunker to avoid the hot sun as much as possible. While we were resting, a chopper landed. Within minutes an important-looking military group made their way toward us, heading for the ARVNs. We still knew our military procedure and stood at attention as they passed us. A U.S. Army general was among the group and said, "You fellas keep up the good work. We are aware of what you guys are doing and what you have to go through."

After they passed Wilson said, "That's General Gettys, the commander of the Americal Division." Most of us knew of the general, but seeing him at a remote LZ was rather strange. Wilson had seen him up close back at Chu Lai and instantly recognized him.

Meanwhile, the general and his staff sat with the ARVNs under the canvas shade. After a few minutes a large pitcher of lemonade arrived at the general's table. The general made a remark, and the lemonade was brought our way. The messenger said, "The general thought you fellas could make better use of this lemonade. He sends this with his compliments." Standing under the hot sun in tattered fatigues, we waved thanks to the general. After moving to a more shady area, we proceeded to enjoy the unexpected refreshment.

The following day our company was ready to move out early. Once again we waited next to a chopper landing pad. A Chinook landed, and some ARVN troops disembarked from the tail end. They were sporting fake smiles to try and mask their fear and uncertainty. I gathered that another major operation was in the works. Soldiers continued to pour out of the chopper. It made me wonder "How many ARVNs can a Chinook carry?" Finally, they all unloaded, and we boarded the chopper and were flown toward Chu Lai.

After we arrived we were taken to the area next to the main PX. We were to have a couple days of stand-down. Billets with cots were available, which meant no guard duty for us. Soon beer and sodas were on the way. After we cleaned up, we did whatever we wanted.

I got comfortable on my cot and closed my eyes. I thought about advice once offered to me about taking R&R (rest and recuperation) when you were at least nine months into your tour of duty. It might be worth getting the paperwork started. Some R&R destinations included Taipei, Taiwan; Hong Kong; Bangkok, Thailand; Singapore; Kuala Lumpur, Malaysia; and Sidney, Australia. The mere thought of these exotic places made me want to go. The opportunity was available, and I knew I would never get another chance, so I requested R&R.

The main PX was a hub of activity. I bought an item or two and went back to the billets. All I wanted to do was to take it easy and relax. That evening I watched the movie *The Good, the Bad and the Ugly*. After that it was off to get some much needed rest.

The next day was more of the same. In late afternoon a trailer load of beer and soda on ice arrived. Out in the boonies we usually could purchase only 33 or Tiger beer. The GIs called Tiger beer Tiger Piss, because it had a bad taste. Another beer was a Korean product called OB. In a base camp, however, GIs consumed American products. There were enough cold drinks to go around on this day.

We sat in groups and talked into the night. Everyone was in good spirits. Included in my group was Tree, the hefty soldier from the weapons platoon. We were sitting outside an empty billet when someone dared him to break a board with his fist. That had probably been the last thing on Tree's mind, but he accepted the challenge.

We followed Tree into the empty billet. He grinned at us, made a fist, and hit the board squarely in the center. The board went flying. We looked at each other for a second, and then—perhaps it was the effect of the alcohol or because we were so used to destroying things—in the next instant we were all kicking and hitting the walls of the empty billets. Others nearby heard the fracas and joined in. We finally stopped, but not until we had destroyed several billets. The top brass didn't appreciate our antics.

The next morning we found ourselves flying north from Chu Lai, destination unknown. We landed on a beach that was white as snow, which caused us to become snow-blind. Luckily, I had a pair of dark glasses. Good thing we hadn't come under fire as we landed, or we could have been very disoriented by the surroundings.

From there we went north and entered a village laid out among large coconut trees. The whole place was very peaceful, and we were told to treat the villagers with respect. Soon kids came around. We weren't too sure what to do. We were used to checking hootches and the surrounding area. The place seemed very secure. The villagers minded their own business. They fished more than farmed. There were rice paddies, but not as many as in other villages.

After a lunch break some of us headed to the east, where we came upon a large inland lagoon with a village on the far side. Some fishermen were working their nets. When we got closer we discovered that two of them were women. They all had muscular bodies. It was strange to see them. Some were teenagers, an age group not usually found in the unfriendly villages. We passed the fishermen and exchanged smiles with them. Out in the lagoon children were swimming and playing in the water. Somehow the scene didn't seem real. It almost seemed staged.

With the kids was an older girl. She was in her early teens, and her name sounded like Charlotte. She was young, but she was smoking a cigarette. As a joke I asked her for some dinky dow. She said, "No dinky dow. I give you own cigarette." She then took out a pouch of tobacco and rolled a cigarette. I took the homemade cigarette and lit it up. I had no taste for it, but I didn't want to hurt her feelings, so I smoked the cigarette.

We spent a few days in the area and then were sent to Hill 54, where we spent a short time. We then received a sudden change of orders to make another combat assault in the mountains to the southwest.

We knew the LZ would be hot, and so we were ready as we airlifted. When the choppers reached our LZ, gunships raked the area with their Gatling guns. Rockets streaked to suspected hostile areas. The LZ was in a clearing of elephant grass, and beyond that there was thick, jungle-type vegetation.

As we descended, we received some fire. After landing we scrambled into the elephant grass and waited for instructions. Our objective was the wood line and farther past that. After getting organized we slowly advanced, moving cautiously. We reached the trees without receiving any casualties. Out in the distance we heard the noise of a battle.

We were on line and ready to continue up a hill, as the noise of battle continued to our west. We knew that an NVA base camp was in the area. Before we continued any farther, however, our orders suddenly changed. We were to be picked up at the same location where we had just been dropped off. By now the area could be considered secured, and we hoped, the enemy was nowhere near.

We proceeded back to the landing area in the tall grass and waited for a Chinook to arrive. A Chinook airlifted out our company, except for Uncle Mickey's fire team. We waited with another company for the next chopper.

18. West Quang Ngai

WHEN THE CHINOOK ARRIVED WE BOARDED with individuals from another company. I don't believe anyone knew where we were headed. The chain of events was happening too fast. One moment we were on the offensive against a sizeable enemy force. The next we were on a big chopper, speeding toward an unknown destination.

We flew south, and the chopper ride was longer than I had expected. We finally descended and landed at the far end of an airstrip. We looked around for the rest of our company, but they were nowhere in sight. The terrain around the airstrip was flat, with mountains to the west.

Within a few minutes the commander of the other company, along with his RTO, came over to us and said, "I understand you guys are part of Bravo Company. Your company is somewhere else. There will be no more chopper flights tonight. You'll be with us for the night. We are Alpha Company Fourth of the Third. In the morning you might rejoin your company. Which one of you is the leader?"

Uncle Mickey spoke up, "I am in charge, sir."

"We are at the Quang Ngai city airstrip and are to defend this place from an expected VC attack. I want your men to take up a position at the far end of the airstrip and dig in well. I'll get you some C rations. How is your ammunition?"

Uncle Mickey knew we always had enough and replied, "We should be okay."

"If you guys need me, I'll be close by. I'll go ahead and send you some additional ammunition. Lord only knows that you might need it."

When the captain left, Uncle Mickey said, "You heard the guy. Dig in well. I don't like the looks of things. Double-check your weapons, and set up claymores and trip flares."

By the time we were through it had become dark. Uncle Mickey sat down next to me asked, "What do you think, Chief?"

"We're as ready as we can get," I said. "One thing in our favor is the large flat area to our front and the concertina wire around the airstrip. We could see Charlie for a long ways, if he came charging. He could try to crawl close to us, but there is no cover for him. Charlie could also try shooting RPGs and rockets, but our flat positions will make it hard for him to score a direct hit. Charlie is good at walking in mortars. I believe that's what he'll do, and he'll follow with a ground attack. We'll just have to be alert."

We stayed up for about another hour before settling in for the night. The captain checked our position and asked if we needed anything. Uncle Mickey said, "We are dug in and set. We'll be waiting for Charlie."

Late in the night the expected mortar rounds came whistling in and exploded around us. We braced ourselves for a ground attack. After a few minutes, shooting erupted on the western sector of the airstrip. Charlie had chosen that area for a ground attack. However, he quickly realized there was too much firepower and withdrew into the darkness. We kept alert for the rest of the night, but nothing else happened.

The next day a chopper picked us up and flew us to our company, who were at some firebase west of Quang Ngai, close to the mountains. It rained, and had in fact, been raining more frequently lately. The heavy monsoon rains would soon be upon us.

Sergeant Jordan had assumed leadership of our platoon for several weeks. Personally, I felt comfortable with his leadership, because he had months of experience. Common sense told you it was better to have someone experienced in the field to lead, no matter what unit you were in. However, we soon had a new platoon leader named Eggleston.

Lieutenant Eggleston was fresh out of Officer Candidate School (OCS) and very inexperienced. Knowing this, he relied heavily on the seasoned veterans. This I felt was a wise decision on his part. We also received several new replacements. Miley, Henson, DeLao, and Anderson were the names of a few.

Early one evening we came under automatic rifle fire followed by satchel charges. Charlie was very near. The satchel charges caused no damage, but they put some new guys on edge. We threw hand grenades past the perimeter. Shortly after the explosions, tear gas came upon us. Someone yelled, "Grab your gas masks. It looks like Charlie is using gas on us!"

This was the first time I had had to use my gas mask. I fumbled with it before finally putting it on. It didn't work. I tried clearing it as instructed back in training. It still didn't work. Luckily, while I was trying to get the mask working, the tear gas dissipated.

Later we learned that one of our own guys had thrown the gas grenade. In the excitement a new guy grabbed whatever was available and threw it. The gas must have drifted back at us. This type of mistake happened at times, and in this instance we were lucky. I felt relieved that it wasn't Charlie who had used the tear gas on us. My gas mask would have been useless.

After checking my mask further, I discovered that the cartridge inside was clogged. Apparently, it had happened long before due to the weather. I had never bothered checking before to see if it worked. This was just another fortunate break for me.

Our daily operations went farther west of Quang Ngai. One evening the company set up a night defensive position next to a large clearing. To the north were trees and other vegetation, and to the south, across a long stretch of rice paddies, were more trees. After we secured a perimeter the resupply chopper arrived. Among other things it brought a rare hot meal and ice cream.

When we finished our unusual and wonderful evening meal we prepared to dig in for the night. Before we could do that a radio message came in, advising us that E Company Fourth of the Third was badly pinned down. Our company had to get to them immediately.

We quickly got ready and waited for the choppers to come. Before long they appeared, twirling in to where smoke grenades marked our positions. There was still a little bit of daylight left.

When the choppers descended, heavy fire erupted from the wood line to the south. All we could do was stay low; we couldn't fight back. We weren't in a proper fighting position because of the way we had set up for the choppers.

The choppers lifted, made a large circle, and attempted to land again. Again, the enemy fire was intense, and once again the pickup was aborted. The choppers made several more attempts to land, without success. Every time they tried, heavy fire rained upon them from the south. Several choppers were badly hit but still functioned. Gunships raked the area of fire, but the firing continued. Our plans to use the choppers had to be aborted, and we would have to proceed on foot instead.

The decision was very unfortunate for our comrades who were pinned down. Word on the radio was that E Company was holding out but Charlie was closing in. Earlier in the day E Company had walked into an enemy base camp, which quickly turned into a hornet's nest. The enemy had E Company trapped in a cross fire, and the company was taking heavy casualties.

We wanted to help E Company. The gunships continued shooting at the suspected source of fire from the south. This gave us the distraction we needed as we ran east. The gunships would take care of Charlie if he tried to cross the large open rice paddies. The thought of our comrades in need outweighed any fears we might have about an ambush.

The whole company was on line as we approached the wood line. We expected Charlie to open up at any second. An individual from the First Platoon was on my right as we took the lead. When we were close to the woods we shot at any place where the enemy might be lurking. The others followed our lead.

At the woods the company split up. Our platoon would attempt to cross the hills directly to our front. The other platoons would make a sweep to the north and south.

When we reached the hills, it was dark. We couldn't see any landmarks. We continued as best and as quickly as we could, making our way through the thick vegetation. Our radio contact was very broken; at times it came through enough for us to understand what was happening. The situation for E Company was grave. It would be a fight to the death for them. They were making a terrific stand and used air support to buy time as Charlie continued his assault on them. Another sketchy report said E Company had lost half their men. The ones still alive were running out of ammunition, and many of them were badly wounded.

Meanwhile, our company frantically made its way in the darkness. It became apparent to us that the platoons going around the hill had the best chance to reach E Company in time. Our platoon eventually reached the summit and continued down the other side, scrambling over large boulders. After an hour or so we finally reached flat terrain.

We were within the proximity of the last known location of E Company. The sporadic sounds of battle reached us from ahead. We maintained as quick a pace as possible to get through some trees. Word soon reached us on the radio that another platoon had reached E Company and was engaging the enemy. Our platoon continued forward, fully expecting to join in the battle. We were in rice paddies when figures appeared out of the darkness in front of us. Someone heard them talking in Vietnamese, so we fired. We paused to hear a message on the radio. E Company had taken a terrible beating and suffered many casualties. Our orders were to remain in position and set up a blocking force. We were to fire at any movement in our direction. Out in the distance we could hear a steady barrage of machine gun fire.

We kept alert for the remainder of the night. I wondered if Hanson or the guy from San Juan Pueblo made it out alive. I could only pray that they both did.

What was left of the enemy slipped away under cover of darkness. That night our company made every attempt to get to E Company quickly. We arrived in time to prevent an even worse disaster, but unfortunately, it was a little too late for the many who died. I wished we could have been airlifted in. However, I also realized we could have suffered many casualties if we had attempted to board the choppers. Either way the situation would have been bad. Afterward, I asked about the two GIs I knew from E Company. Hanson died, and I couldn't get a definitive answer on the fellow from San Juan Pueblo.

A Presidential Unit Citation was awarded to E Company Fourth of the Third Infantry for what happened there. The citation reads:

The Reconnaissance Platoon, Company E, 4th Battalion, 3rd Infantry, 11th Light Infantry Brigade, distinguished itself by extraordinary heroism in action against a hostile force near the hamlet of Phuoc Loc, Quang Ngai, Republic of Vietnam on 6 and 7 September 1968. The platoon of 27 men was conducting a combat sweep operation on 6 September when it became engaged with a battalion-sized enemy force entrenched in fortified defensive positions. Exposed to the heavy automatic weapons and small arms fire from the estimated 400-man enemy force, the men of the Reconnaissance Platoon gallantly fought against the numerical odds and established defensive positions. Maintaining their positions, integrity, men of the platoon, with complete disregard for their own safety, braved the heavy fire to bring their fallen comrades within the perimeter. Although under heavy fire and repeated attacks from the enemy, the men of the Reconnaissance Platoon valorously held their positions, directed air strikes and repulsed all enemy efforts to overrun their defensive positions.

The platoon was able to engage the enemy force until reinforcements arrived during the early morning hours of 7 September. A sweep of the battlefield on the morning of 7 September revealed that the Reconnaissance Platoon had killed 48 enemy soldiers. Intelligence from captured prisoners indicated that the enemy force had suffered 88 casualties, rendering it ineffective as a fighting force. The Reconnaissance Platoon is credited with spoiling an impending attack on the city of Quang Ngai by discovering and inflicting heavy losses on one of the key enemy forces poised for attack, thereby sparing the free world forces and the city of Quang Ngai much loss of life, equipment and personal property.

The heroic actions of the men of the platoon aided in the defeat of major enemy forces which had been poised for attacks on the major cities of Quang Ngai province. The gallantry, devotion to duty of the men of the Reconnaissance Platoon, against numerically superior enemy forces, are in keeping with the highest traditions of the United States Army and reflects great credit upon themselves and the Armed Forces of the United States.

The small valley where E Company had been pinned down was still considered very hostile. Charlie was nearby. We spent three days searching the area. A village near the battle site bore signs of the ravages of war. Many livestock were dead, and hootches and vegetation had been destroyed.

During this time we received no resupply for three days. We soon exhausted our extra supply of C rations, and some GIs were getting desperate. They wanted to kill a large pig out in the rice paddies. However, no one knew how to skin and butcher the animal. When asked, I declined. I knew how to do it, but I wasn't in the mood. When the larger animals became out of the question, the men turned to some chickens nearby.

Miley came over, lugging his M-79, and asked, "Do you think a shotgun shell in the grenade launcher will kill some chickens?"

Henson and DeLao urged him to find out by shooting into the middle of a flock of chickens.

"Why not, I should at least get one of them," Miley concluded. With that he fired into the flock. Feathers flew everywhere, but not one chicken was killed.

DeLao ended up wringing a chicken's neck. After removing the feathers, DeLao said, "It's your turn, Chief. Cook the chicken for us."

I replied, "I guess I have no choice. I'll get a fire going and boil the bird in a steel pot."

As I was preparing the chicken, Hump came around, wondering what we were doing. He laughed at us. "I hope you don't plan on cooking the bird. If you do, I hope you guys know what you are doing."

After the chicken boiled for an hour or two, someone threw in some rice. Every now and then Hump came around to observe how I was cooking the chicken. Of course, there was nothing to it. You just made sure the water didn't boil away. After another half hour, Hump took out his survival knife, poked at the chicken, and declared, "It's ready."

We took our canteen cups and served ourselves. The meal wasn't bad at all. Hump then came over and served himself some food. He chuckled and said, "Anytime you guys need some cooking advice, let me know."

He had had nothing to do with cooking the chicken, but that was Hump. He always had a laugh or two. Brooks often kidded Hump about his claim to have played semipro football, referring to him as "Hump the semipro."

We remained in the area for a few more days before going east. Charlie frequently took sniper shots at us to let us know he was there. This kept us alert and always anticipating the worst. We eventually came upon a fire base atop a steep hill. It was manned by the ARVN and was in their AO.

Eventually we made another combat assault to the southwest, where we continued our daily routine of checking out villages and surrounding areas. We were now somewhere west of Duc Pho.

Jordan, Hadaway, Whitaker, H. P., Brooks, Nevins, Willingham, Watts, Fields, Uncle Mickey, and some others were close to serving their time. They would be leaving within a few weeks, which meant the inevitable was about to happen. The guys I had arrived with, as well as I, would soon be assuming leadership roles. I kept that thought in mind, but I still walked point a lot.

One day while I was walking point, I heard automatic rifle fire behind me. We took up a defensive position next to a large river and waited. After a few minutes the all-clear message came to the front element. A new guy named Rader had shot a VC.

Rader was known as a friendly, likable soldier. One day new replacements had arrived on the resupply chopper, and he was one of them. The chopper had to make a quick exit, and when it took off he was still on board. The chopper was well into the air when Rader decided to jump. He landed quite hard. He was all right but had a badly bruised ankle.

Off to our right as we continued on the trail was a gigantic water wheel. It seemed to go all the way across the large river. It wasn't functioning, but the size of the thing fascinated me. We continued until we reached our night defensive position.

When we set up for the evening, I found out what had happened with Rader. He had slid down an embankment and come face to face with a VC. At that moment, Rader explained, "We looked at each other for a split second, before I shot him dead."

Rader beat the guy to the draw but felt bad about the incident. He was a very devoted spiritualist, and in a sense, he believed a lot in the supernatural. That evening Rader sat next to me as we heated up our C rations in makeshift stoves and said, "You're an Indian, and you'll probably know where I come from."

"What do you mean?" I asked.

"My belief is somewhat in the supernatural and stuff like that. You probably know what I mean."

"Maybe I know what you are talking about. What are you trying to say?"

"In my religion, we don't believe in killing. What happened today is bothering me."

"If that is the case, why are you in Nam and the infantry? I thought conscientious objectors got out of going to wars."

"I know. Someone promised me a noncombat job in the rear. So much for promises. I didn't fight it when I had to go to the field."

Getting back to his first question, I answered, "Rader, we all believe in the Creator in our own ways. Indians are no different. Most of our beliefs are similar to what the Bible teaches. We know of the supernatural. We are aware of certain situations and avoid them. I believe we are all here because that is the way our course of life is set. We have no control over it. Until I came to this place, I never took the power of prayer seriously. Now I know that is what keeps me going on a daily basis. As for what happened to you today, think about it for a moment. Would you rather it had been you that got killed? This place doesn't give you very much time to react to situations. At times you make split-second decisions. That is what you did. You exercised the most basic human instinct. The will to survive."

19. Arc Lights

OUR NEW AO APPEARED TO BE NORTHWEST of Duc Pho, after we spent a few days south of there. Now we continued west toward the mountains and a narrow valley. Soon the rice paddy terrain was ending and the valley was directly ahead.

During a lunch break I looked at the mountains looming straight ahead. I said to Wilson, "The mountains are very close. I wonder if we might be conducting operations there again."

Wilson shrugged. "Who knows from day to day what we will do. You know how it is. We are here now, but within the next few hours we might be making another combat assault. We all thought we might be operating south of Duc Pho for a while. But we ended up here rather quickly. To tell you straight, I wouldn't be surprised if we end up humping all over those mountains."

That evening the company set up a defensive position in the area. Then our orders changed. We were to leave the area immediately, so we quickly packed up and left. We continued in an easterly direction and ended up about five klicks from the mountains, where we set up a night defensive position.

Jordan explained our situation, "There is to be a B-52 strike in the mountains exactly where we are headed. To be on the safe side, you have to be at least three miles from the strike. That is why we left in a hurry."

This was to be my first experience with an actual B-52 strike. Someone said such strikes were called Arc Lights. I had often wondered about the B52s. On many occasions we had looked up in the night sky and observed them on their way north.

When it became dark the B-52 assault began. The mountains to the west lit up, followed by a loud thundering sound. Then I knew why a B-52 strike was called Arc Lights, for it resembled an arc welder striking an arc to create a brilliant light. We were about three miles away, but the ground shook and vibrated around us. It was an exhilarating experience. It seemed impossible for anyone to survive such a strike.

In the morning we waited once again in the rice paddies for choppers to pick us up. When they did we flew toward the site of the B-52 strike. Our mission was to assess the amount of damage. The choppers soon dropped us off on a mountain peak in the midst of a very devastated area.

Going south, we came across a scene of complete annihilation. There was nothing but scattered debris over a wide area. It looked as though someone had twisted and snapped off some large mahogany trees, as all that remained were the stumps. We searched a large area, and it appeared that nothing on the surface had survived. Even if the NVA were underground, the explosions would have caused casualties. We spent the night nearby.

The following day a chopper dropped off two Chieu Hois. The former enemy soldiers then led the company away from the devastated area. Supposedly they knew of a large cache of weapons hidden in these mountains. The new terrain we traveled through was the usual thick jungle-type vegetation found in the mountains. For the remainder of the day we went up one ridge and down the other, doubling back a time or two.

This seeming wild-goose chase was setting the guys on edge. It was bad enough to hump in the flat area, but doing it in the mountains was twice as hard. The hot weather caused us to gulp down water, which raised concerns that we might run out. We hadn't come across any streams.

When we set up for the night, Sergeant Jordan updated our situation. He said, "You guys might have heard that the Chieu Hois are looking for a cache of weapons. Now, I understand that they are trying to locate larger weapons hidden in these mountains. The devastation is confusing them. Meanwhile, we have to continue following them. We'll also get some water on the resupply chopper."

The next day we went down a hill and entered a heavily fortified area, an enemy base camp abandoned for some time. There appeared to be no recent enemy activity. From there we followed the Chieu Hois down a hill until we eventually reached a small valley. The Chieu Hois checked out the area thoroughly, and soon they pointed to a sandy creek bed. The company then set up a defensive perimeter around the area.

Brooks and I shared a defensive position nearby and kept a lookout to our front. After a while I took out my camera and snapped some pictures. One was of Brooks standing with the M-60 machine gun. I told him, "Let's hope that the film won't be ruined by the wet weather. I heard from my brother back home that some film I sent him was ruined."

Meanwhile, the Chieu Hois dug around in the sand. Within an hour there was a buzz of excitement. They found what they were leading us all over the mountains for, some parts of a large gun wrapped in plastic and buried in the sand. It was a 105 Howitzer, disassembled, along with the tires. Also uncovered were many 105 rounds and various small arms, along with ammunition. Later a flying crane shuttled the confiscated weapons and ammunition to Chu Lai in a large net.

The big gun along with the small weapons and ammunition was a major discovery. Further evidence revealed that the large gun and cache of small arms were going to be used in an attack against one of the big base camps. In a later issue of the *Stars and Stripes,* I learned that the big gun had come from a nearby base camp overrun by the VC years earlier.

We operated in the area for another week, encountering very little enemy activity. One day we searched an area full of large boulders among heavy overgrowth. A trail led past some boulders and into trees. Lieutenant Eggleston, the platoon leader, decided that we should investigate the trail further.

When the point element went past the large boulders, Lieutenant Eggleston found himself next to someone who happened upon a hornet's nest. The angered bees immediately attacked the unlucky GI, who frantically dashed past the platoon leader. However, the lieutenant had no time to react himself and was swarmed and stung repeatedly by the bees.

I was about fifty meters away when the incident occurred. I could see the hornets flying in circles. They were larger than bumble bees, and the sight of them sent a shudder through me. We had no recourse but to remain very still. After several minutes, we knew something had to be done for the men in pain. Cautiously, we moved the hurt men away from the hornets, who were now flying higher in the air. Our platoon leader was the one who needed the most medical attention and had to be evacuated. Doc Walker mentioned that the hornet stings could be fatal. Yet another danger in Nam, and one that we were totally unaware of.

The following day we waited in the rice paddies for choppers to take us on another combat assault. I was a now a team leader. I stood with my rifle above my head and guided in a chopper. I believe we went just north of Duc Pho.

From there we worked our way back to LZ Bronco, where I believed we might be spending more time. Because the frequency of the rains was increasing, it was good to have the better shelter a base camp afforded. That evening as I stood in chow line, I recognized one of the cooks as a guy from basic training whose name was Smith.

After eating, I decided to pay a visit to LZ Bronco's barber shop. When I entered the place I saw that the barber was Vietnamese. He was cutting someone's hair, so I sat and waited. A sign on the wall read "Don't Pay the Barber Any More Than 50 Cents." I could tell that the man receiving a haircut was a rear echelon soldier. Compared to the tattered rags I had on his starched fatigues appeared especially neat. When the barber was finished the guy reached into his wallet, gave the barber a bill, and said, "Keep the change." The barber was all smiles.

The barber wasn't very friendly toward me. He knew that I was an infantry soldier by my appearance. When he was through I handed him a fifty-cent MPC. He looked at the paper money, making a sour facial expression and mumbling something. I interpreted it to mean I was a cheapskate. I didn't like his attitude and felt like giving him a horizontal butt stroke with my rifle. Instead, I just pointed at the sign and said, "That's all you get from me, fool."

Our sector of the perimeter around LZ Bronco had received mortar fire for several weeks. The rounds were landing close to and sometimes damaging places of importance. However, the ambushes sent out nightly couldn't pinpoint Charlie's position. He was too sly. He sent rounds into the perimeter without walking them in. He fired his rounds and quickly left the area.

One night Charlie's luck ran out. Another platoon surprised him and wiped out a mortar squad as he prepared to send rounds into the perimeter. A routine check of the bodies revealed one to be the barber. This was no surprise to us. It was common knowledge that some of the local population worked inside base camps by day and moonlighted as VC by night.

After a short rest we headed to the mountains southwest of Duc Pho. We were ordered to sweep the foothills for anything unusual. The closer we got to the mountains, the more sparse the population became. We had to be careful of the marshy areas, as certain parts of the terrain were swamplike. A stretch of rice paddies we crossed made us feel like we were walking on gelatin. The ground moved with us as we tried to maintain our balance. We were lucky none of us sunk into the deep mud.

From the hills we were to cross relatively easy terrain to Highway One. However, the constant rains had caused some streams to rise. This was unexpected, but the swollen streams still had to be negotiated. We had no time to go around them, even if that had been possible. Fortunately, the water flowed slowly at the streams and wasn't too deep. We were able to cross them without any problems, until we reached the last one. It appeared to be a lot deeper and would be more difficult to ford. Again we had no choice and had to take a chance.

We slowly went into the water as it steadily became deeper and deeper. Soon the water was chest high. I carried my rifle above my head as the rising water created a floating sensation. I was concerned for some shorter members of the platoon and hoped that the water wouldn't get any deeper. It didn't, but the water did reach some soldiers' chins. Later we would cross other streams of similar depth.

By now it was raining almost every day. Jordan, Uncle Mickey, and some others had left us to go back to the world. I missed them all. They were a good bunch of guys. I was glad that they had made it back to the world in one piece. Uncle Mickey was a top individual and a close friend. Sergeant Jordan was a very good leader. I learned combat smarts from him. He had a lot of confidence and knew how to handle difficult situations. Hadaway took over as platoon sergeant when Jordan left. Lieutenant Eggleston was our platoon leader, but Hadaway provided much of the expertise.

I was now a team leader. I knew what to do and performed my duties as others before me had done. The important thing was to have everyone ready to fight in case of enemy engagement.

Our operations took us south of Duc Pho to the area around LZ Thunder. The terrain in this area was the same as around Duc Pho, with rice paddies scattered among hills. LZ Thunder sat atop a very large hill about five miles south of Duc Pho. Halfway up the hill was an engineer battalion. These guys cleared Highway One of mines on a daily basis, among other duties.

While we were at LZ Thunder, Hadaway left the platoon to go back to the world. With his departure I felt we had lost the last of the good leaders. I never hesitated on the countless times when he said, "Chief, move out when we get you cover fire." At times I disagreed with his attitude toward the villagers, but overall he was a very good leader. When he left he waved good-bye to the guys and walked toward me. We shook hands, and I said, "Good luck, Hadaway, you were a good leader and inspiration."

Hadaway replied, "Good luck, Chief. Take care, and don't be surprised if you take over the platoon." He might be right. I now knew how to read a map and use the radio, and I knew the terrain features and what to expect from each. I was now a team leader and squad leader. Most of the old guys were gone. Only Whitaker, Willingham, and Nevins were still with us. Guthrie had left in the early part of October.

During this time Lieutenant Eggleston went back to the rear for some reason and put Whitaker in charge of the platoon. I was the platoon sergeant, although some others had seniority.

Our bodies were tired and weary as we made our way to the bunkers one day after climbing a hill in a driving rainstorm. I heard someone say, "The bunker isn't exactly a Waldorf-Astoria, but it'll do just as well."

However, we would not be able to enjoy dry bunkers that night. Whitaker came over and said, "I'm sorry, but we have to go out on ambush tonight." The news didn't go over very well with the guys. They fell silent. Having to climb the large hill after a wet day in the field had lowered our morale even further. For the past few weeks we had spent a lot of time going on ambush. The constant routine was starting to take its toll and threatened our level of alertness.

We had very little time to rest. After a hot meal we got ready to go out again. Meanwhile, the rain fell at a steady rate. We reached the main gate at dark, when Whitaker had a change of mind and held up the platoon. He called me over and said, "Chief, what do you think of us going out a few meters and taking it easy?"

"I don't get you," I replied. "What's on your mind?"

"For the past few weeks we have constantly been on the go. It's starting to affect the guys' morale and alertness. I'm going to tell the guards at the main gate that we'll spend the night in the bunker up ahead."

"I hear you. Let's do it."

Our platoon spent the night in a bunker a few meters past the entrance. This type of incident might not have been within strict military procedures, but I'm sure it was repeated time and time again throughout the country. We were exhausted and needed to be ready and alert for Charlie when out in the boonies.

We operated in the LZ Thunder area for a few more weeks. During that time Whitaker left us. With his departure all the old guys were gone. Lieutenant Eggleston was still our platoon leader, and I remained platoon sergeant. This didn't matter to one guy with seniority over me; another was visibly upset. I didn't say anything, although I would gladly have given him the responsibility.

Our operations took us north to LZ Liz, which was close to Highway One. Here, the villagers often came around to the base camp. One unusual item they sold was blocks of ice. This I felt was strange in a tropical setting. They put the ice in sawdust and transported it in large blocks. The ice wasn't too clean, but this didn't matter. We bought it to cool off our sodas and beer.

One afternoon, as we enjoyed our cold sodas and beer, our platoon received a package from back in the world. Harlow had sent the usual canned goodies and included a couple cans of Coors beer for me to enjoy. The timing couldn't have been better. I placed the two cans of Coors in the ice, and after a couple of hours I took out the beer and shared it with some others. Needless to say, it made my day.

There were steady changes as time went by, as our platoon now consisted of all new guys. At LZ Liz I shared a bunker with Dozier, Henson, and Miley. Dozier, a black soldier, became Hump's machine gun assistant. Henson and Miley, both white, were close friends. Other replacements were Smith and Cretens, both white. Smith, who was from Tennessee, was to become an RTO, and Cretens served as the new medic. I became close to both of them.

During this time I drank beer only in moderation. I already knew what kind of feeling a joint produced and how it made the negative feelings go away. However, I never found a need to use the stuff and just didn't trust it. I had already decided that this and other types of drugs were bad for you. At the time, I erroneously felt that alcohol was different.

In the morning we were getting ready to go on another patrol south of LZ Liz, when I joked to Rader, "I have a bad premonition about getting shot today."

Rader immediately became concerned and replied, "Don't say that. Remember, I believe in that sort of stuff."

"Not to worry. I'm only kidding," I reassured him.

Walking through the rice paddies, we passed a small hill and continued south until we eventually encountered more dense terrain dotted with small clearings. Charlie fired a few rounds at us as we entered one clearing. It seemed to be only one sniper. The lieutenant held up the platoon and waited in place. After he discussed the situation with me, we all fired our weapons toward the sniper. He quieted down. I thought of what I had said to Rader earlier and started to use more caution.

My duties as platoon sergeant weren't all that bad. I received messages from the platoon leader and relayed them to the squad leaders. I also took care of the guys' needs, making sure they were properly supplied. Every day the RTO radioed in a list of their needs, and the resupply chopper would bring them. Being platoon sergeant also meant that I was next in command. I would take over the platoon in the absence of the platoon leader.

On one operation we went farther west of LZ Liz toward the mountains. When we came under heavy fire at one point, Smith and I found cover behind a pile of dirt. He was shaken as he looked at me and admitted, "I've never been shot at like this before. It's weird."

"Just remain cool. It seems like Charlie is playing games with us."

Lieutenant Eggleston crawled over to us and said, "I think they are shooting from the big coconut trees across the paddies."

"That's correct," I answered.

This was a test of Eggleston's leadership as well as mine. Lieutenant Eggleston announced, "I'm not taking any chances. Send the M-79 man over."

Soon grenade rounds were fired at the suspected area. I then yelled for Henson and two others who were close to me. "Get ready to move out when the lieutenant gets us some cover fire! Make sure one of you has a LAW [light antitank weapon]."

As the cover fire raked the trees, we ran to the right, making our way through the bushes to where we could see the coconut trees. From there Henson fired the LAW. With deadly accuracy the rocket slammed into the coconut trees and exploded noisily. We then assaulted the position, and Charlie suffered one casualty.

After the hostilities were over I walked over to Smith and said, "I know how you felt. You never quite get used to it. At times it's a lot worse. Sometimes you are pinned down for hours or get caught in a minefield."

Lieutenant Eggleston was glad that we had experience in handling bad situations. I recommended to him that it's best to go straight at the enemy if at all possible.

Eventually we ended up back at LZ Bronco. That evening someone invited me to an NCO club. I wasn't an NCO, but I went with him to another part of the base. The club was nothing fancy. It was just something put together to accommodate the NCOs. We spent the better part of the evening there with members of other infantry units.

We arrived back at our battalion late and were feeling the effects of the alcohol. When I found my tent, I stumbled inside looking for my cot. When I found it, someone was sleeping on it. I told the guy, "Hey fella, you're sleeping on my cot. Go find your own."

The guy mumbled something and turned over. I repeated, "This is my cot, get off," kicking the side of it.

The guy sprang at me like a cat. Within the next instant we were wrestling among cots full of guys. He was very strong. We traded a few punches, and then some guys broke us up. After the brief fracas, I recognized him. "You're Moreno from the First Platoon. What are you doing in our tent?"

"And you're the Chief. Hell, I thought I was in my own tent."

We both had been out late that night and were in the same state of inebriation. No one was hurt, and we both laughed as he staggered out to find his tent.

Anderson then yelled from the far end of the tent, "Settle down, Chief. You can use the cot next to me." I'm sure Anderson still gets a good chuckle about the whole incident.

In the morning it took several attempts to wake me up. Unbeknownst to me, Lieutenant Eggleston had earlier received word from the CO to have the platoon ready at first light. Our platoon would be the lead platoon. Although I was dragging my butt, still feeling the effects of the alcohol, I was ready to go within minutes.

Eggleston came over and said, "The CO is really pissed off at you. He claims you're holding up the company."

"Hell, I had no way of knowing we were leaving today," I retorted. "I thought we were going to stay another night. I'm as ready as I'll ever be. The CO will just have to live with it."

Another platoon took the lead. When we left the main gate we began south and then continued east. There was some VC mortar activity from this direction, and we were to search the area thoroughly. At first my hangover was terrible. All I wanted to do was sit and rest. Fortunately, my problem cleared up soon enough. The heat and our movement caused me to drink gallons of water. I sweated all the alcohol out of my system.

20. Responsibility

THE RAINY SEASON, WHICH OCCURRED in the northern part of South Vietnam from late August to December, was now upon us in full force. Most days it rained a steady drizzle. You tried to keep as dry as possible, but it was a losing battle. Some guys wore rain jackets and even rain pants, but they made you perspire to the point where you became wet anyway. We collected plastic bags or pieces of plastic, which were used to wrap anything valuable that could get wet. I had at least four pieces of plastic secured with a piece of duct tape around my wallet. You did whatever it took to keep your valuables dry.

Soon the steady rain caused the lowlands to become flooded. Many villagers in an area north of Duc Pho were forced to move to higher ground. The situation reminded me of nature movies in which animals huddled on the only piece of land around in similar instances. The villagers did what they had to; I'm sure that it had happened many times in the past.

We shifted our operations to the mountains to the west. One day we set up a night defensive position atop a large hill. After the resupply chopper left, some guys built a fire with the empty C ration boxes. It was just cold enough to be uncomfortable, and the fire was welcomed.

The fire roared, and we scavenged whatever fuel we could to keep it going. The warmth felt good as we stood next to it. Someone made hot chocolate, which we all shared. At times like these a packet of hot chocolate mix became a coveted item. Only certain C ration meals had the packets, however. After that everyone hoped for a meal with a packet of hot chocolate.

The rain became very uncomfortable, chilling you to the bones at night. I finally broke down and acquired a gray raincoat with a hood, which everyone else already had. The raincoat was rather bulky, but it did keep me warm.

After a few weeks in the rain we arrived back at LZ Bronco. When we were settled in Lieutenant Eggleston came around with a bottle of cognac. I had never had cognac in my life and just took a sip.

Everyone talked in groups as the rain pounded on the tent. The trenches around the tents were soon filled with water. The CP group sat off to the side and joined in our own conversation. Eventually another bottle of cognac was passed around.

"We had some close calls," Lieutenant Eggleston said. "I'm glad that you guys knew what to do."

"The guys we relied heavily on are gone," Ladd replied. "Now it is our turn. It has been an eternity, but we are also getting on the short side. Soon it will be someone else's turn, and so on. I'll be glad to stay around here and keep away from Pinkville."

Lieutenant Eggleston turned to me. "Where is this place called Pinkville? I heard it mentioned a time or two."

"What Ladd is trying to say," I replied, "is that we have a better chance with Charlie shooting at us. When we were in the Pinkville area we lost many guys to mines and booby traps. That place is nothing but death. I hope we stay away from there."

Jones, a red-haired country boy from Tennessee, then approached us, the alcohol already affecting him. He had hit the cognac quite hard, and it put him in a happy mood. He whooped and hollered as loud as he could as he did back flips. The lieutenant advised him to take it easy, but it didn't do much good. We just allowed him to let off some steam.

Our operations continued around Duc Pho, and we avoided the flooded area. During this time Lieutenant Eggleston was rotated back to the rear. This came as no surprise to me. I had a feeling he would be leaving. When we were at the battalion he said, "Chief, I'll be leaving the platoon in a couple of days. I won't be with you guys when you go back out in the field. I just want you to know that I honestly feel that I don't belong out there. For the past few weeks you have been at my side and helped make the decisions. I strongly feel that you are the only one capable of leading the platoon. You know the situation out there. You belong out there. I told the company commander that you would be in charge after I leave."

I had a very good rapport with Lieutenant Eggleston, although I agreed that he didn't belong in the field. He had the necessary training to do his duties, but he never developed a feel for the boonies. I'd still give him a passing grade, especially because he allowed seasoned veterans to make crucial decisions.

Lieutenant Eggleston was right about me belonging out in the field to a certain extent. Throughout my tour of duty, I felt more freedom out in the field. I couldn't see myself being in the rear and putting up with the rear echelon routine. I had felt that way, however, when I had no responsibility. Now I was in a top leadership position, and the responsibilities were great. Yes, I had reached the top, although I would have just as soon let someone else have the responsibility.

I also knew my being in this role wasn't by luck or chance. Until this time I had had many different leaders. Somehow they all had thought alike and steered me to this position. I had been a team leader, squad leader, and platoon sergeant and now was a platoon leader.

I'm sure many GIs felt as I did when chosen to lead a combat platoon. Many times it happened overnight. One day you were content to follow orders, the next day you were bestowed with a tremendous responsibility. The scenario might be best related through Sergeant O'Neil's expression in the movie *Platoon*. There is that certain look on his face when Captain Harris says, "Sergeant O'Neil, you have the Second Platoon."

It's very important not to show your misgivings to your platoon, however. You have to come across with confidence to be able to carry out the responsibilities. As in anything you do, sooner or later you get used to the leadership role.

I also thought of my new responsibility from my Jicarilla Apache way. When I was in high school the subject of being a leader came up in a conversation with my aunt and uncle. They explained what it meant to be a leader in our traditional way.

In the Jicarilla language a leader of a group of people is referred to as

Nahn Tahn. The short translation of Nahn Tahn is leader. A more in-depth translation, however, describes it as someone who is also an orator. He tells his people what happened in battle or what is about to happen to them next.

My aunt mentioned that in the old days being Nahn Tahn was something to be feared. Only the very strong took on the responsibility. One had to set a good example and ensure that the needs of everyone in his group were met before he thought of himself. He must never be corrupted or gain wealth from his position. The main criteria were that he never retreat in battle and he show a lot of courage. He had to be the first one into a conflict, and if need be, he would fight single-handedly with an enemy leader. If one wanted to be a leader he had to follow what was expected of him. To do otherwise meant a terrible fate for the individual.

My aunt once told me a rather humorous story of a Nahn Tahn. She said, "When I was a young girl my elders told me this story. They told of a time in the old days when we still fought enemies to survive. It seems that there was a Nahn Tahn that took his position to the extreme. One day, while seated next to a fire a hot coal somehow landed on his bare leg. Instead of swiping the coal away he just let it burn into his skin. His wife, standing nearby and noticing his bravado, came rushing over and swiped away the hot coal." My aunt laughed and said, "That's a foolhardy way to be Nahn Tahn. That's going a little too far."

In a sense, I was now a Nahn Tahn, although under circumstances different from the old days. However, I knew that the criteria would still apply, especially in a battle. I also knew that now, more than ever, I would need the help of my Creator in the dark days ahead.

I took on the responsibility, thinking it would be temporary and another leader would arrive shortly. My rank was specialist fourth class. Keeping the arrangement we had had before, although it was a bit unusual, I had two subordinates who were sergeants. We operated in the Duc Pho area and south to LZ Charlie Brown. It was raining most of the time, and our main priority was to keep our weapons dry at all cost. We used plastic bags to accomplish this task.

I often think of those days as a depressing time, not so much from being out in the field but from the rain constantly pounding on you and seeming to work its way into your soul. No matter where you turned you couldn't get much relief from the wet conditions. We sloshed in the rain and did our best to carry out our operations. In a firefight, it was not too surprising for someone's weapon to malfunction. Frequently we would spend more time in hootches, just to keep out of the rain. Sometimes we went several days without seeing sunshine. To this day a stretch of rainy days brings back bad memories of those times.

Even though our situation couldn't be controlled, the GI was always resourceful and found a way to overcome any obstacle. When in the boonies we found a way to keep out of the rain for a few hours. When a perimeter was secured we set up a makeshift tent with our ponchos. We tied a knot where the head went, placed about a four-foot stick there, and then tied the four sides of the poncho to the ground. We blew up our air mattresses and put them inside these "tents." The water would run down the sides of the makeshift tent, and the air mattress would protect you from the water on the ground. We found some temporary relief from the wetness in this manner.

Some new replacements were Kent, Whitt, Lacina, Hadley, and Norman, all white soldiers. With them we continued the daily routine of checking villages and conducting night ambushes.

During this time Captain Davis departed the company, and Lieutenant Fox assumed temporary command. He was a bit green and didn't seem to possess the ability to lead men. One day when we were back at LZ Bronco, Lieutenant Fox assembled the platoon leaders together in the mess hall and announced, "Platoon leaders, have your guys ready to go. In the morning we're making another combat assault. We have to build a temporary LZ in the mountains west of here. We will be in NVA domain and have to work quickly to secure a strong perimeter. The plans are to have the big guns talking by nightfall."

In the morning we were airborne and headed west into the dense forest of the mountains. The farther west you went the denser the terrain became. We landed in a small clearing atop one of the many ridges. The terrain was very dense, similar to that farther north.

When we disembarked, we secured a small perimeter in the clearing. Lieutenant Fox came over and asked me for advice on where to set up defensive positions. I walked around with him and pointed out the possible avenues of enemy approach and our avenues of escape. We then set up positions to cover the approaches.

Meanwhile, choppers brought in 105 howitzers, artillery personnel, combat engineers, materials, supplies, and so forth. We hustled to make fighting positions out of sandbags and culverts that were cut in half. The big guns soon were working and sent out artillery rounds west into the Central Highlands.

The area to the front of our perimeter was thick with vegetation that had to be cleared. It had to be hacked out with a machete, which would take some time. Before we could start, Lieutenant Fox came around and told us about an alternative plan. "Chief, have your guys assist the engineers with bangalore torpedoes to clear the jungle."

"What the hell is a bangalore torpedo?" I asked.

"You'll know when you see them. For now, get some guys to work with the engineers."

I found out that a bangalore torpedo was a long, metal cylinder filled with explosives. The cylinders could be joined to make the "torpedo" as long as you needed. We attached one section after another and pushed it into the jungle as far as we could. Then the bangalore torpedo was detonated. The huge explosion cleared a large portion of jungle all at once. We repeated this throughout the afternoon and into the night. Eventually we cleared a large area in front of our positions.

I asked Lieutenant Fox, "What's the name of this new LZ, and how long are we going to be here?"

"It's LZ Cork," he answered. "We might be here a week or two. I want to thank you for helping me set up defensive positions. You might not realize it, but you've been a great help."

When it was dark, LPs and OPs were set up well away from the perimeter, which we secured over the next few days. The artillery rounds kept going off, and every now and then there was a fire mission.

After about two weeks the temporary LZ was abandoned. Before leaving we destroyed everything, including cases of hand grenades and other unused ammunition. We then flew back to Duc Pho.

21. Stripes

OUR COMPANY EVENTUALLY ended up at LZ Charlie Brown. The place was on a strip of land next to the sea, separated from the mainland by a channel. Across the channel was another small base called Hardstand, manned by the U.S. Navy.

Navy personnel ferried us across the channel on a landing craft. From there we walked up an incline. Across the channel to the west we could see a large village next to the ocean. The place, Sa Huyn, was a fishing village. Along the seashore were many small Vietnamese boats as well as larger fishing boats.

My platoon was assigned to bunkers on the south side of the perimeter, directly across from the village. When it became dark someone mentioned that Vietnamese girls were in the perimeter, so I checked out the area with a couple of guys. When we inquired around it seemed that some guys were indeed hiding girls. When I went to the CP group, a company RTO named Culberson called me over. "I heard that you guys were asking around about some gook girls," he said.

"I'm just checking out what someone told me."

"There are girls inside," he admitted. "They came across the channel in boats when it got dark."

"Does the CO know of this?" I asked.

Culberson nodded and said, "Yeah, he does."

I didn't reply and headed back to my bunker. Culberson was supposed to be an Indian or part Indian. He was with the CO group, and I had been aware of him for several weeks. However, I never paid much attention to him, because he came across as the "kiss ass" type. Arriving back at my platoon, I learned that the guys already knew of the girls. I told them that the CO knew about the girls, so we'd just let it be. I cautioned them to be more alert. Some guys thought Lieutenant Fox should take charge and get the girls out of the perimeter, but that didn't happen.

After that, the girls came across the channel in boats every evening. I say girls, but as old as some looked, the GIs must have been desperate. None of them had the beauty that many young women of the country had. They used heavy makeup to hide their age. These shenanigans, I assumed, must have been going on for a long time. Every new unit on the LZ just went along with it. As far as I knew, none of my guys took part, but you never know.

While there, we made several combat assaults south of the village. On one occasion there was heavy contact during the initial chopper landings. Several VCs were eliminated by the combined effort of the ground troops and choppers.

Our operations now took us back and forth from Duc Pho to Charlie Brown. We made more combat assaults to give Charlie an idea of our mobility. He didn't know what to expect from us; we were here one moment and miles away the next.

Our radio code for the company changed again. It became Duncan Yeoman, and it is the only one I remember, probably because of the obscurity of it. My reaction upon hearing it for the first time was, Duncan what? Also during this time the local vendors got word that the military MPC system was to change. Many Vietnamese vendors had hoarded huge amounts of GI MPCs over the years. Now they were frantically exchanging them for their own currency, knowing the MPCs would soon become worthless. In the end many villagers got stuck with the worthless MPCs.

One day on an operation west of Duc Pho we took a break on an old railroad track. The rains had let up for a few days. As we sat in place we observed a procession of some sort, heading our way from the south. As it got closer it appeared to be a funeral procession. In front were Buddhist monks followed by men carrying a large wooden box. A large group of villagers followed behind. The CO became aware of the situation while the procession was still some distance away. He said, "What's that procession headed your way?"

"It appears to be a funeral procession," Smith replied.

"Don't take anything for granted. Remember the recent firefights in this area. Perhaps there is a VC body inside, or there might be weapons. Do what you have to do to check out the box."

We knew that it might be immoral to do so, but the CO was right. We motioned to the monks that we were going to look in the box. The people realized what we were about to do and all spoke at once in protest. The monks remained silent and motioned to allow us to search through the contents of the box. No weapons were inside, but there was the dead body of a young man. We assumed it to be a VC and let the CO know.

After that incident, we returned to LZ Bronco for the night. Back at camp that afternoon, I walked with the CP group to the mess hall. On the way I saw a GI unloading something out of a jeep. When I took a closer look at him, I strongly suspected him to be a Navajo Indian. I didn't get to talk to him, however, as he was leaving in a hurry.

Later that night I met the GI at the C Company tents. When I said hello to him in Navajo, he immediately responded in Navajo. I knew basically what he said. The Jicarilla Apache and Navajo languages are similar enough for one to understand the other. However, I had to tell him I was Jicarilla Apache but knew what he was saying.

We sat on a cot and talked for about an hour or two. It was good to talk to another person who shared a common heritage. He took the liberty of talking in Navajo every now and then. I knew he just had to speak his language, having been away from it all these months, and I welcomed it. I thought of the many Navajo friends I grew up with in the boarding school back home. Through the years I would continue to make many Navajo friends.

As we talked I realized he was also a leader within his platoon and was also called Chief. This gave me a good feeling, knowing that another individual lived up to the name. Before leaving we shook hands with the understanding we would meet again. However, I never saw him again.

We were operating around LZ Thunder when we received a new company commander, Captain Pryor. As soldiers go, he knew how to lead men into battle. He was the type who took charge of a situation, and that is what he did with our company. First, he assembled the platoon leaders. He reminded us of our responsibilities and said that he wouldn't hesitate to relieve us if we failed. My initial reaction to the way Captain Pryor operated was admiration. I thought that we had leadership for a change, and I began to feel more comfortable.

On one operation soon after, we left LZ Thunder and went about a mile north on Highway One. From there we headed east through rice paddies, thick vegetation, and coconut trees among hedgerows. From the highway the company strung out in a long line and slowly advanced eastward.

Our weapons were at the ready as we made our way toward the South China Sea. Intelligence reports said the place was infested with VC. Our orders were to push the VC toward the ARVN troops to our front. As we advanced we couldn't make up our minds which was worse—to make contact with Charlie or to have the ARVNs close by in a combat situation.

Suddenly shooting erupted a long way ahead, which made us even more wary. After a while we heard more shooting from the same place. We continued to check anything suspicious and to move forward. About a half hour later we heard more shots. They sounded different and were spaced at regular intervals. We stayed in a long line and kept in sight of each other by going slow. As we got close to the ocean we spotted bodies on the ground, directly in front of us. I warned the platoon not to move the bodies. If they were VC, they might have a live grenade in hand.

When we reached the bodies we had weapons at the ready and held up. There were about a couple dozen corpses scattered across the ground. We looked closer and someone said, "Look at their hands. They are tied behind their backs. What do you think, Chief?"

"It seems they were all executed," I replied, looking at the bodies. "Someone shot all of them in the back of the head. That explains the last series of shots. I would assume we chased these gooks into the ARVN's lap. Then they were executed by them. These people treat each other far worse than the GIs treat them."

"I wonder where the ARVNs are," Smith said.

"Hopefully, they are far away. I don't want them shooting at us."

We continued toward the ocean. As soon as we reached the beach area we held up in place and took a break. After that we searched the hootches in the area.

I was inside one when I heard a commotion outside, near the ocean. A large crowd of villagers was gathered around something. The Kit Carson scout, my RTO, and I went to investigate, pushing our way through the crowd of people. Some people were digging in the sand. Several ARVN soldiers were jabbering away as they stood next to the ones digging. Within a few minutes the shovels struck something metallic, which caused the ARVN soldiers to become very excited. A couple of them took over digging in the sand.

The digging continued until an upside-down fifty-five-gallon barrel was uncovered. As the barrel was lifted up, the ARVN soldiers had their rifles at the ready. Inside the barrel was a badly shot-up VC. He was barely alive. Suddenly he shouted as loud as he could. With that, his life, whatever was left of it, abruptly ended with a burst of fire from an ARVN soldier.

Afterward I asked the Kit Carson scout, "What VC say?"

"VC say, 'Long live Ho Chi Minh.'"

During this time I received my orders for R&R. In anticipation of this, I already had in hand a check from my bank back home. I put De Lao, a Chicano, in charge of the platoon. I told him, "The company will be at Bronco for a couple of days. Ladd should be back from R&R shortly. He'll be in charge when he gets back."

De Lao replied, "I know what to do, even if we go back to the field. Just forget about this place for a few days."

After that I hopped on the first chopper to Chu Lai, and from there I flew to Da Nang. Da Nang was one of several places where the out-country processing took place. The first person I ran into there was Ladd. I asked him cheerfully, "Ladd, what are you doing here? I thought you might be on your way back from some exotic place."

Ladd looked at me and replied, "I'll just put everything out in the open. The first night I was here someone stole most of my money. I didn't have enough to go anywhere out of country and also didn't want to go back to the field, so I just hung around here with this guy (pointing out another GI). The same thing happened to him. Anyway, we ended up having a good time. I'll be leaving later this afternoon."

At Da Nang I had no problem getting my check converted into U.S. currency. I followed Wilson's advice and chose to go to Taipei, Taiwan.

The following evening about a hundred GIs made the long flight toward the island nation. When we approached the city it was night. Below us was a large array of lights, which added to our excitement aboard the plane. Taipei appeared to be a very large city from the air.

When we landed we went straight to the in-country orientation center. There we converted our money to Taiwanese currency, called NTs. The exchange ratio was forty NTs to every U.S. dollar. When I left the place, I felt very rich with all the one-hundred-NT bills I had. One of my first purchases was some civilian clothes.

Taipei was a large city that never went to sleep. Because it was night, the city was lit up with bright neon lights everywhere I looked. A bus took me to a hotel I chose at the orientation center. On the way I noticed all the signs were in Chinese, and I didn't know what they said. I could tell where the bars and restaurants were, though. I put most of my money in the hotel safe, believing that was the wise thing to do.

Most of my time in Taipei was passed in carefree spending. I checked out some clubs, which were different from the bars. The girls at the clubs engaged you in conversation and didn't solicit you for anything else. On the other hand, when entering a bar, you found many girls waiting inside to solicit you for whatever. The favorite nightclub of GIs was the one called Sea Dragon, operated by the U.S. Navy.

The food in Taipei was mainly Chinese, so I usually ordered American food through room service. Another place to get American food was the Sea Dragon. There one could get an authentic American cheeseburger with french fries. I tried some Chinese food, but it was spicier and prepared differently from the kind you found in the states.

One day a friendly, middle-aged Taiwanese took the time to take me on a tour of the city. We spent an afternoon looking at museums and the main attractions of the city. We even sat through a western movie that was in the English language. There I realized that the Nationalist Chinese were very patriotic people. Before the movie started they all stood at attention for the playing of their national anthem. I stood with them.

While in Taiwan I also got to see the surrounding countryside. I became acquainted with a cab driver, who offered to take me to the mountains. One thing worth mentioning is the traffic. There seemed to be no traffic lights. Instead, the first driver to reach an intersection honked his horn for the right of way. That's all you heard at the crowded intersections. Miraculously, there were no collisions, particularly amazing with the large volume of bicycles on the roads. If the system worked for them, then let it be.

As we cruised on the open road I sat with the breeze blowing in my face. The driver looked at me and said, "You look like Taiwanese."

"The Vietnamese people also say I look like them," I replied. "I'm an American Indian from the United States."

"I know of the Indians. In school we studied them."

"You speak good English and seem to know a lot."

"I'm going to the university and working part time. I'm also like the Indians. You might say I'm a Taiwanese Indian."

"I don't understand."

"My people were the original inhabitants of the Island of Formosa, now called Taiwan. When the Communists forced Chiang Kai-shek out of the Chinese mainland they came to Formosa. After that they took over our lands and forced us into the mountains. Now you understand why I say I'm like you."

"I understand. From now on we are brothers."

The driver smiled big. At his first opportunity he pulled over to a vendor by the road. He bought two bottles of Taiwanese beer, handed me one, and said, "I drink to that."

Our destination was somewhere high in the mountains. The driver parked below, and from there we walked toward the mountains. I wondered if we would climb all the way to the top. That would be no problem, as that was what I had been doing for months. As I walked with my new friend, an individual on a motorcycle rushed by us and waited up ahead. He appeared to be taking pictures of us with a camera. When we reached a railroad track, we stopped and waited. From there someone pushed us up the mountain in a railcar. This I thought was rather strange.

At the top were members of my friend's people. They were referred to as Aborigines. They, like the American Indians, were a source of interest for tourists. Most of the tourists seemed to be Japanese. The Aborigines dressed in their traditional attire as they posed for photographs. For about an hour or two we sat at a table and drank some beer. Close by was a tramway that took tourists across a deep valley to the top of another mountain. I was relaxed as I visited with my friend's people, feeling a closeness to them.

We then went back down the hill on the railcar, whereupon the individual on the motorcycle came over to us. He had taken photographs of us in various stages of going up and on top of the mountain. I went ahead and purchased the photographs. That was the highlight of my time in Taiwan. All too soon the R&R ended.

De Lao and Ladd were still around Duc Pho when I arrived back. They had nothing major to report, and everything seemed routine. The air remained damp from all the rain. I found it very hard to be back in the field, and I still had about three months remaining. I understood then why it was best to take R&R when you were getting short. I realized then that my time to go home was getting near. My devil-may-care attitude was fading. Now I knew how the guys before us felt as their time to go home approached.

One evening on LZ Thunder the CO and platoon leaders met with the brigade and battalion commanders to discuss battle strategy. The top brass were colonels, whose staff all consisted of commissioned officers. I was the only leader who had no commission. All the rest were out of OCS or West Point. The main thing going for me was my knowledge of the terrain. When I stood among the top brass, I realized that here I was, discussing battle strategy with the top brass, when I had never expected to be a leader. That meeting was a highlight of my military duty.

That night we developed a plan of action to deal with a company of VC operating north of Duc Pho. Our plan was to have our company airlifted early in the morning into the area. With some luck we might make contact with them.

After the meeting, Captain Pryor met with his platoon leaders. He said, "I hope we can meet up with those bastards. I haven't tasted VC blood in a long time." The captain had had a previous tour with the Twenty-fifth Infantry Division in Tay Nihn.

At daybreak we were flown north in formation aboard a dozen choppers, leaving LZ Thunder as scheduled. The gunships that accompanied us soon raked out the LZ. There were no large rice paddies in the area, so we were forced to land in clearings among the hedgerows. Parts of the platoon landed in different clearings, which caused temporary chaos. It took some time before we regrouped. Luckily, we received no hostile fire in our sector. If Charlie was around, he was well concealed. Choppers overhead had a clear view and flew around in circles.

We were still bunched in a clearing when a chopper threw a smoke grenade into it. Another chopper then landed next to the colored smoke. The individual who stepped out of the chopper was the battalion commander. He was very upset as he came over to us and barked, "Who is in charge of this outfit?"

I stepped forward and said, "I am, sir."

"What's going on here? Why are the men bunched up like this?"

I had no clear answer but replied, "We are just getting ready to move to the west."

"What is your rank, soldier?"

"Spec Four, sir."

"A specialist fourth class leading a platoon. Well, just get your men spaced and start moving. Charlie is around. See if you can flush him out to us."

"Yes, sir, will do."

We then advanced from hedgerow to hedgerow, careful of anything suspicious. The command from the chopper overhead was to keep moving. Suddenly, a short burst of automatic fire went off to the rear, followed by another burst. After a few seconds word came that a new replacement had been attacked by a water buffalo. We held up in place.

When my RTO and I arrived at the scene of the shooting, someone pointed to a dead water buffalo. "What happened?" I asked.

The person replied, "The new guy was bringing up the rear when the animal attacked. It threw him up in the air, but he managed to roll and dodge the animal. That was when someone shot the animal."

I went over to the new replacement and asked, "You all right?"

He was visibly shaken but replied, "I think so."

I then cautioned the guys, "This is a prized animal to the villagers. Today, we apparently had no choice and shot it. That won't make it any clearer to them. They'll still be resentful toward us and probably aid the VC against us."

The CO then called on the radio and asked for a report. I told him about the water-buffalo incident and said that we were continuing west. The CO reported that the choppers had spotted some suspected VC moving away from us. The choppers began raking the area to our front with sure fire.

The operation turned out to be not as successful as we had hoped, but several suspected VC were killed. We lingered in the area for another week. Charlie was around, but he avoided contact.

Around the middle of November we returned to the brigade base camp. We were ordered into a company formation, which happened only when awards were given out. The CO talked to us and gave us an idea of what the brigade and division had accomplished. Some Combat Infantryman's Badges (CIBs), Purple Hearts, and other awards were issued. After these awards, several of us received orders that we were now sergeants in the U.S. Army.

Along with the orders I received sergeant stripe pins to put on my collar. That day I felt a great sense of pride and accomplishment. I never expected to be a sergeant when I entered the army. Now I had orders in my hand stating just that. I also knew that I had earned the rank.

It took a little time before I got used to being called sergeant or sarge. Some called me Sergeant TeCube. Most of the time I still went by Chief or Sergeant Chief. This had more meaning. According to my traditional beliefs, I had now earned the right to be called Chief.

After getting the new rank I went with the new NCOs to an NCO club to celebrate. Jenkins was one, I felt, who truly deserved the stripes. A southern boy, Jenkins was an individual I admired, and he had the respect of his men. At the club I took care not to overcelebrate and just absorbed the atmosphere. Most of us had been together all these many months. When we were seated at a table, some guys from another outfit joined us. One made a familiar comment: "You look like an Indian."

"That's right. I'm Jicarilla Apache from New Mexico."

"Is that right. We have a guy in our outfit who is also an Apache."

"Do you know what tribe he is?"

"I could swear he said he was a Mescalero Apache." I became very interested. One of them tried, unsuccessfully, to find the Apache.

We now had a new platoon leader, Lieutenant Porter. Early on we realized that he was his own man. He did and said whatever he wanted. He held nothing back and often told you exactly how he felt. This frank attitude turned off most of the guys. He and I had one thing in common. We were familiar with rodeos and the western way of life. He mentioned that he was a bull rider and followed the rodeo circuit. I said that I had tried riding bulls a time or two.

The next time we left LZ Bronco, Lieutenant Porter was in charge. I was again the platoon sergeant. We made our way south on Highway One through a small gap south of Duc Pho. We conducted operations in the large open rice paddy area. The CO had ordered us to check the area thoroughly, because Charlie had been harassing an ARVN outpost and planting mines nearby on Highway One.

The villagers weren't as friendly here, which probably meant they sympathized more with the VC. However, we didn't find anything useful in the villages and encountered no hostility. After several days we found ourselves back close to Highway One.

We took a break next to a village on the highway. The platoon leader and I sat with the CP group a ways from the village. After a while some villagers and prostitutes came around selling their wares or themselves. We had rested for an hour when we noticed a large crowd gathered around a hootch.

After a few minutes Smith went to find out what was happening. The crowd of villagers, especially the smaller kids, was trying to peek into the windows of the hootch. After a few minutes, Smith returned, laughing. "All those people are weird," he said, shaking his head.

"What do you mean, weird? What's going on?" I wanted to know.

"The people are fighting to look into the windows to see what the prostitutes and some of our guys are doing."

"What about our guys, don't they know they are putting on a show for them?"

"That's just it, they don't seem to care. Everyone is having a good time and laughing up a storm. I guess we've been here too long." We found the whole incident hilarious.

That night we assumed we would be inside LZ Thunder, but instead we continued past it and on toward the sea. Sniper fire occasionally came from the northeast, but it was nothing significant. We established a company perimeter on a small incline among hedgerows, and the platoon CP group set up inside the perimeter.

We were ready to call it a night, when suddenly a burst of automatic rifle fire interrupted the silence. Another short burst followed. Instantly, we were on guard, ready for further action. I told the platoon leader I was going to investigate. Lieutenant Porter said, "I'm going with you. Smith, call the CO to advise of the situation."

We made our way to the east end of the perimeter, where the guys were on full alert. Henson said in a low voice, "Lacina shot at something in the dark. He thinks they were gooks." Henson and Lacina were part of an LP to the east. We had the guys maintain the high state of alert as we talked to Lacina, who pointed into the darkness to where he took the shots. He said, "We were ready to set up, when we heard noises. I saw something moving in our direction. I just shot at the thing and backed off."

I put my rifle on automatic and said, "I'm going to see what's out there."

"I'm going with you," Lieutenant Porter answered. "Lacina and Henson, follow us."

"Watch out, Chief," Henson cautioned. "Remember, you are getting short."

"I hear you," I replied, "but we have to do what we have to. Thanks for your concern, and you also be careful."

I slowly made my way in the darkness toward the spot Lacina indicated. Lieutenant Porter was directly behind me, followed by Lacina and Henson. We moved among hedgerows, which made it darker. When I had advanced about thirty meters in I had a feeling we would either come upon a dead VC or be fired upon. With my finger ready to pull the trigger, I whispered to keep low. I continued, and within another meter I spotted a dark shape on the trail, directly in front of us. I was convinced Lacina had shot a VC.

I held up and whispered, "Sir, something is lying on the trail. You guys be ready for anything."

Lieutenant Porter whispered back, "Go ahead, but be careful."

When I cautiously reached the figure it turned out to be a dead cow. We sat in place for a long while, looking out in the darkness, not saying a word. When we returned to the perimeter, the other guys had a good laugh about the incident.

I sat with Lieutenant Porter. "Normally and especially when GIs are in the area, the livestock are penned up at night," I explained. "I wonder if Charlie isn't having himself a good laugh."

Lieutenant Porter's reply was characteristically blunt. "I don't give a damn. We weren't scared to take him on tonight."

The next day we continued our operation to the north, ending up at an abandoned base camp, LZ Carentan. It was the original headquarters of the Eleventh Brigade. We stayed out of the camp and behind the old concertina wires. In all probability, Charlie had mined the place. I surveyed out position. To the northwest was LZ Bronco, to the west was a large open area that was flooded, to the east was the sea, and to the south, more rice paddies. In the morning we headed toward LZ Bronco and eventually turned west, avoiding the flooded area and working our way back to Highway One. After another day or so we were back at LZ Thunder.

No matter how long we were in the field, we never got used to the constant movement, night ambushes, and LPs. It felt good to be back inside a secured place.

At LZ Thunder, Rader somehow brought up his religious beliefs again. He explained to Lieutenant Porter what he had told me earlier about the supernatural. Lieutenant Porter wasn't impressed, however.

He turned to me and spat, "I don't know about you, but I say fuck that kind of religion." Henson and I just looked at each other.

When Lieutenant Porter left, Henson said, "The guy says what he thinks." That type of attitude eventually put Lieutenant Porter on the wrong side of Captain Pryor.

One night our platoon went on ambush west of LZ Thunder, with Lieutenant Porter in charge. Prior to leaving we plotted the ambush site on his map. I had a very good idea of where we were to go.

When ready we moved out, heading down the large hill and on past Highway One. We continued west and passed an ARVN outpost. From there we went southwest until reaching a large trail, which joined two heavily wooded areas.

Before reaching the ambush site, the platoon leader and I disagreed on our exact location, so we held up next to some trees. In the darkness we whispered to each other. "I think we should go farther to the east," I said.

Lieutenant Porter disagreed and suggested, "Let's get under a poncho and make sure." After looking at map we still disagreed.

Lieutenant Porter was the leader and had the final say. He then told the point man where to go. Suddenly rifle fire came our way. Most of the rounds went over our heads as we stayed low. So Charlie wouldn't know our exact location, I advised the guys to hold their fire. I said quietly to Lieutenant Porter, "From the shots we're receiving, I believe Charlie is farther west from where our ambush was to be."

"I'm going to call in some rounds on him," the platoon leader replied.

"That might be a good idea," I agreed, "but you have to be sure of your exact position."

The shooting continued as we debated under a poncho again. Lieutenant Porter's grid coordinates and mine still opposed each other. He pointed to the place where Charlie was supposed to be firing from. "We can't call artillery in there, that's our position," I said.

Meanwhile the shots were hitting to our left, meaning Charlie still didn't know our exact position, and the guys were becoming aware of our disagreement. It was futile to try to reason with Lieutenant Porter, because it was clear that he was going to have his way anyway. "If you want to call in rounds, at least call in a marking round first," I advised.

Lieutenant Porter did call in the rounds. When they came, they exploded all around us. The lieutenant frantically called off the fire mission. We were lucky no one was hurt by the rain of artillery. We had dodged another bullet, but this time it was from our own hands.

The rounds did serve their purpose in a different manner. Charlie hastily retreated from the area. After that we silently moved our position and kept a 50 percent alert for the rest of the night. At first light we made our way back to LZ Thunder. Before we entered the LZ, Lieutenant Porter talked to the guys. He said he was sorry for the mistake and wanted us to not tell anyone know about the incident. I knew the guys were very upset. I also knew what they would do about it.

The company was to move out that morning with our platoon in the lead. Within an hour we were ready by the main gate. Before we left, Captain Pryor came around, visibly upset. He pointed at Lieutenant Porter and said, "You're through." Then he pointed at me. "Chief, you have the Third Platoon again." Someone had told the captain about our narrow escape. I knew this would happen and let it be at that.

22. Getting Short

ONCE AGAIN I WAS AT THE HELM of the Third Platoon. This time I already knew what to do. Captain Pryor briefed me on where we were to go that day—our plan was to move in a southerly direction and eventually, by that afternoon, into the mountains.

From the base of the hill we went southeast along Highway One. One klick farther we turned and steadily made our way through the rice paddies toward the mountains. The broad valley around us, dominated by rice paddies, became narrower as we continued. It ended at the base of the mountains, giving way to thick, canopied, junglelike terrain.

The terrain became much more difficult to negotiate. We started up a steep slope thick with vegetation, with no trail to follow. Here I advised the point team, "Keep to the left of this draw. It's going to get harder as we go. Be sure you have a machete. Charlie won't be a problem here. If we run into a trail or the terrain changes be careful."

There was no way to keep your bearings in the thick jungle. After a while there was no sunlight coming through the trees. The hill became steeper as we continued upward, and the air even seemed less plentiful. I wasn't too sure of where we were as the terrain roughened. We took frequent breaks during the steady climb. Earlier I had observed a small saddle in the mountains. Now as we made our way up, I had the point man veer more to the left, hoping to come out at the saddle. If we missed it, we could continue to climb for a long time.

We were lucky to be able to move at all here. The point man had no idea of where to go and just followed my directions. I had a gut feeling we would be coming to a clearing in the direction we were headed. If we didn't find one, we would be stuck in the jungle for the night. My fears weren't of the NVA but, instead, of getting caught in the darkness.

We continued upward and to my great relief eventually saw patches of blue sky ahead. My gamble had paid off. I advised the point man to hold up when he was close to a clearing. When he did, I went past him to check the area myself. We had reached the saddle I had spotted earlier. A wind was blowing in our direction, carrying no clues of anything hostile, such as the smell of human waste that emanated from all NVA base camps. My platoon crossed to the far end of the clearing. The other platoons humped their way up the hill and into the clearing, very exhausted. Climbing through the jungle without any daylight was a very demanding experience.

Once we were settled in Captain Pryor called me over to his CP group. I wondered what he might want. Perhaps choppers would pick us up. Anything was possible. We met in the open, away from the rest of the company. Getting right to the point, he said, "I called you over to commend you on getting us here. I thought we would never get out of the thick terrain. How did you manage to find this place?"

"To tell you the truth, I had my doubts. I just relied on my instincts and had a little bit of luck."

Captain Pryor continued, "Well I'm glad you got us here. I also had my doubts. There's another thing I want to say. To be honest, you have shown good leadership. The army needs men like you."

I looked at him, surprised. "What are you trying to say?"

"Have you ever thought of making the army a career?"

"I never gave it serious thought. I would just as soon put in my time and get out."

"If you want," the captain added, "I could get you a commission, but you might have to put in more time."

"I appreciate your confidence. I don't think I could put in more time."

The captain persisted. "I want you to think about it, Chief."

There was still some daylight left, and we still had to reach our night position. After a good rest, we continued south until the point man came upon a large trail.

The CO told us, "The trail is a main branch of the Ho Chi Minh trail on the map. The NVA often use this trail as a resupply route. Keep a sharp lookout for signs of recent use."

With that thought in mind I advised the point man, "Go on the trail, and be on the lookout for anything that is not right. If you see fresh, turned dirt or broken twigs or whatever, hold up. This is supposed to be NVA territory. Mines and booby traps won't be too much of a worry, but you never know. If anything watch out for an ambush."

When we reached a bend in the trail it was late in the day. Here, the CO advised us to go left up an incline. Our night defensive position would be a short distance farther. The sun was just above the horizon when the last of the company made their way into the perimeter. The day had been an exhausting one. Guys rested in place before digging foxholes and settling in for the night.

My platoon couldn't get too comfortable, as we had to go on ambush that night. We were ordered to go farther up the trail about a klick. Another ambush would go in the opposite direction. If we made contact, we were try to get back to the perimeter ASAP.

When it got dark we left the perimeter and went south on the trail. The dense jungle canopy all around made it even darker. We eventually found a clearing just before the trail went deeper into the jungle. This seemed like a good position to set up the ambush. I had the guys set up claymores to cover the trail and told them to watch the thick growth ahead carefully, as it was a possible avenue of approach of the enemy. The tall elephant grass to the left of the trail would give us good cover. We set up guards to cover both sides of the trail and one to cover the rear.

When everyone set in for the night I checked the guard positions. We had received new replacements, and I wanted to make sure they knew what to do. After checking I went back to the CP group but didn't go to sleep right away. Smith and I sat in the tall grass and talked quietly for a while. A strong breeze blowing north to south would prevent the enemy from hearing us.

The moon was already well above the horizon, making its way through the clouds. It illuminated the area well enough so that we could see up the trail. The tall grass we crouched in afforded excellent concealment.

"Chief, you want something to munch on?" Smith said. "I received a package back at LZ Thunder. I still have some goodies."

"Sure, why not, as long as it's not the Cs."

Smith then reached into his rucksack and took out a box of Chicken in a Biskit and an aerosol can of processed cheese. We sat there whispering as we munched, before going off to sleep.

The next day we continued in a southwesterly direction, looking for signs of NVA activities. Eventually we reached a more open area. The place was still very sparsely populated, and we spent very little time in any one place. The terrain gradually turned to rice paddies, although we were still in the mountains. At this point the platoons split up, but all continued in a southerly direction. My platoon made a sweep to the southwest and then back to the east. After finding nothing definite we rendezvoused with the company for the night.

We eventually ended up on a mountain slope overlooking the South China Sea. Here the rice paddies were terraced all the way to the bottom of the mountain. We then made our way down the incline to Highway One.

After reaching the highway, we went north toward the village of Sa Huyn. Our destination was LZ Charlie Brown. Before long a landing craft arrived and transported our weary bodies across the channel. From there we walked to the outpost. During this operation the weather had cleared up for a few days, but now the steady rains returned. It rained hard as we settled into our bunkers.

I thought of the last time we were here and how some guys had taken advantage of Lieutenant Fox. Now we had a company commander who stressed discipline. That night no girls came across the channel, and none would the whole time we were there. I knew the CO had something to do with this difference.

The following day we stayed in the bunkers as the weather turned from bad to worse. The rain hit the bunkers in large sheets, like someone throwing buckets of water on them. At the village all the boats were secured in place. The storm had become a typhoon. There was nothing to do except wait it out.

Out in the ocean a U.S. Navy barge came loose from another ship and beached next to the village. Huge waves pounded the barge for a few days, eventually spilling its cargo onto the beach. The villagers helped themselves to all of the supplies under the cover of the bad weather. The stormy weather didn't let up for a couple of weeks. This was the worst rain we had seen.

During this time I rotated our squad or team leaders. Vic, who at first was the all-American boy, had changed for the worse, becoming rebellious. I felt he tried very hard to be a bad boy and had succeeded. At times he took part in mistreating villagers. He was also a sergeant, so I gave him the responsibility that went with the rank.

After I informed Vic that he would be leading a squad, he replied, "I don't want to be a leader. Let someone else."

"Sorry about that," I said, "but the responsibility goes with the rank."

"I don't give a damn about rank," he cursed. "I don't want to be a damn leader. If you want to take my stripes, take it."

"Suit yourself, I'll do just that."

"Go ahead, take the stripes. I told you I don't give a damn. Just take it." Vic stalked off.

After that I assigned someone else to be squad leader. Henson, who was standing nearby, came over and said, "Chief, you have a very tough job. Just hang in there."

I sighed. "I know, it's bad enough worrying about the enemy. Something like this could mess up your whole day. Thanks for the words of support."

In the morning our plans changed. Instead of making a combat assault in choppers, we ferried across the channel and went down Highway One. We went past the village and toward the sea and were soon in formation with fire teams abreast going across the rice paddies. The company was making a sweep to push Charlie toward another unit to the east. When we received occasional sniper fire we answered with our own volley. Charlie played this game for the rest of the day, until a chopper surprised him. We later learned that he left two bodies behind.

After spending another day in the rain, we made it to LZ Thunder. We sat in our bunkers as the rain pounded on the roof. I had heard nothing from the CO about my platoon going out for the night. I was sure we wouldn't. We sat in groups enjoying a hot meal and wearing dry fatigues. It felt good to sit under shelter with the rain pouring down outside.

However, just at that moment, the CO came over and announced, "Chief, your platoon is to go out on ambush for the night. Have them ready to go when it gets dark. I'll give you the coordinates after you're through eating."

This news didn't go over too well with the guys. Leaving the perimeter wasn't as bad as knowing you'd soon be soaking wet again. We had all been looking forward to getting a good sleep in dry fatigues.

The ambush site was to be southeast of LZ Thunder. When the time came to leave it was still raining. I understood how the guys felt and let them gripe as we prepared to move out. I advised the platoon that we would be going all the way down the hill. Faking an ambush admittedly did cross my mind, but I knew that we had to go all the way. I agreed with the CO that Charlie might be out tonight. It was worth a shot.

It was dark when we reached Highway One. We set the ambush on a trail leading from a small village. We bedded down in the rain as best as we could, but the saturated ground afforded little comfort. I wrapped myself in a poncho and stayed awake thinking of the guys. I had a tremendous responsibility for their well-being. I prayed that I would continue to lead them wisely. The incentive of ridding the countryside of Communist domination had died in me months ago. Our survival was now my priority.

Survival. When in the Pinkville area, we suffered many casualties from mines and booby traps. Around here the greater danger came from sniper fire. At times we came under intense fire, but we survived the hostilities by using common sense and not taking unnecessary chances. I had now been out in the field about ten months. I knew what to expect from various terrain features. When a possible ambush site loomed ahead, grenade rounds were used before advancing. This strategy worked well for us. We had had no major casualties for a long time.

In the platoon CP group we did not pull guard duty but instead went on radio watch. Four of us took turns listening to the radio at night. I couldn't sleep, so when my turn for radio watch came around that rainy night I was still awake. After the watch I went into the half sleep that I had become so accustomed to.

At daybreak we reascended the hill. The company was to move out again that day, and we barely had time for some hot chow before leaving. As we hurried about, I managed to ask the CO where we were headed this time.

"Back down the hill and to the east," he said. "We have to make a large sweep to the north. If you remember, on a previous operation we netted a bunch of VC in this area. We hope to do the same thing. I'm somewhat surprised you didn't make contact last night."

"For some reason I also thought we were going to," I admitted.

My platoon brought up the rear as we made our way down the hill. When we were close to the ocean, we went on line. Going on line as a company through hedgerows was not an easy task. The sweep we had conducted earlier and farther north was in more open terrain. After an hour the platoons to the west were making faster progress. I kept my platoon moving steadily to the north, using the map I carried. Every now and then I checked my coordinates. The CO became concerned with the way the platoons were splitting apart. He called, and Smith relayed our grid coordinates.

The CO replied, "In that case, you should be about four hundred meters to the southeast. We'll hold up until we spot you."

For the rest of the day we continued the sweep. That night we set up near the abandoned base camp we had visited before, LZ Carentan. For the next two days we conducted a thorough search of the whole area. After that we continued northwest in the direction of LZ Bronco. The wet weather seemed to limit Charlie's activities, although he still set mines on the road.

All units now concentrated on LZ Bronco and its surrounding region, especially Highway One. When we set up some ambushes in this area, Charlie was not around. He was already wise to our intentions. On some occasions other units were more successful.

From Highway One, we went west to the foothills of the large mountains, traveling through valleys and hills, always on the move. Such constant humping tested your endurance and your ability to find something extra within yourself. Taylor, a new replacement, complained openly as we were climbing one hill. He was exhausted and was having trouble finding extra energy. We soon took a break, sitting on the trail to eat.

We later rested on an open grassy slope. Below was a narrow valley. Farther up the slope were thick trees. Whitt asked me, "Chief, where we headed today?"

I reached into a pocket for my map, which was encased in plastic. I pointed at the map. "See the red lines made by a china marker? We will go southwest into the hills, make a swing through this valley, and head back into the hills to the southeast. I'll show you the grid coordinates of where we stand. It's very important to know how to call in air support in case you are in a bind." We were still on the first leg of our plans for the day.

While we took a break, Taylor was still whining and gave his team leader some back talk. I had been aware of Taylor when he arrived in the platoon. At that time we had been operating in the lowlands. The going hadn't been as tough there, but he still complained, as some did. I believed that he was used to having his way and had never experienced tough conditions. He hadn't yet realized that here in Nam, he was no longer a boy. Now that we were in the hills, Taylor was being tested.

I went over to him and said, "I know what you're up to. You want me to call in a chopper to take you in. That's not going to happen. You don't get out of the field just for being tired."

"I don't care," he muttered. "I can't go any farther. My feet hurt like hell."

"Taylor, you will continue," I said patiently. "We all went through the same thing. There is such a thing as a second wind. Here in Nam at times you find a third wind. You think you have it bad now, but there are situations ten times as bad. Get your act together, and start doing your part in the platoon. We all have to work as a team. When we move out, be ready to move or stay on the trail."

Taylor mumbled something to himself as I left. When we continued after our break, he thought I was bluffing and just sat there.

We let him sit there and left. If I had given in, before long everyone would be sitting, just to get out of the field. We finally reached the top of the hill and began our descent down the other side. Halfway down someone said, "Taylor is coming along behind us. He must have thought it over."

Someone else added, "Hell, there's nothing to think over. The poor guy knows Charlie is out there. That's all the incentive he needs."

When we reached the valley floor we found many abandoned hootches but no villagers. The whole population had apparently moved elsewhere. Before continuing farther south, we came under sniper fire from the east. The CO advised us, "Go ahead and check out the sniper fire, and if you run into anything hot, we'll be close by. If you don't meet any resistance, continue east until you reach the top of the hills. That's where we will set up for the night. The rest of us will continue to the south, swing east, and go north to meet up with you. Either way we'll be in close proximity in case we need each other."

When we reached the approximate origin of the sniper fire, Charlie was nowhere to be seen. This was what we had suspected. I knew he might want us to follow him. Charlie might be waiting around the next bend.

We advanced cautiously and approached a point where several different trails went into thicker terrain. I warned the point man, "We have been lucky with mines and booby traps lately. Don't take anything for granted. If you see anything suspicious, hold up. This includes possible ambush sites. Charlie might be waiting up ahead."

As we inched forward, thoughts of Pinkville were on my mind. This time I was not on point, but that didn't lessen my concern for the point man and the ones up front.

Within a few minutes the point man stopped at a log. Brittenham, the team leader, told him to step carefully over it. After doing so, the point man saw a canister buried loosely in the dirt, covered with twigs and leaves. It looked like a freshly buried mine. The rest of us cautiously avoided it; down the trail a safe distance we held up. I then had a GI blow up the suspected mine.

That was the first mine we had encountered in a long time. Perhaps the rainy season had forced caused Charlie to use mines in this area. I prayed that wasn't the case and that this was an isolated incident.

We eventually entered a grassy open area and continued until reaching the approximate rendezvous site. As the drizzle turned into a steady rain, we set up a defensive position and waited for the rest of the company. Within an hour all the platoons had arrived.

When a perimeter was in place the CO told us to forget about an ambush that night. There was nothing we could do about the rain. Instead, each platoon was to send out two LPs. We were allowed to take it easy for the rest of the day.

I made a tent with my poncho and blew up my air mattress. The rain poured down relentlessly, but I stayed dry. I took out a pen and paper to write some letters but was unable to concentrate under the makeshift tent. I became drowsy but stayed in a half-awake state to make sure everyone took care of his responsibilities.

The rain hitting the tent brought back memories of my childhood. I thought of when I was very young and lived with my grandmother in a canvas tent. When it started to rain, you could see the raindrops hit the tent, forming spots. After a while the whole tent would be wet. If you touched the tent, it would start to leak.

After a while, I drifted off into a deep sleep. My guardian angel must have allowed me to do this. Sometime, maybe hours, later, I woke up in total darkness. The rain had subsided. I made my way outside the tent and saw Smith watching the radio. He whispered to me, "We knew you were exhausted and let you get some rest. The platoon is okay, and guards are in place."

Our operation next took us farther south of Duc Pho. On top of a large mountain we were resupplied and spent the night there. In the morning the CO told me, "The company will go east. Your platoon will follow the Second Platoon. A squad from the First Platoon will set up an ambush at our night position. We just might catch Charlie out in the open."

About an hour after we left, we heard shooting from the rear. As hoped, Charlie had checked our previous night's position. The squad left behind said that Charlie received casualties and fled down the hill to the west. Sometimes this strategy worked.

That incident changed our plans. Now my platoon was ordered south, the others were to go down each side of the mountain, and we were all to meet somewhere at the base of the mountains. After making sure Charlie was gone, we started down the mountain slope, necessarily taking our time. Out of necessity and due to the heavy pack carried, one went down such an incline at a slow pace.

I told the platoon as we marched, "We know Charlie is definitely in these mountains. The CO wants us to check as much of this place as possible. We will go down and at the same time look for signs of enemy activities. We just might run into something."

"What if the something is a battalion of NVAs?" someone asked.

"Then it'll just mess up our whole day."

Trees covered the mountain slope. The going had to be slow, so we took time to check for signs of a base camp, weapons, and food caches. The trail we were on was overgrown with grass and appeared unused. I knew at our rate we would barely make our rendezvous point before dark. The small trail we followed broadened, and other trails branched off.

Suddenly someone screamed behind us. There was no gunfire or explosion, so I thought someone had stepped on a punji stake. Barreto, a Puerto Rican soldier, came running down the hill, a swarm of bees following him. He was screaming in pain and had left his rifle and gear behind. The others who had been next to him were also running down, and soon we all were racing down the hill as fast as we could. We managed to get away from the bees and sat still as they flew angrily around in large circles. These were the same type of gigantic bees that had attacked Lieutenant Eggleston a while back. After they finally flew away, we crept back to retrieve Barreto's gear and weapons. A Medivac chopper then came and evacuated him.

I called the CO and reported the incident with the bees. I also advised him that we were delayed and probably wouldn't get to the rendezvous point on time. The CO told me not to worry and to radio our coordinates at dark.

The darkness caught us on a steep mountain slope in a grassy area. The trail we were on was the only decent place to bed down. We set up claymores to cover the front and back and also set up a guard position at each end of the trail.

I found a spot on the trail and bedded down, as did the rest. Overhead, the night sky became partly cloudy after some rain. Soon you could see the stars through openings in the clouds. I felt comfortable that Charlie was nowhere close by and slept. Later that night I was awakened to pull radio watch. By that time most of the clouds were gone, and a full moon had emerged. I sat looking down the slope and at the guard positions.

I was now wide awake as I sat in place. After a while a shadow started covering the moon. I had spent a lot of time out at night, but I had never witnessed a lunar eclipse. Now one was unfolding in front of my eyes. I forgot about my immediate situation and fully concentrated on the moon.

Soon the moon was half covered, and the surrounding area became increasingly darker. Before long the moon was completely covered and turned a reddish color. I thought of waking the guys but decided against it. I also thought that perhaps one might not be allowed to watch this type of event in my traditional ways, as we were taught to be aware of unnatural changes in the moon. I continued to watch, though, because I had never been told otherwise. It was well over an hour before the moon slowly started coming into view again. As my radio watch ended, I sat in wonder at what I had just witnessed.

23. Bangkok

BEFORE NOON WE REJOINED THE COMPANY at the base of the mountains. From there we made our way back to Duc Pho, where Meehan, Montieth, and Norman joined the platoon. Within a few weeks, like all of us before, they would be thoroughly used to the routine. GIs had a tour of duty of one year. As they reached their departure dates, others behind them would take over the responsibilities. There is much to learn about the field and a limited time to do so. In Nam circumstances did not allow you to drag your feet. As I've mentioned, leadership often changed overnight.

One day while back on LZ Bronco my eyeglasses broke, so I had to go to Chu Lai for another pair. That same afternoon I boarded a Chinook chopper, in the center of which was some large cargo. One other GI was on board, an infantryman like myself and also with the Eleventh Brigade. As we were flown north I looked out the small window and could see the South China Sea. Soon the familiar area of Task Force Barker came into view below. That place instantly brought back bad memories of a time that now seemed very long ago. The Chinook then banked and headed west toward the mountains. I did not care for the detour but sat patiently.

We flew over a mountain chain before the chopper landed at a small base camp. The cargo in the center was removed, and we took off again. From there we flew northeast over the mountains toward the sea. Within minutes we were hovering over the Chu Lai base and then landing next to the airstrip. I knew my way around and the location of the battalion. I also knew I might have to pull sergeant of the guards duty while there.

Earlier someone had told me of an Eleventh Brigade Guest House around the main PX area. After asking around I found the place. When I walked in I recognized the guy in charge, Sergeant Harris. He also recognized me and said, "Hello there, Chief, what brings you here?"

"I need a place to stay for the next two days," I said. "I didn't know you ran this place. I thought you might be back at the world."

"Well, I'm still here, but I'll be gone shortly. You came to the right place. I know you don't want to put up with the crap at the battalion. What are you in Chu Lai for?"

I stood in front of him and replied, "I need a new pair of glasses."

Sergeant Harris laughed and said, "In that case, how did you find this place? I know, if you can find your way in the dark, you should be able to find your way here." He pointed in several directions and added, "There is a mess hall over there where you can get some good chow. Over there you can catch a movie most nights. To the west of it is an EM club. I know you are now an NCO, but this place is better than the NCO clubs."

I relaxed on a bunk and thought of being a short timer. The time to go home was now approaching. Back home it would be hunting season. The crisp autumn air would be a sign that winter was near. I longed to be with my uncle and cousins as they got meat for the winter.

For the past several months I had chased an adversary who was as crafty as the deer. The only difference was that he also stalked you and fought back. I eluded him, because I thought as he did. However, I was not home free yet. I would be back in the field soon enough, but for now I had a few days to myself.

At the mess hall I recognized a GI from basic training named Garren. Later, he came over to where I sat and said, "I thought that might be you, TeCube, but I wasn't too sure."

"It's good to see you, Garren," I greeted him. "How long have you been here?"

"I arrived in September. How about you?"

"I've been here since January and am getting short."

"You went to Ft. Polk. You must have spent a lot of time out in the boonies?"

"That's right," I replied. "For the past many months we've chased

Charlie from one end of the Americal Division AO to the other. He's a crafty little devil, and you have to think like him."

That evening I visited the EM club that Sergeant Harris had recommended. The main show featured a band, dancing girls, and a black comedian. The heavyset comedian, named J. R., was very good. He had a routine that could rival the best.

In the morning an eye specialist ordered me some new glasses. I would have to wait a day for another pair. Having no further business, I went to the USO and continued taking it easy. That night I watched *Hang 'Em High*, a Clint Eastwood movie.

After a couple of days in Chu Lai, I rejoined the company around Duc Pho. The CO advised me about some new VC mortar activity. Intelligence suspected them to be operating from the area west of Duc Pho. We spent the next few days in the region setting ambushes, hoping to catch Charlie in the act. The rain let up for a few days, but the weather remained very humid.

During this time a new guy named Couch joined our platoon. He arrived in Nam by way of an instant NCO program from the states, the only individual to join our platoon in that manner. The program trained individuals to take combat leadership responsibilities. That being the case, I had him head a fire team immediately.

Almost from the beginning there were problems with Couch. He believed his training in the states superceded what we did. He often chose to do his own thing. The CO quickly became aware of this. Early on, I had good rapport with him, however, even buying a Fraternal Order of Eagles watch from him.

Soon our differences of opinion started to surface. He became more insubordinate and defiant. One day everything came to a head when he refused to obey a direct order. After trading strong words we were ready to fight each other. The CO saw us from a distance. He knew what was about to happen and called on the radio.

"What is going on over there?"

"Nothing the platoon can't handle," I reported. "We're all right."

"From what we can see, you guys are about to tear each other apart.

Just cool it. Save all your energy for Charlie. We'll get to the bottom of this later."

We decided to settle this matter between Couch and me one way or another later on, and we left it at that. However, the CO learned what happened and that Couch had disobeyed a direct order. He threatened to give Couch an Article 15 for refusing the order. Before long the CO phased him out of the company.

When we were back at LZ Bronco I went to the First of the Twentieth Battalion sector, located farther east of our battalion. There I ran into Ulenkott, my buddy from Ft. Polk. He was very glad to see me and exclaimed, "TeCube! It's good to see that you are still in one piece."

"That goes for you too," I said, smiling. "I see you have a job in the rear. How's everything with your outfit?"

"Oh, we continue to chase Charlie and catch him every now and then."

Ulenkott and I caught up on what had happened to guys from Ft. Polk. Stuart had gone back to the world about a week after we went to the field. He received a Million Dollar Wound, shrapnel wounds that were bad enough to go back to the world but not enough to mess him up for life. Burke had died when he dove into the sea and hit his head on a rock. I told Ulenkott about Hanson's death with C Company. I learned that Lee still carried an M-60 for D 4/3. With only a few weeks left in-country, we both agreed that it was important to keep a positive attitude. It didn't seem possible, but we were getting there.

When I arrived back at my battalion I learned that my friend Tex, who had gone AWOL about two weeks before, was hiding somewhere in the base camp. I needed to talk to him before he got himself in serious trouble. He and I had arrived in the company together and had gone through a lot during all these months. A court-martial wasn't worth it after spending so much time in the field. I checked the Third of the First Battalion, but I had no luck in finding him. Finally, all I could do was leave word with some guys who knew him that he should contact me.

The company remained at LZ Bronco for another day awaiting further orders. The captain advised the platoon leaders about a VC unit operating somewhere south of LZ Thunder. It was probably the same unit we had joined with the ARVNs to destroy earlier. Odds were that we would be going after them again.

That evening I felt weak after the evening meal. I lay down on my cot and soon began to feel the chills. It felt like malaria. Ladd noticed my condition and urged me to see the medic. I didn't argue with Ladd. When I got to the dispensary I was burning up; at the same time I had chills. A medic took my temperature and immediately became concerned. "Your temperature is 105," he said. "It has to be lowered immediately, but we can't do that here. The last chopper has left for Chu Lai. We can call in a Medivac."

I thought about the ice bath. I wanted no part of it. I said, "Forget the Medivac. I'll take my chances here."

The medic shrugged. "Suit yourself. We can only give you some pills. Hopefully, it will lower your temperature somewhat."

Instead of taking a couple as he suggested I took four and left the place. Back at my tent, De Lao and Ladd were waiting. I told them, "Take care of things. You guys know what to do. The CO has us on standby for a possible combat assault south of LZ Thunder. I got the chills bad. The medics say my temperature is extreme."

I then wrapped myself with my poncho and poncho liner. De Lao said, "Here, Chief, you can also use my poncho liner."

"Thanks, good buddy."

I then covered myself with his poncho liner and shivered in the darkness. I experienced alternating chills and fever for a long time before I drifted off to sleep. I woke up at daybreak. My high fever was gone, and I felt 100 percent normal. To this day I never found out what brought on the high fever.

The following day we made a combat assault southeast of LZ Thunder, where a heavy concentration of VC had been reported. Other companies, including the ARVN, also took part in the operation. At dawn we were already in the air heading south in choppers.

After landing in rice paddies our objective was to push Charlie north toward the ARVNs. As we swept north, we came under minimal sniper fire. I heard shooting to the north that sounded like the executions by the ARVNs in an earlier operation. By its conclusion, the operation was successful. We had bagged a few VC, although not the whole unit, as we had hoped.

After a few days we were back on LZ Charlie Brown, staying in the same bunkers as before. The rains were letting up, and there were actually days when it didn't rain at all. For the next couple of days we filled sandbags. Kids from across the channel helped us in this task. Some guys filled sandbags closer to the channel. When I checked on them, Karaba and others had burrowed into the sand and made caves. This was their way of escaping the hot sun.

"Get out of the caves," I warned them. "The sand might cave in on you. Don't take stupid chances."

I left them at that. A few minutes later I received word that Karaba was trapped in the sand. When I saw his predicament I told the others, "Remove the sand with your hands. Remember not to move him when you free him. This is what I warned you guys about." When Karaba was freed, he was injured and couldn't move. A Medivac chopper took him to Chu Lai. That was the last time I ever saw him.

Several weeks earlier I had put in for a seven-day leave, although I didn't believe that it would actually be granted. While at LZ Charlie Brown, I learned that my leave had indeed been approved. I already had gotten a check from home to be on the safe side. I left Ladd in charge of the platoon. Fenstermaker had also received orders for R&R the same day, so that afternoon we boarded the resupply chopper and went to Chu Lai.

It was close to Christmas, and Bob Hope was going to be in Chu Lai for a Christmas show. Knowing this, Fenstermaker and I had second thoughts about going anywhere. We wanted to stay around for Bob Hope's show, a once in a lifetime opportunity. We were torn, but the lure of visiting an exotic country was stronger, so we continued on to Da Nang.

Before we did, we met two members from the company CP group. They told us, "The CO sent us here to try to get Bob Hope to come to LZ Charlie Brown or Hardstand."

Fenstermaker snorted. "You guys have to be joking. There is no way you can get Bob Hope to go out in the boonies."

The guys were serious, however. We bid them good luck as we continued to Da Nang. Having been there before, I already knew the procedure and advised Fenstermaker what to do. "I'm going back to Taipei, Taiwan," I told him. "I kind of liked the place."

"I'm thinking of going to Bangkok, Thailand. Chief, why don't you come along?"

I also was leaning toward Hong Kong, but I ended up going to Bangkok with Fenstermaker. On the flight there, I sat with two Mohawk Indians from the Marine Corps. The flight detoured around the southern tip of South Vietnam before heading toward Thailand. When I looked out the window, I could see many outposts below. Some were very large, others were just a speck, but all clearly indicated how large the U.S. involvement had become. I read somewhere that the U.S. military commitment was then at half a million men.

When we approached Bangkok, I noticed that the surrounding countryside was flat, not what I had imagined. After we landed we went by bus to an orientation center where we filled out forms and chose a hotel. We also got a packet from Tommy's Tourist Agency. As we filled out the forms, local people gave us generous samples of a Thai beer called Singha.

After the orientation we were taken by bus to our hotels; on the way the bus stopped at different hotels. At each stop free glasses or bottles of beer were given to us. At one stop a GI was handed a bottle of beer and told, "Take beer and share it. Not worry about germs, alcohol in beer kill them."

At our hotel, Fenstermaker and I each got a bottle of rum along with the free beer. After that, as advised, we hired a cab driver for the week. The cab driver, named Max, agreed to take us anywhere we wanted anytime. He first took us to a place to buy some civilian clothes. It was strange to see the driver on the right side of the car; the traffic also went in the opposite direction from what we were used to.

When we arrived at the clothing store, again we were given free beer. It was becoming apparent that locals wanted to get GIs loaded as quickly as possible, to make it easier to take advantage of us. Fenstermaker and I realized this and took it easy on the beer. Max, our cab driver, also warned us about the beer. Evidently it was more potent than the beer we were used to.

The city of Bangkok featured a vast array of night life in its so-called red-light district. It was a place where one had to be careful. The GIS were advised to stay instead in the districts set aside for them. To go elsewhere meant taking your chances.

It was the Christmas season, and the hotel we stayed at had a decorated Christmas tree, Santa Claus, and a Nativity scene in the lobby. It was strange to celebrate Christmas in a tropical setting. I just couldn't get used to it.

The hotels provided tours to various places, so we took advantage of some. The hotel personnel, all native people, spoke good English. One afternoon we toured Bangkok in a boat, using the many canals that served as roads. The place looked like Venice, only in a tropical setting. There was much to do but too little time for everything we wanted to do. We took in whatever we could, including Thai boxing. One place we missed was the Bridge on the River Kwai. Bangkok was the experience of a lifetime. All too soon we had to return to the war.

Arriving back at LZ Bronco, Fenstermaker went back into the field the same day. I didn't go with him. I had only about two weeks left in-country. In my absence a new platoon leader had arrived. An elderly sergeant who had been temporary top sergeant now had a rear echelon job.

I was ready to rejoin the platoon, but this sergeant thought otherwise. He said, "Chief, it's not worth going back into the field. You have just two weeks left in-country. You'll be leaving the field in a week anyway. Why risk your life anymore? I can find something for you to do."

Normally I wouldn't have even considered his offer. I always felt more freedom out in the field. In this case, however, I knew he was right. I had to accept that I no longer belonged out there. I would stay around the base camp.

My decision was the opposite of what I had told some guys several weeks earlier. At that time I had a crazy notion to extend my tour of duty by joining the Long Range Reconnaissance Patrol (LRRP). I talked to some LRRP members and thought I could handle the duty. They made it sound uncomplicated. "We don't do anything while around a base camp. We go out in a small group every now and then. A chopper takes us far into the boonies and lets us off. After that we remain hidden for a week or two. We look out for NVA activities and get picked up again. We avoid contact if at all possible."

In reality, however, the LRRPs had a very dangerous task. Their main objective was to detect large enemy movements out in the boonies and to report them. You heard of them sometimes fighting their way out of life-and-death situations, and sometimes none of them made it. The main reason I thought about joining the LRRPs was to get an early out from the army, which you received if you extended your tour of duty four months in Vietnam.

When the guys heard I wanted to extend, they all told me it just wasn't worth it. After an evening meal Brittenham, Lacina, and others called me over to where they sat. Brittenham said, "Chief, we heard you wanted to extend a few months. All the guys are against it. We're telling you it's not worth it, even for another day."

They were serious, and it made me seriously think it over. I was confident I would make it back to the world, but there was no guarantee it would be in one piece. I thought of Lieutenant Lewis and how he chose not to live with both legs missing. The possibility of spending the rest of your life in that condition was very real in Nam, and I didn't know if I had the courage to do so. After that conversation I thought only of going home.

When I returned to LZ Bronco some guys told me of an incident that really depressed me. While I was away Vic had killed himself. One night some guys had been in the far bunker smoking dinky dow. Everyone was having a good time and joking. Vic had given no clue of his intentions. He merely picked up his rifle and stepped outside, and after a few seconds the rifle went off. He shot himself in the head and died instantly. When I heard the news I thought of the first time Vic and I had met and how well we had hit it off. I also thought of how he had slowly changed over time. The war made you do strange things, often for the worse.

While I was away the guys had taken part in several firefights in the LZ Charlie Brown area. Wilson told me about one harrowing incident. "We were operating west of Charlie Brown with the First of the First Cavalry. I was standing in front of an APC when a rocket came slamming in. It hit the dirt in front of the APC. The explosion sent dirt and me flying. It scared the daylights out of me. I'm too short for this sort of thing."

They also told me what happened with the two GIs who were sent to Chu Lai to attract some entertainment. Somehow they persuaded a touring group to put on a show at LZ Hardstand. The afternoon of the show most of the guys went across the channel to watch it. For security reasons the entertainment took place during the day.

When the show started Charlie got bold. He started crossing the channel to LZ Charlie Brown on the south side. This was why tight security was left behind, as Charlie could never be underestimated. The guys on security waited until Charlie was in the middle of the channel. Then they opened up on him. Over a dozen VC were destroyed.

Winston was also at LZ Bronco during my last weeks, having left the field with foot problems several weeks earlier. He limped on one crutch as he came over to me and said, "How you doing, Chief? When you going back to the field?"

"Not this time, good buddy," I replied, somewhat regretfully. "The field is a thing of the past for me. We have to start processing out of country in another week. Meanwhile, I'll be making myself scarce around here. How's that foot of yours coming along? Every time I see you, it doesn't seem to be getting any better."

Winston looked around and then leaned closer. "I have something to tell you, Chief. There is nothing wrong with my foot. All this time I've been putting on an act. I had some bad jives a while back in the field. I thought of what you told me about going back to the world with a leg or arm missing. To tell you the truth it scared me. That's when I knew I had to get out of the field. Do you blame me?"

"Not really, given the way the war ended up for us," I answered. "More power to you, to survive any way you can."

Our conversation turned, as many did during that time, to home and upcoming good-byes. "We're almost there. I'll sure be glad to get home," Winston said wistfully. "When I do I'm going to catch up on all the sleep I missed and forget this place. What about you, Chief?"

"I agree with you on the sleep." I paused and shook my head. "I don't think, though, that I can ever forget this place. It took too much out of us. We spent a lifetime here."

"I know what you mean. We went through a lot. You helped us out of many tough situations. I'll never forget you, Chief."

"That's goes for me too. I'll never forget the guys."

The distance from LZ Bronco to LZ Charlie Brown was about ten miles. On one occasion I rode shotgun for a vehicle that was part of a convoy to LZ Charlie Brown. When we drove down Highway One, I thought of the many miles I had already walked on this same road. Now I was cruising along, passing the villagers. I thought of them and how their lives hadn't changed much, and probably wouldn't, no matter the outcome of the war. I had my rifle ready and watched for possible ambush sites. When we reached LZ Hardstand, we ferried across and drove up the incline to LZ Charlie Brown.

Lacina recognized me and called, "Look who's back!"

That day a new first sergeant for the company arrived. Captain Pryor introduced a solidly built black man with a Mohawk haircut. The guy had a no-nonsense approach to matters and made a speech to the company. I listened and was glad that I wouldn't be working with him.

I had little time to spend with the guys, as the convoy had to be back at LZ Bronco before dark. However, I managed to chat with them a bit and to hear what was going on.

De Lao, a platoon sergeant at times, told me, "We are doing okay. Some new guys got a good taste of the field. The other day we were pinned down south of the village."

Some others added, "There is talk of the company going back to the place you guys call Pinkville."

That news made me uneasy for the guys. I didn't realize how attached I had become to them. I said, "If that is true, avoid using main trails, especially when leaving the villages. Don't take unnecessary chances. Shoot all the firepower available into suspected places. You guys hang in there." I told them I hoped to see them at LZ Bronco before I left.

The convoy then departed and headed back to LZ Bronco. The shadows were getting long as we drove past a suspected ambush site. I cautioned the driver about the location and kept a close watch as we drove by. After that it was mostly rice paddies on either side of us, and we eventually made it back to LZ Bronco safely.

Within a few days the guys returning to the states came in from the field to process out of country. Wilson, Ladd, Reddy, Hump, and Geary were among them. Others from different platoons included Moreno, Longoria, Jenkins, and Tregarten.

Wilson confided to me, "Boy, I thought I'd never make it back to the world. A few days ago we ran into some bad stuff and had to fight our way out of a gook ambush." Charlie had set up a horseshoe ambush southeast of LZ Thunder. The guys had been badly pinned down, but the choppers came quickly and got them out of the jam.

Orders for our next duty station in the states arrived. My orders were to report to the Eighteenth Airborne Corps at Ft. Bragg, North Carolina. I felt good about that. It was better than going back to Ft. Polk.

24. Farewell

THE LENGTHY OUT-COUNTRY PROCESSING began at the battalion. Here we turned in whatever combat gear we could, except for our weapons and ammunition. Everything issued us at Chu Lai had endured an enormous amount of wear and tear and was now mostly junk. My rucksack had a couple of holes courtesy of Charlie. I put a finger through one hole, thinking of how lucky I was to be in one piece.

The time to leave the battalion was near. Some of us went to a tailor by the main gate and had the proprietor sew new combat fatigues to our specifications. We had combat patches along with a Task Force Barker patch sewn on the fatigues. I hoped to take the fatigues home as a memento of my time in Vietnam. I also had sergeant stripes sewn on.

I patiently spent time giving a new pair of combat boots a good shine. When through I set them off to the side under some items and went to the mess hall. An REMF must have been watching from a distance. When I left, he came and took my new shoes. In my traditional ways, we call such individuals coyotes. They are on the sly side and wait until the proper moment to take advantage of a situation. I was issued a replacement pair of boots.

We were soon ready to leave for Chu Lai. On our last night at LZ Bronco, several of us went to an NCO club close to the airstrip. Others from our company were already there when we arrived, including Moreno and Tregarten. Tree was flashing his usual wide smile with his handlebar moustache.

The evening was filled with excitement and anticipation. No one overindulged in the alcohol. We exchanged addresses and had pictures taken in groups. We held up our glasses and made toasts to each other. In the morning we would be leaving a Vietnam that held both good and bad memories.

Early the following morning we loaded onto a c-130 and headed north. Wilson had left a day earlier. I sat on the side of the plane facing the South China Sea. Within minutes I recognized LZ Uptight and the surrounding area below. I already knew that was one place I would never forget. What happened in the rice paddies and beaches down there would forever be etched in my mind. That was the place where many young men gave up their lives for a cause that turned bitter. The promised South Vietnamese aid was never really there. As a result the GIs out in the boonies became frustrated with the lack of help. Many also became bitter, because they felt that there was no real reason to be out there. Some wrote letters to their congressmen to let them know their feelings, and many others continued to die.

I looked out toward Pinkville. I thought about the many times I had walked point there. I also thought about the company going back there very soon. At that moment, I felt a great sense of relief about not extending my tour of duty.

At Chu Lai we turned in our weapons and ammunition at the battalion sector. Then we headed to the main PX area, where we conducted our out-country processing. To clear the brigade and division took about three days. We waited in many long lines, but no one griped during this time. Thoughts of going home overshadowed any inconveniences of waiting.

As we waited, the guys from Ft. Polk met up again after a full year. We shared our experiences, which were very similar. When we shook hands there was a genuine feeling of having made it through the hard times. Some of us had made sergeant. The sad part was that many comrades we had arrived with were gone. We completed the out-country processing at Chu Lai, and it was then time to say farewell to the Americal Division. During my tour of duty I had gained a great sense of pride from being part of the division. Throughout the year my company was with each of the main elements of the division. We were part of the 11th Brigade. At times we were attached to the 196th, the 198th, and the 1st of the 1st Cavalry. Right before leaving, we were thanked for having served with distinction. A special mention was made of the infantry personnel.

When ready we flew farther south to Cam Rahn Bay. This was the point of departure for our trip back to the world. We still had on jungle fatigues but would change to Class A attire for our trip home. When the time came to change, however, I decided not to do so. I ended up wearing my fatigues back to the states, as I didn't want to take the chance that they would be stolen before I left.

Before departure, our duffel bags were checked for illegal items. One set of fatigues I had had specially made at LZ Bronco was confiscated. I was glad that I had chosen to wear the other. After inspection we hauled our bags to a large waiting area. After that it was a matter of waiting for our flight, which was due within an hour.

While we waited we talked of what we were going to do when we got home. I sat with Hagberg and Voss from the Ft. Polk training days. Both were now sergeants.

Hagberg proclaimed the same thing others had said before, "When I get home all I'm going to do is sleep."

"I don't really know what I'll be doing," I answered. "I'll just be glad to get a good cheeseburger and a Coke."

Voss added, "All I know is we lost a year of our lives. I have a lot of catching up to do. I don't even know what the popular songs are now."

Within an hour a plane approached and landed. It was a commercial jet. Everyone thought it was our Freedom Bird and let out a large yell. It turned out that the plane was for another group of soldiers who also waited nearby. After the fresh troops unloaded, the other group boarded the plane and left. It was just our luck, that our plane was delayed for a couple more hours. This left more time to kill.

Tired of sitting, I took a walk to try and find something to eat or drink. On the way I passed new recruits who looked at me in my jungle fatigues and bush hat. They had the same look as my group when we had arrived in-country.

One approached me and said, "What is it like here?"

"It depends," I told him. "If you are noninfantry, it won't be as bad as if you are infantry. Use common sense. If you are infantry you will pray a lot to get through the year."

Our Freedom Bird finally arrived after several more delays. We waited for the fresh troops to get off before we boarded. We left the new replacements alone. Some of us did offer words of encouragement. We all knew how tough the year ahead would be for them.

We boarded the plane, a Scandinavian aircraft, and left for the world around midnight, excited to be flying into the darkness. I didn't feel a true sense of relief until we were well away from the coastline. There were no movies during the flight, but that didn't matter.

I soon drifted off to sleep, knowing we had a stopover in Japan. On the way there we again crossed the International Date Line. This time we gained a day, which meant that we would arrive at Ft. Lewis, Washington, on the same day and time as when we left Cam Rahn Bay.

After our brief stopover in Japan, we continued our journey. Around midnight the plane arrived at Ft. Lewis. The date was January 15, 1969. The cold air greeted us as we left the plane, and we were glad to be wearing field jackets issued us at Cam Rahn Bay. From the airport we went to a center to clean up and put on Class A attire. A steak dinner was ready for anyone who wanted one. I don't believe anyone had the steak dinner. Instead, everyone was anxious to get to the Sea-Tac Airport.

We were home. It was good to be back in the good old U S of A.

The airport was located between Seattle and Tacoma. There I bought a ticket for Los Angeles. My first stop would be to visit a sister who lived north of there. After I purchased my ticket, I waited for my flight with the others. Each time the flight numbers sounded over the intercom, someone would leave. As each person departed, we shook his hand and wished him the best.

When I heard my flight number, I did the same and left for the L.A. International Airport. The flight was swift, and I was soon walking down the corridors of the huge airport. My first thought was of getting something to eat, so I found a restaurant and ordered some American food.

When the food arrived a strange thing happened to me. Reality hit me. For the past year I had lived in a very violent world, and I began, slowly, to accept that I had truly escaped it. I really was back in the states. I tried to use my utensils to eat, but my hands started to shake. Trying to use both hands to drink the cup of coffee was futile. After several attempts I gave up and left the place without eating.

When I arrived at my sister's home I called Harlow, who lived in Huntington Beach. He came over the following day, and we went to a quiet place to talk. There I told Harlow about my experience at the airport. He said, "You know, Chief, I also had a similar experience. I think we had a lot of violence built up inside. It was hard for us to accept reality. We did things over there that we normally won't do here. Perhaps that had something to do with it. It takes time, but you start to get over the feeling."

I replied, "I think you are right. We are really afraid of ourselves or rather what we know we are capable of doing. When the airport incident happened I had to take a double shot of hard liquor to settle me down."

Harlow was silent for a minute, and then asked, in an upbeat tone, "Anyway, what are your plans? Me, I'm back into getting a college degree. I have a couple of years, and that is my goal."

"For the present nothing matters," I replied. "I'm back in the world. I'll be at Ft. Bragg, North Carolina, after my leave. I have no plans after that. I can only say that for the rest of my life, I hope I never hurt another human being."

"That's how I feel," Harlow admitted. "Let's keep in touch."

A few days later I headed for home. I didn't rush it, as just being back in the United States was good enough for me. When I arrived it was dark. My hometown appeared no different than it had been the day I left. My aunt and uncle were very glad to see me, especially my aunt, who gave me a good hug with tears in her eyes.

There was no welcome-back committee or parade. Life just went on as usual as I made my presence known around town. During this time many people I knew or was vaguely acquainted with acknowledged me with a handshake or a verbal comment. A middle-aged Jicarilla Apache woman asked me what I thought of my experience in the war. I was truthful with her, as I replied, "The war was a very frustrating experience. I feel we had no business there."

Surprisingly, she knew more about world affairs than I thought she did. She emphatically stated, "We have to stop Communism. If we don't they will take over the rest of the countries there."

"That's what we went for, but it's not that easy," I told her. "The people themselves didn't help us do that. They helped the enemy a lot."

"Well at least you tried. Some things we don't know around here."

Before I left for Ft. Bragg my aunt and uncle had the same medicine man come over to bless me again. The ceremony this time was to bring me back into the people. After a month's leave I left for my new duty station.

I was unaware of how much the Vietnam War would affect me in the years ahead.

Epilogue

THE YEAR IN NAM tested each GI on an individual basis. We found out a lot about ourselves, both positive and negative. We realized we could do things we never thought possible.

Many GIs came home to a public that didn't understand what they had just gone through and what many others were still going through overseas. The returning GIs believed that the growing hostility toward the war was directed at them, which was unfair, because they had had nothing to do with the political decisions that had been made.

As infantry personnel we tried our best to do what we trained for—to aid the South Vietnamese government in getting rid of the Communist threat. However, a corrupt government in South Vietnam failed to keep the trust of its people. As a result, many Vietnamese people sympathized with the Communist cause.

It was very important for the American soldiers to gain the trust of the local people. To win the war we had to focus on them and gain their favor. But this was not to be. When I arrived there, the situation created by other units before us was irreversible. The villagers in the outlying areas already greatly mistrusted the GIs. They wanted to be left alone to run their own affairs. The Communists wanted to dominate them and control the countryside.

South Vietnam's army, the ARVN, had no real desire to fight the Communists. The United States and its allies willingly provided men to help them in combat. Instead, we ended up doing the majority of the fighting. The villagers in the countryside never totally supported the Allied effort. This lack of support, the enemy's patience in waiting out the war, and the antiwar protests were the key reasons why we lost. In the end the effort to rid Vietnam of Communist aggression failed.

Many GIs lost their lives or were maimed in the war. Many more lives were changed forever. From the infantry standpoint, at times the animal within us took over. Those who refused to allow the animal to control them went on with their lives. Others let the animal loose at times but learned to cope with it after a few years. Still others let the animal completely dominate them, and to this day they are still fighting themselves. For me it was bad enough, but it could have been worse.

So, from the infantry standpoint, we all died. None of us came back the same person he was beforehand. We had gone through too much for that to be possible. It was bad enough to see fellow soldiers get killed, but the hardships we went through and the violent world we lived in would forever change us. Some of us became more aggressive or more reserved. Some became dependent on drugs and alcohol without realizing it. For some it was best to forget the war, act as though it had never happened. For others it was best to talk about it with those who shared the same experiences. Some of us felt a need to write about the war.

In the words of Teddy Roosevelt, "It is not the critic who counts; . . . the credit belongs to the man who is actually in the arena, whose face is marred by dust and sweat and blood." In this sense, the U.S. military won. We won the vast majority of skirmishes, large or small. However, there was no way of holding on to the territory won. The enemy quickly regained it as soon as we left.

I've also read somewhere that the Vietnam War was very costly for the former Soviet Union. During the war the Soviets supplied the majority of military aid to North Vietnam, which caused the former Soviet Union economic hardships it never recovered from. This, along with the Soviets' invasion of Afghanistan, their own "Vietnam," caused Communism to collapse in the Soviet Union. This was a great victory for those of us who still relate to the Vietnam War.

From an American Indian perspective the war had similarities to our past. We found we still had a bridge to it. In many instances the warrior in us naturally took over. As a result we performed with pride and dignity.

The Vietnamese people gave us a new perspective about ourselves. I for one believed that life might have been a little hard on me as I grew up. However, after seeing what some Vietnamese kids endured, I became more thankful for what I had. The kids there didn't have much of a future. When they came of age, they had a choice between fighting for the South Vietnamese government or for the Communists. Many of the kids were also homeless and had no one to take them in and care for them. In general, here in the United States someone will always take you in and give you something to eat, a stark contrast between our two cultures.

When the reality of war sank in, I found the only way to get through was with prayers. There are no statistics, but I'm sure the phrase "There are no atheists in combat" holds true. One has to be in this situation to truly understand.

In closing, I thank my Creator for being with me every step of the way.

WINNERS OF THE NORTH AMERICAN INDIAN
PROSE AWARD

Boarding School Seasons:
American Indian Families, 1900–1940
Brenda J. Child

Claiming Breath
Diane Glancy

They Called It Prairie Light:
The Story of Chilocco Indian School
K. Tsianina Lomawaima

Son of Two Bloods
Vincent L. Mendoza

All My Sins Are Relatives
W. S. Penn

Completing the Circle
Virginia Driving Hawk Sneve

Year in Nam: A Native
American Soldier's Story
Leroy TeCube